The Life and Times of
THE LATE DEMON RUM

Other books by J. C. Furnas

Novels

THE PROPHET'S CHAMBER
MANY PEOPLE PRIZE IT
THE DEVIL'S RAINBOW

Non-fiction

ANATOMY OF PARADISE
VOYAGE TO WINDWARD
GOODBYE TO UNCLE TOM
THE ROAD TO HARPER'S FERRY

The Life and Times of

THE LATE
DEMON RUM

By J. C. FURNAS

G. P. Putnam's Sons

NEW YORK

46200

To
my good friend
who bears watching
C_2H_5OH

CONTENTS

Illustrations will be found following page 128

INTRODUCTION

Allentown, N.J., 1800: The local tavern-keeper tots up the
bill for the members of the Presbytery of New Brunswick,
New Jersey, come thither to install the Rev. John Cornell as
minister of the local Presbyterian congregation: Dinner, feed
for their horses—and four large bowls of punch, a pint of
brandy, one "go" of grog, two bottles of wine, three and a
half bottles of beer. Such pot-tossing at an occasion of
churchly flavor can have caused no comment then, for it was
very much the expected thing six generations ago.

Washington, D.C., 1913: William Jennings Bryan, giving
his first official luncheon as Secretary of State in farewell to
James Bryce, the most respected ambassador Britain ever sent
to the United States, signalizes Temperance principles by
serving only water and unfermented grape juice as drinks.
(The Russian ambassador, forewarned, has put away his usual
ration of Bordeaux before setting forth.) This omission of
wines and liquors got as much attention from the press as the
White House luncheon several years before to which President Theodore Roosevelt had invited Booker T. Washington, the eminent Negro leader. But the reaction was by no
means all ridicule of a grandstanding breach of conventional
hospitality. Many felt and said that Bryan had done just right
to stick by his principles, never mind how it struck them
godless furriners.

For in the 113 years between that dinner at Allentown and
the Great Commoner's sharklike smile of welcome to his
polyglot guests, the American approach to alcoholic drinks
had greatly changed. Indeed many not unintelligent and
progressive-minded persons had actually come to believe that
Prohibition was not only right and advisable but feasible.

9

With justification the Drys had been chanting victory for a generation: The Rev. Dr. Lyman Abbott, a relatively mild detractor of the Demon Rum, wrote: "This cause has no other side . . . the drinking traffic . . . [is] without either defence or defender." A Dry exulting over Abraham Lincoln's teetotalism hailed "coming days when drink will be banished from the daily life of respectable people, and when a drunkard will be a curiosity. . . . Because the world is awakening from its alcoholic stupor, we now seem to be approaching the end of the temperance controversy."

Something went very wrong with this prospect of The Good Time Coming. National Prohibition lived only fourteen years. Now, two generations after it went into effect, drunkards are still anything but a curiosity. Certainly, with so many women tippling along with their men, a higher proportion of the population now "drink" than did in 1865 when Prohibition was only a well-meant experiment in a few states.

On trial it became a nationwide, calamitous mistake and we are well rid of it. How sour it went, how it was got rid of, does not concern this book. Many books have already dealt with the failure of Prohibition to consolidate its victory. Some are valuable but all are fragmentary and do little to reorient today's drinker in his current difficulty: Whether old enough to remember speakeasies or not, he is still doing his drinking, whether temperate or excessive, in the shadow of the old ideas, emotions and folklore that begot Prohibition. Outworn theories and anachronistic shames make it hard for him to judge his indulgence intelligently.

The best way to shake off these dead hands, to cure that cultural hangover, to smother those faint, persistent strains of "Father, Dear Father, Come Home With Me Now," is intimately to understand the cumulative error from its beginnings. No doubt the prime beginning was the first hangover, likely in Neolithic times. We have no details. Much detail, however, most of it now sounding queer, is available in the case of the United States, so we may confine ourselves to that. The Quakers, that always catalytic sect, had the most to do with starting it.

The Life and Times of
THE LATE DEMON RUM

1

GOOD CREATURE
OF GOD

ೲ

. . . 'Twas honest old Noah first planted the Vine,
And mended his Morals by drinking its Wine;
And justly the drinking of water decry'd;
For he knew that all Mankind, by drinking it dy'd. . . .

From this Piece of History plainly we find
That Water's good neither for Body nor Mind;
That Virtue & Safety in Wine-bibbing's found
While all that drink Water deserve to be drown'd. . . .

—BENJAMIN FRANKLIN,
"A Drinking Song" (c.1745)

NEARLY two hundred years ago one Jacob Lindley was a robust young member of the Religious Society of Friends with the Quaker knack of plain, clear speech. Shortly before the American Revolution the Spirit moved him to rise in meeting in Philadelphia and express a momentous "concern." One might say that *spirits* moved him, for what he protested about was being "oppress'd with the smell of rum from the breaths of those who sat round him."

Another Friend present at this meeting was Anthony Benezet—imaginative schoolmaster-reformer, indeed a Quaker saint of the same order as John Woolman, and one of the most fertile minds in North America in that century. With sober good will this self-styled "Lover of Mankind" bent his great if unostentatious abilities to having and spreading salutary ideas. His original teaching methods anticipated the educational reforms of later generations. His pleas for "the poor wild Indians" were intelligently humane. His emotional writings about Negro slavery were germinal in the British as well as the American movements toward Emancipation and Abolition. And at the very season when young Jacob got that one whiff too many from his elders, Anthony, always scenting social morbidities and exploring ways to reduce them, was writing a strong anti-alcohol pamphlet published later (1774) as *The Mighty Destroyer Displayed, in Some Account of the Dreadful Havock made by the mistaken Use as well as Abuse of Distilled Spirituous Liquors.*

In principle any Friend may speak up in meeting any time. Local feeling, however, usually determines whose prestige qualifies him or her to do so, and who should keep a meek silence. Many present may have found Jacob pesumptuous. But Anthony took him home to dinner and invited him to collaborate on *The Mighty Destroyer*. Though later eminent among Friends, Jacob was then obscure and maybe diffident. Yet his had been the latest and strongest expression of growing Quaker uneasiness about the Demon Rum, and his innocent vigor may have deepened Anthony's resolve to make his copy for the printer strong and hot. When it went to press, for the first time in North America the Demon had been roundly, deliberately, conspicuously—and not at all undeservedly—denounced as a general menace to body, soul and civilization.

The skein thus begun lengthened and tangled until, 150 years later, it had hogtied and blindered the United States into making a continent-wide fool of itself. The calamitous results—major financing for organized crime; pandemic public and private hypocrisy; queer fiscal and emotional handicaps—will still mar several generations yet to come. To those born since Repeal—the eldest such have already passed thirty! —this phenomenon of Temperance-cum-Prohibition must sound like one of those factual fantasies, such as the Children's Crusade, that historians can never make credible. Yet it was real—witness the lasting scars—and in its own times and places had a certain validity.

§§

[American dram-drinking] is a deeper curse than ever afflicted any nation . . . worse than the yellow fever, or the negro slavery, because apparently more irremediable.
                                        —CAPTAIN BASIL HALL, R.N. (1827)

The notion of Quakers with rum on their breaths in meeting or anywhere else is startling nowadays. But this was the early 1770's. As yet John Wesley's English Methodists were the only body of Westerners apt to think it wrong casually to take "strong waters," and Bishop Francis Asbury's tooth-gritting efforts to spread that idea in the Colonies had barely begun. It was still usual among Quakers as well as "worldly" persons to put on the breakfast table decanters, wineglasses and sugar for guests to mix their morning dram with, and unless young Jacob was having olfactory delusions, Quaker hosts often set a good example on First Day as well as the other six. John Woolman stocked rum in his New Jersey village store as a matter of course; the chief rum importers in the neighborhood were also Quakers; and members of his monthly meeting were not infrequently obliged to accept discipline for drunkenness.

In many other segments of our Founding Fathers' America the morning dram was taken for granted like breakfast orange juice now. The custom owed something to the dram of whiskey on which the Highland Scot counted to set the system going after the stagnation of sleep. It also reflected the Colonists' belief that a pre-breakfast jolt of something highly alcoholic, often known as "bitters" because of the allegedly medicinal drugs sometimes steeped in it, warded off the chills and fever of the prevalent malaria. Never mind its ancestry, the "eye-opener" of spirits—peach brandy, applejack, rye whiskey from domestic crops; rum from the West Indies or, presently, made from West Indian molasses in Colonial stills —became a hygienic institution. It went west with the necessary copper tubing, seed-rye and apple- and peach-seedlings. (Indian corn was no great success as raw material for malt for Colonial beer; but in due season it rivaled rye in the mash tub as ancestor of "corn" and bourbon.)

New York City's breakfast tables around 1800 provided cherry brandy as well as cider and sangaree (sweetened wine punch) plus tea and coffee. On the old place in the Blue Grass the grandfather of Carry Nation—destined to be the hatchet-wielding terror of Kansas speakeasies—never let a morning pass without mixing a pre-breakfast hot toddy, offering a hygienic spoonful to each member of the family, adult or child, then, having done his duty by his nearest and dearest, drinking the rest himself with no notion that he was damaging and polluting God's image. As late as 1861, long after Temperance was well established, "Bull Run" Russell, the great early British war correspondent, found the pre-breakfast cocktail or julep still lively on both Chesapeake Bay steamers and Louisiana plantations. Simpler folks just had a straight snort of anything handy without trimmings. According to recent theory (details later) the first thing in the morning on an empty stomach is the most damaging time to take hard liquor. Indeed, consistently to feel the need of such a morning "phlegm-cutter" is now considered a pre-monitory symptom of alcoholism. But our forebears had their own theories and practices to match, and clung long to the late-medieval notion that alcohol deserved its splendid name, *aqua vitae*, water of life, given it by the alchemists who first distilled it in potable quantity in the West.

It burned the mouth like flameless fire and, once swallowed, diffused through body and soul (or so it felt) a sense of heightened well-being all too readily mistaken for an intensification of life itself. The euphoria that went with heavy dosage of wine and beer among peoples ignorant of distilling had already got alcohol associated with the divine. Now our ancestors were panacea-minded, and any item new in their pharmacopoeia—quinine, tobacco, sassafras, whatnot—was likely to be thought sovereign for many ills and used as such without experimental tests. As a scientific novelty of impressive potency, alcoholic "hott waters" were inevitably hailed as good for practically everything: "It sloweth age," wrote a contemporary sage of alcohol; "it strengtheneth youth; it helpeth digestion; it cutteth flegme; it abandoneth melancholie; it relisheth the heart; it lighteneth the mind; it quickeneth the spirits; it strengtheneth the hydropsie; it healeth the strangurie; it pounceth the stone; it expelleth the gravel; it puffeth away ventositie; it keepeth and preserveth the head from whirling, the eyes from dazzling, the tong from lisping, the mouth from snaffling, the teeth from chattering, and the throat from rattling; it keepeth the weason from stiffling, the stomach from wambling, and the heart from swelling; it keepeth the hands from shivering, the sinews from shrinking, the veins from crumbling, the bones from aching, and the marrow from soaking."

Nobody wants his weason to stiffle or his stomach to

wamble unnecessarily. Such weighty advice from the august and learned was bound eventually to permeate all layers of society, particularly since the effects of small quantities of spirits on the system are rapid and marked.

෴

"Mr. Edward . . . just took part of a bowl of punch with a friend at the Flying Horse—but that's no more than the parson himself might do—and there's Deacon Whitleather, he never sits down to dinner without a stiff horn of something to wash it down."

—*The Drunkard*, II, 2

Spirits probably came to the Colonies with the first English and Dutch settlers. Dutchmen of that day seldom went far without their "genever" (gin) that was a major contribution to civilization—and to human misery. If only for medicinal use some kind of *aqua vitae* was doubtless shipped in the English vessels founding Jamestown and Plymouth. Among the Puritans sailing in the *Arbella* to set up the Massachusetts Bay Colony was a servant girl who "near killed herself" by taking too much "strong waters" against seasickness. English distilling was soon advanced enough to warrant founding the Distillers' Company to control it, and spirits-drinking among the lower orders in port towns was rapidly increasing. In another forty years the horrors of Hogarth's "Gin Lane" were disgracing most English cities. Hence the first taxes to discourage sale of spirits by making milder tipples a better bargain; and that short-lived ban on spirits in Georgia, the newly founded colony for rehabilitating debtor-prisoners and other presumably worthy persons in hard luck. The other Colonies set up no barriers to the influx of spirits as their trade with the rum-minded West Indies grew important. And presently came another source of hard liquor in immigrant Scots and Scots-Irish whose affection for pot-stills and long-standing skill in making whiskey of barley malt led them soon to try other grains where barley was lacking.

Relative lack of spirits in early times did not mean that the Colonists meekly put up with water during their pioneering hardships. Nobody reared in Europe was likely to do that except from dire necessity. The British tavern and table drinks of the day were beers of varying strengths; cider and its cousin perry (made from pears); wines for those able to afford imports. Naturally the earliest settlers, who were just Dutchmen or Englishmen transplanted, tried to supply themselves with those items. Their mistrust of water was often good hygiene, for the risk of pollution was high. But that probably had little to do with it. Predominant was another pseudoscientific notion of medieval flavor: the false association, based on naïve analogy, of the "strength" of one's drink with the strength of one's body. Water—flavorless, colorless, proverbially weak—was suspected of diluting physical vigor and settling cold on the stomach; whereas it stood to reason that "jolly good ale and old" warmed and strengthened. Economic snobbishness heightened this hydrophobia, for to have only water to drink was to confess extreme poverty. When stuck with water as the only drink available, the self-respecting Colonist mixed in molasses, vinegar or sassafras to mask the implied disgrace to his purse and insult to his palate. Some of these values survive in the British waiter's reluctance to believe that Americans mean it when asking for water with a meal.

Barrels and barrels of beer went to sea with every ship out of Bristol, R.I. (and Bristol, England, for that matter), because the hands expected a quart a day to keep them fit; a minor reason was their belief that anything alcoholic helped to ward off scurvy. Early students at Harvard expected the same supply, so a brewery was one of the College's first projects; for the same reason a brewhouse was annexed to the great mansion that William Penn built for himself in his new colony.

Benjamin Franklin's fellow printer in London in the 1750's was convinced that to keep up efficiency—he did not mention keeping up self-respect too, but the issue was likely there—he needed five pints of strong beer spaced through the working day. Crèvecoeur, the intellectual theorist about

American democracy, had such ideas in mind when remarking how hard the Negro slaves of the South had to work under a sun as hot as Africa's without "the cordials of any cheering liquor."

Before distilling was vouchsafed them the Colonists struggled ingeniously to produce potable beer from mashed pumpkin or molasses flavored with sassafras, wild hops, spruce or pine twigs, with a result that may have been rather like the root beer of modern commerce. For traditional flavor they imported malt from home at considerable expense. Visiting dignitaries from Holland thought the beer brewed in New Amsterdam worthy of old Amsterdam itself. In a land where wild grapes flourished, some eventually proving to make good wine, the Huguenots fleeing Louis XIV were the only settlers making serious efforts of that sort; the others came from countries without strong traditions of vine-growing. Much of the new country from Virginia northward was well suited to apple trees, however, and they recalled the home tradition of cider to great effect. Cider flooded the middle and northern Colonies, largely replacing beer as the principal tavern and table drink:

> For Planters' Cellars, you must know,
> Seldom with good *October* [ale] flow,
> But Perry Quince and Apple Juice
> Spout from the Tap like any Sluice.

wrote a rhyming observer of eighteenth-century Maryland.

The Hutchinsons of Milford, New Hampshire, hundreds of miles northward, whose offspring would sing for Temperance and Abolitionist crusades, put down at least 100 barrels of hard cider yearly as household supply. In nearby Derry, a barrel lasted the family of young Horace Greeley, eventually editor of the great New York *Tribune,* hardly a week; anybody dropping in had his mug filled again and again, "until everybody was about as full as he could hold . . . whole families died drunkards and vagabond paupers from the impetus first given by cider-swilling in their rural homes." Old-timers round Albany, New York, recalled how women and children

as well as men drank cider as freely as if it had been water
from the well. And mark, this was not the ferment-proofed
stuff still familiar at Hallowe'en time. The alcoholic content
of the cool, tingly tipple in those barrels could run up toward
that of light European table wines.

Now if the strength of beer and cider was good for labor-
ers, artisans, seamen and mankind generally, how much better the strikingly stronger effects of rum—originally known as
"killdevil" in its native West Indies—or applejack or whiskey.
It took time and bulk of liquid for beer or cider to make a
harvest hand feel "strengthened"—meaning cheered up and
slightly tiddly. Wine was rather more effective but disproportionately expensive, and still required more ounces per quota
of effect than was obtainable from hard stuff. Applying the
strength analogy to the utmost, farmers in New England,
New Jersey and Pennsylvania began to set a jug of rum somewhat cut with molasses under a bush at the edge of the hay-
field where each mower took a swig each time he came round,
believing that it lightened their toil in physiological as well
as psychological effect. The handling of the scythes might get
riskily wild as the day wore on, but both hands and employers were long since convinced that such work demanded liquid fuel.

Conversely it surprised nobody to read in the newspapers
about the untimely deaths of certain rash workmen taking
cold water after a hard summer day's work. The only safe way
to fool with water was to blunt its deleterious powers by
heavy dilution with spirits. So the trades as well as farming
floated on alcohol. The custom of workingmen knocking off
for rum at the boss's expense at 11 A.M. and 4 P.M. was so well
established in Portland, Maine, that the city hall bell was officially rung at those hours. P. T. Barnum recalled that folks'
cellars round Fairfield, Connecticut, held not only cider but
an apple brandy known as "gumption," which was copiously
drunk in "all the hat and comb shops [in Danbury]." A new
journeyman owed his shopmates drinks "to pay his footing."
A new coat called for "sponging" by the same method. And
at funerals not only the mourners and family but the offici-
ating clergy drank copiously. Well after the Civil War an old

Yankee minister recalling seeing the glasses and decanters conveniently placed not only on the table but on the closed lid of the coffin itself. That sort of thing had not waited for the advent of spirits, however. The company mourning an eminent Boston widow soaked up some fifty gallons of Madeira in 1678. A less elegant barrel of beer for the funeral of a Philadelphian cost his widow eighteen shillings in 1781. And well into that time, New England towns felt bound to supply wine or cider at public expense for pauper funerals because proper respect for the dead meant tippling as well as coffin-burial.

Indeed most occasions involving parsons called for considerable elbow bending. Not only at funerals, weddings and christenings but at purely ecclesiastical rites of passage, such as convocations, synods and installations (as at Allentown), gatherings of fishers-of-men called for sideboards loaded with spirits as briskly patronized as if they had been fishers-of-mackerel. The ensuing "spillings of water and sugar and liquor," said the Rev. Dr. Lyman Beecher, champion Presbyterian theologian of his day and one of the pillars of early Temperance, "looked and smelled like the bar of a very active grogshop." A York State minister making rounds of pastoral calls often came home pretty how-come-ye-so because each household visited was supposed to offer him a drink—and he to drink it. According to a venerable minister of the last knee-breeched generation, such folkways had sent half the preachers round Albany to drunkards' graves. And in spite of Asbury's war on spirits, dram drinking was scandalously prevalent among the Methodist preachers of the Old Northwest, Tennessee and Kentucky in the early nineteenth century.

Though the Colonies soon had commercial distilling, it met heavy competition from household stills, which were long as legal as skillets. In the upper South, professional distillers went from plantation to plantation supervising conversion of the local lavish peach crops into the peach brandy on which the first mint juleps were based; in the fall they sometimes used persimmons, which sounds delightful. (Jerseymen are said to have bypassed the still by letting hard cider freeze in

the keg, then boring into the still-liquid core to drain off the
alcohol concentrated into "Jersey lightning.") In old Albany
—which probably drank no more than other towns but got
special attention as York State's hotbed of Temperance—
"pastors and people . . . vied in the production of the best
cherry, and raspberry, and strawberry brandy" given not only
to adults but to children for worms and bellyaches and to
dispel the bone-searching chill of meetinghouses unheated in
winter. The Rev. John Marsh, a great Temperance crusader,
recalled being a small boy in Rhode Island and crying from
the cold in meeting, then going home to a mug of flip (hot
rum, sugar, beer and nutmeg) that made the room spin so
fast he had to hold on to the chair.

Fuddled parsons, tipsy urchins, sound strange to us reared
in the shadow of militant Temperance. But the dosing of
small fry with alcohol is still a problem in some countries,
notably certain parts of France, where the schoolchild often
gets a good slug of Calvados to strengthen him for the day—
and send him to sleep in class. (Not long ago I saw in a Nor-
man post office a health poster of a little girl, maybe four
years old, saying: "I grow fast because I drink neither wine
nor beer nor cider.") None of this picture of booze and our
forefathers makes sense unless one keeps in mind that they
saw alcohol not primarily as a potential menace, as we were
taught to, but as one of those "creatures of God" that the
New Testament pronounced "good, and nothing to be refused if it be received with thanksgiving"—that is, enjoyed
like the other innocent gifts of God and used as socio-physio-
logical-psychological convenience when indicated.

They even thought supply of drink an essential public service. The New England tavern was basically a community institution like meetinghouse, school or mill. Selectmen licensed it partly to control local opportunity for tippling,
true, but also to ensure that its necessary, important function—"entertainment" of man and beast away from home
—was in responsible and capable hands. Hence New England's chosen tavern-keepers were not unlikely to be deacons
of the church, or at least particularly zealous members. In at
least one Yankee village successive local rum sellers were

addressed as "deacon" because, though not actually thus distinguished, the original licensee had been an especially impressive specimen of deacon. For reasonable payment both two- and four-legged travelers were entitled to food and shelter, and Two Legs, it was assumed, had as much right to strong drink to repair the fatigues of the road as Four Legs had to oats and hay.

Drink being good for the worthily weary, whether from toil or lawful travel, the tavern also catered to local good citizens—miller, blacksmith, wheelwright, the local lawyer if there was one, the parson on occasion, for keep it perpetually in mind that nobody yet saw anything unrespectable about drinking as such. Indeed, wives might sometimes come along for an evening treat of flip or toddy. Only flagrant drunkenness drew social or legal penalty. The disorderly drunk wound up in stocks or lockup as much because he was a dangerous nuisance as because local opinion disapproved of excess. On both grounds the landlord's license often forbade him to serve those signally abusing drink. The selectmen might guide his judgment by an official list of "common drunkards"—a sort of scarlet letter "D" canceling normal privileges at the tavern somewhat like the modern Finnish system of licensing citizens to drink and revoking it if they overdo.

Such early devices to curb the Demon suffered from the same drawbacks, however, as any that followed: They could not rule out sluggish or venal administration. Tavern-keepers, bent on popularity and profit per drink, tended to give the customer the benefit of the doubt. Selectmen grew slack about supervision, like the justice of the peace-millowner in Erie County, New York, who swore to the good character of a license applicant soon after firing him from the mill for embezzling. Even in New England where community responsibility was strong—and the tradition of minding one's own business weak—the town sot reeling out of the bar after several too many was a common sight. In at least one Massachusetts township in the 1820's the list of "posted drunkards" was so long that a stranger mistook it for the local roster of eligible voters. And instead of remaining a town club and caravanserai, certain taverns in large settlements, where social stratification was well begun, became the headquarters of sordid political cliques led by or toadied to by landlords all too willing to serve frowsy lushes belonging to the crowd. Enter the classic Tammany-type precinct-boss-saloonkeeper cynically exploiting society's enjoyment of his bar—the man who did more than any other to bring about Prohibition. Well before the Revolution John Adams was already denouncing him.

Those times had some primitive teetotalism. Jonathan Edwards, greatest Yankee theologian, abstained after the age of twenty. Benezet eschewed alcohol for tea, and was thankful that he had so chosen when young. Senator Felix Grundy of Tennessee, born in 1777, could boast that he had never touched liquor. In the same generation Dr. Charles Jewett's brother stuck to cold water simply because spirits revolted him. The general picture was pretty Rum-soaked, however, as Abraham Lincoln eloquently reminded his fellow members of the Washingtonian [teetotal] Society of Springfield, Illinois: when "we first opened our eyes . . . we found intoxicating liquors recognized by everybody and repudiated by nobody . . ." given to babies at birth and men on deathbeds, while "to have a rolling or a raising, a husking or a hoedown, anywhere without it was probably insufferable"—an adjective explained by Judge Thomas Hertell of New York City in a pamphlet of 1819: Lack of booze on such occasions was taken to imply "meanness or parsimony."

Lincoln might also have listed marriages, militia musters, elections, auctions. Local justices' and sheriffs' courts were held at taverns and heavy drinking went with such trials as a matter of course. The Louisiana legislature of 1814 required the keeper of every jail in the state to allow each prisoner a gill of whiskey daily. It came free with meals at inns and on early steamboats. In prosperous houses in New York City spirits-and-water was "the universal table drink." Down South, whiskey or brandy-and-water washed dinner down and then was taken straight to help digestion. Cherries were steeped in rum* to be taken to ward off cold; nursing moth-

* Hence the old-fashioned name "rum cherry" for the wild black cherry (*Prunus serotina*) of the Eastern forest.

ers took rum-and-milk. Purchasers in crossroads stores were usually entitled to a free snort from the jug—an anticipation of trading stamps. Since the store counter served as stand-up bar, "grocery" and "groggery" grew synonymous. Even after Temperance was well under way the stores of relatively staid Stockbridge, Massachusetts, annually sold ten quarts of spirits per capita in the township in addition to consumption at taverns. The Rev. Dr. Nathaniel Prime of Long Island, an influential early Temperance parson, thought the groceries' effect worse than that of taverns because they sold larger drinks at lower prices, openly violating regulations against allowing drinking on the premises. And the Whiskey Rebellion made it rowdily clear how much the pioneer economy of Western Pennsylvania depended on home distilling as the most sensible way to transport a rye crop to market by packhorse.

ϾᏩᏅ

. . . if it be the design of Providence to extirpate these savages in order to make room for the cultivators of the earth, it seems not improbable that rum may be the appointed means.

—BENJAMIN FRANKLIN, *Autobiography*

That same Monongahela rye was further notable in the young nation's history as key item of the Indian trade. Among the red men, Rum really was a demon. New Amsterdam, Providence Plantations and other early Colonies soon forbade sale of drink to Indians within the settlements, not from regard for the red man's welfare but because he was a menace when under the influence. Spirits, when they became available, soon eclipsed gunpowder, textiles and hardware in the back-country fur trade because, far less bulky than beer or wine, they were more easily transported over bad trails and frequent portages; and Indians preferred them anyway because their aim in drinking was to get fighting, blind, passing-out drunk as soon as possible. So the stronger the stuff they got for their peltry, the better they liked it.

The Seneca, for instance, canoed their annual catch of beaver and so on down the Allegheny to Pittsburgh and fetched back mainly whiskey. For days and weeks thereafter, until every keg was empty, their home villages were one murderous frenzy of intratribal riot between both sexes. A horrified witness of such a jollification in French Canada mentioned husbands bashing in wives' heads, mothers throwing

children into the river or the fire. Franklin said that a minor debauch of the sort that he saw in 1753 after an intertribal council at Carlisle, Pennsylvania, with "[the Indians'] dark-colored bodies half-naked, seen only by the gloomy light of the bonfire, running after and beating one another with firebrands, formed a scene the most resembling hell . . . that could well be imagined."

Well-meant official efforts to keep spirits away from the Indians failed because the upcountry was too diffuse and remote for effective policing. The governor of North Carolina explained in 1717 that the local frontiersmen, too many of them transported criminals or ne'er-do-wells, made a practice of getting the Indians drunk and cheating them in trade, which too often meant revenge-murder after the victims sobered up and learned the score. "The rum ruins us," an eminent Iroquois chief told the Colonial government of Pennsylvania. "These wicked whiskey sellers . . . bring thirty or forty cags [kegs] . . . and make us drink, and get all the skins that should go to pay the debts we have contracted." Much the same complaint was made about South Carolina and Georgia traders by Chief Eneisteegoe in 1768.

After the corroboree that Franklin described, the hungover participants explained that the Great Spirit had made everything of some use, and when He made Rum, He said: "Let this be for the Indians to get drunk with," so that was the way it had to be. That does not satisfy modern scientific speculation. Anthropologists have made some illuminating guesses as to why Indians were so notoriously gluttonous about alcohol:

Contrary to the usual impression, North America was not altogether innocent of the stuff when whites first intruded. There were corn-beers here and there south of the Rio Grande; the Indians of what is now Mexico also fermented maguey sap into pulque. But in the bulk of what is now the United States and Canada, neither carbohydrate-rich squash nor abundant wild grapes and berries had inspired fermented drinks. The cataclysmic passion for alcohol of the Colonists' Indians stayed latent until whites arrived. Doctors marvel at its intensity. A Yale physiologist once likened it to a congenital drug addiction common to a whole race. Yet it was not peculiar to the red man. The Polynesians, who also had not known alcohol at all, behaved much the same way when first encountering spirits. Indeed, says Donald Horton in an analysis of a hundred-odd assorted cultures, " 'Moderate' drinking in the European sense . . . is relatively rare. . . . Drinking to 'excess' is characteristic of primitive peoples." Nor are all Indians equally helpless in the Demon's insidious presence. Among the Northwest tribes (who gave us the word "hooch," from "hoochino," the name of their foul-tasting moonshine) Lemert found individuals, usually among the better born and more responsible, able to break away from the local tradition of drinking oneself blind whenever possible. Some go teetotal, others are even capable of take-it-or-leave-it moderation—a temperance probably due to psychological rather than physiological deviance.

Actually, it looks as if the eastern Indians' genius for alcoholic excess had emotional grounds. Many widely separated tribes put high value on trances, ecstatic hallucinations, self-transcending vertigo. In their view such states connote quasi-magical power over environment, a supernal self-aggrandizement, a glorious intimacy with the universe. Some Indian peoples arrive at these ends by fasting and self-torture, things already familiar to us as religious exercises leading to mystical experience; others by mass dancing and singing, also familiar; still others by drugs—peyote, Jimson weed, hallucinogenic mushrooms—to induce a grandiose ecstasy. Northwest Indian children are known to trot after automobiles snuffing up the dizzy-making exhaust gases—a modern version of the Greek oracle's method of preparing to prophesy. William James tells of "laughing gas" (nitrous oxide) used to bring on allegedly "genuine mystical revelations," and, even nearer the problem of the Indian debauches, says that "the sway of alcohol over mankind is unquestionably due to its power to stimulate the mystical faculties of human nature. . . . The drunken consciousness is one bit of the mystic consciousness. . . ." Consider the Papago Indians of Arizona who "hymn the glories of dizziness. The words [of their language] which mean 'drunken' and 'dizzy' are . . . sacred and poetic, for the trance of drunkenness is akin to the trance of vision." Certain other Indian tribes are almost as explicit about it.

To us it is perverse thus to mistake temporary poisoning, however euphoric, for identification with the Cosmos. The Indian seems to be too practical to look for degeneracy or unworthiness in the gift horse's mouth. He yearns for the ecstasy, never mind the context. Prayer, peyote, the trader's rotgut, hydrocarbon fumes—anything leading to such feelings is all the same to him. One good swig to start with, and no reluctance to lose self-control, no fear of disaster to his own interests, deters him, any more than they deter the compulsive alcoholic. There is a difference, however, in the Indian's lack of shame about it afterward. Hence, Lemert points out, solitary drinking hardly appears among his Northwest tribes. Any bottle available is shared till empty. What is shameful about being whirled out of oneself so gloriously?

Others, notably Horton, ascribe the destructive drinking of the eastern Indians to strains arising from their traditions against showing emotion and from the dislocating effects of their frontier contacts with white things and ways of doing. Alcohol deadens the cautionary, don't-do-it function of the brain first. So the Iroquois or Cherokee brave, trained to dead-panned dignity and impassive courtesy to all yet apprehensive, maybe unconsciously, of white encroachment on both hunting ground and cultural traditions, found whiskey a trigger releasing his pent-up anxieties and hostilities, which he proceeded to take out on the first thing handy—so he wrecked his hut or crippled his wife or ran down the first man he laid eyes on and beat his brains out.

A likely theory, nor does it preclude the previous one. Both are extreme but recognizable accountings for traits observed in many Indian peoples between Alaska and the Everglades. They do much to clear the Indian of that postulated genetic lack denying him a Western-style resistance to alcohol. He still has every right to reproach the white man for unscrupulously exploiting this cultural weakness. But, though the Indian's own leaders were soon well aware of the danger, as their protests to white intruders showed, they were too few and too late in taking the next logical step—rallying their people against the traders' cynicism, the Colonial governments' laxity, and their own irresponsibility.

The ruin of the seaboard tribes was almost total, that of the trans-Appalachian tribes ominously far advanced, when abortive resistance finally appeared. The backbone of Pontiac's great anti-white conspiracy of 1763 was a folk-hero known only as the "Delaware Prophet," who had visions and eloquently warned the Indians of the old Northwest against witchcraft and the harm inevitable when red men took up white ways and things, liquor worst of all. Under his widespread influence Indian consumption of firewater seems actually to have slacked off for a while. Pontiac's fall doubtless discredited this holy coadjutor's teachings. But much the same pattern reappeared thirty-odd years later on the upper Allegheny where Quaker missionaries were telling the Seneca what bad medicine liquor was. Maybe the great annual wing-ding after the canoes got back from Pittsburgh that spring had been even more lurid than usual. Anyway it so well illus-trated what the Quakers had been saying that Cornplanter, able leader of the Seneca segment of the Iroquois, secured a general agreement to forswear whiskey and assigned two young chiefs to police it.

Their hand was soon strengthened by Cornplanter's elder half brother, Handsome Lake, a fainéant hereditary chief up to then renowned mainly for drunkenness, chronic invalidism and psychotic withdrawals. After a fit of lethargic despair about his alcoholism he apparently died—only to revive after a prolonged, deathlike trance to tell of a mystical journey he had been taking into the afterworld where angels let him know emphatically that liquor was anathema to the Great Spirit. Out of his *Pilgrim's Progress*-like visions—for instance, of the souls of drunks being forced to swallow molten lead— he created a new Indian religion called "the Good Message" that decked out old Iroquois beliefs in Quakerish trimmings such as renunciation of war as well as alcohol. Between these doctrines and the watchfulness of Cornplanter's young deputies this self-imposed Prohibition also had fair success, and the jugs on the Pittsburgh traders' counters began to pour sugar-water instead of whiskey for a while.

At much the same time Little Turtle, a stabler and more statesmanlike chief of the Miamis in Ohio, was imploring the new-formed state governments west of the mountains to bar the Demon from the Indian trade. Presently President Jeffer-son sent Handsome Lake on a peace-minded mission among the restless tribes of the Old Northwest, which is thought to have strongly influenced the famous "Shawnee Prophet," who soon repeated the Delaware Prophet's career. This por-tentous, one-eyed figure was also brother (twin) of his peo-ple's ablest chief, Tecumseh; had been chronically alcoholic; saw visions, took a journey into the hereafter, taught that Indians should renounce rum and got many to do so at least temporarily; supplied the emotional core of a great league of Indian tribes against the whites. . . .

All the Shawnee Prophet accomplished in the long run was to make William Henry Harrison hero of Tippecanoe in 1811 and President of the United States in 1841. Handsome Lake's Good Message survives as the living religion of several thousand Iroquois in the States and Canada. It is nevertheless difficult to see him as a really constructive Indian like Sequoia. Some of his other ideas were deplorable: Jefferson, who entertained and endorsed him, may have been unaware that the Good Message also opposed schooling for Indians and encouraged the detection and knifing of witches. Cornplanter himself sometimes took a dim view of his turbulent half brother's goings-on. And it was not his but Little Turtle's approach that proved to have a continent-wide future when a federal law of 1834 forbade sale of liquor to Indians under federal jurisdiction.

It was poorly enough enforced, of course, but its passage was ominous—it was Uncle Sam's first experiment in direct war on the Demon, hence forerunner of the Volstead Act. Such efforts to keep alcohol away from Indians raise the question whether, as is widely assumed, the Demon Rum was a major cause of their catastrophic decline in numbers. It may well have been. Certainly deaths occurring in those lurid debauches did their population-curve no good. The survivors' weakened condition probably increased their susceptibility to exotic diseases. And as Horton suggests, the "doctored" trade-liquor that they mostly got may have poisoned or weakened many.

In any case, the Colonists *thought* that Rum was killing off the Indians. So to some extent—how much is necessarily unclear, but consider the example of Benezet—seeing what the stuff did to red men suggested to many imaginative and respectable whites that it might also be bad for white men. The drunkenness of the Indians surviving on Long Island was one thing that set the great Lyman Beecher on the Demon's trail. A generation later the same hapless people moved Walt Whitman to write of the "awful lesson . . . which may be learned from the consequences of the burning firewater upon . . .

the poor Indians." Earlier viewers-with-alarm began to see
that redskins were by no means alone in drinking themselves
and families into disaster. May this be why the mother-and-
daughter movements of Temperance and Prohibition were
American-born? Heavy abuse of alcohol had been widespread
since Noah's. Gin Lane was only one of many noisome quarters whence the rise of distilling accentuated the ills of alcohol. But only the North American Colonists had so striking a
view of a whole race of high visibility at least apparently
drinking itself to death.

2

STILL WATERS
RUN DEEP

... much is said about the prudent use of spirits, but we might as well speak of the prudent use of the plague—of fire handed prudently round among powder—of poison taken prudently every day. . . .

—LYMAN BEECHER, *Six Sermons*

Mr. Swell-Gut, the brewer, said that [Mr. Scorch-Gut, the distiller] was Scorch-Gut by name, and Scorch-Gut by nature; for his dam'd Devil's Piss burnt out the entrails of three fourths of the King's Subjects.

—*The Tavern Scuffle, or The Club in an Uproar* (1726)

LATE IN 1885 a redoubtable group of women invaded Christ-Church burial ground in Philadelphia to dedicate a memorial tablet on the grave of Benjamin Rush, M.D., dead since 1815. Many aspects of this extraordinary man command respect: He was a signer of the Declaration of Independence; pioneer in humanity toward the insane; early foe of slavery; surgeon general of the Middle Department of the Continental Army; dedicated physician and hero of Philadelphia's yellow fever epidemics. . . . But none of these claims on the nation's gratitude was what had brought the ladies there. As representatives of the National Woman's Christian Temperance Union they were celebrating the centennial of Rush's *Inquiry into the Effect of Ardent Spirits* and him as "instaurator of the American Temperance Reform."

As often happened, the WCTU had its facts only partly right. The *Inquiry* came out at least as early as 1784. And they might as well have called Jefferson "founder of the United States" because he drafted the great Declaration. Rush was highly important to the birth of Temperance, true. But so were his tutors in the subject, the Quakers and the Methodists. By 1771, Francis Asbury, the Methodist St. Paul, also a friend of Rush's, had landed in the Colonies and was

37

doing his best to ram down American Methodists' throats John Wesley's longstanding strictures against the makers and sellers—and drinkers—of spirits. We have already seen Benezet, whom Rush knew and admired, stirring up the Quakers in the early 1770's with writings that often sound like a rough draft of Rush. Friend Anthony zealously assembled bits from British doctors calling spirits downright poison; describing alcoholics' stomachs as like leather dried before a fire; averring that the guts of hogs fed on spent mash from distilleries were so vitiated that they were too weak for sausage casings, and their meat, however heavily salted, would not keep well. He denied that Rum was necessary for heavy labor, citing one Joshua Evans of Haddonfield, New Jersey, a Quaker-dominated settlement, who had paid his harvest hands sixpence extra a day in lieu of strong drink, paced them himself in the field and found his crop handled as well as it ever had been with the help of Rum. Anthony also touched on the Indian problem and the stupidity of Colonial governments' encouragement of booze because it brought in tax revenue. And, doing his duty by his fellow man's soul, he deplored the despiritualizing effects of Rum, making its victim "prophane and abandoned, and to the last degree regardless of [his] duty to God."

By the mid-1770's, however, Rush had published against current abuse of spirits, which makes him close to a charter member of the club. As august, contentious and widely acquainted physician, he was unquestionably the first American to lend high medical prestige to the anti-Rum cause. As Presbyterian and highly placed sage—son-in-law of the patrician Stocktons of New Jersey, friend and correspondent of Jefferson, John Adams and other great names—he could command a hearing where worthy but less venerable sectarians like Quakers and Methodists could not. As one of the day's ablest lecturers and publicists, he originated or elaborated most of Temperance's best propaganda tricks. His bent for molding public opinion had already kept him continually in print on the organization of armies, though he had never been a soldier; the practice of swearing witnesses, though he was no lawyer; the design of hospitals, in which he was better

qualified—anything that roused his catholic interest, sometimes even including medicine. Most notably it was he who
moved Thomas Paine to write *Common Sense* and acted as
editorial adviser during its genesis. Obviously once this man
threw his gift of gab and sense of omniscience into the scale
the Demon Rum would never be the same again. Nor was he;
to this day much of the folklore and many clinical notions
about alcohol—even some sound ones—can be traced back to
this severe and often wrongheaded savant who predicted in
1788 that by 1915 a drunkard would be "as infamous as a lyar
or thief, and the use of spirits as uncommon in families as
. . . arsenic or . . . hemlock."

Even the best medicine was then ninety parts presumption
and bedside manner; nine parts rule-of-thumb experience;
and one part responsible knowledge. That was unavoidable:
Chemistry was still primitive, biology hardly existed, medieval or ancient Greek theories still dominated medical thinking, if that is the word. Rush gets only part of the blame for
the clinical outrageousness of his teachings. Yet it is clear that
he liked to throw his weight around among less imaginative
colleagues and was too fond of being an innovator or, failing
that, sponsor of others' innovations. That was fine when the
new idea happened to be Jenner's use of cowpox to inocu-
late against smallpox, or the assumption that all psychoses
have a somatic basis—to which, indeed, modern psychiatry is
tending to return. But his self-confidence was deplorable
when, just as eagerly, he recommended calamitous therapy:
horseback riding for the tuberculous, or heavy bleeding and
purging for yellow fever. He was specially proud of a patient
who survived both Yellow Jack and taking 150 grains of
calomel and losing over a gallon of blood in six days. Such
heroic treatment unquestionably killed some of the slightly
less robust who might otherwise have pulled through.

The only sound drug therapy in his *Inquiry* is its preference for daily doses of "Jesuits' bark" (quinine) to daily
alcoholic bitters against "intermittent fevers" (malaria).
Maybe the least sound advice therein is its recommendation
of opium instead of Rum to alleviate "spasmodic affections of
the stomach and bowels" because opium is *less likely than*

alcohol to lead to addiction. Rush also taught that men long exposed to wet and cold could ward off fevers by not only taking spirits internally but also by pouring half a pint of Rum into each boot. Science also owes to the *Inquiry* the curious notion that alcoholic excess so crisps the victim's hair that wigmakers find it useless. Nobody else inside or outside Rush's profession had any better grasp of medicine at the time, however, so his masterful pontificatings did as well as any to erode the treacherous old idea that strong drink was essentially strengthening, hence good for you by definition.

His attack was common-sensical: "Look at the horse; with every muscle of his body swelled from morning to night in the plow . . . does he make signs for a draft of toddy or a glass of spirits to enable him to cleave the ground or climb a hill? —No—he requires nothing but cold water and substantial food. There is no nourishment in ardent spirits." It would be several generations before biochemistry would learn enough to reverse this denial of the food value of alcohol. But Rush does deserve credit for being brilliantly right ahead of his time in calling drunkenness an "odious disease," describing its progressive stages with style as well as timeless accuracy:

> 1. Unusual garrulity. 2. Unusual silence. . . . 3. Captiousness and a disposition to Quarrel. 4. Uncommon good humour, and an insipid simpering, or laugh. 5. Profane swearing and cursing. 6. A disclosure of his own or other people's secrets. 7. A rude disposition to tell those persons in company whom they know, their faults. 8. Certain immodest actions . . . this sign of the first stage of drunkenness sometimes appears in women, who, when sober, are uniformly remarkable for chaste and decent manners. . . .

He also created the don't-spare-any-details technique that subsequent Temperance lecturers, some with medical degrees, many without, would borrow and perfect. He proclaimed that the "habitual use of ardent spirits" leads to poor appetite, liver obstruction, jaundice, dropsy, diabetes, plus "Rum-buds . . . fetid breath . . . disgusting belchings . . . Epilepsy, Gout . . . Madness. . . ." Nor could one fend off such troubles by avoiding overt drunkenness: Many "destroyed by spirits . . . were never completely intoxicated during the whole of their lives." How this came about was clear, as autopsy showed contractions of the fiber of stomach and bowels, abscesses, gangrenous spots in the viscera, ossification of the blood vessels and tendons. . . . It needed only the lecturer's pointer lingering lovingly on a brilliantly colored portrait of a hobnailed liver. Rush went on into the case of a certain Philadelphian of high standing who stuck to toddy for years but finally began to crave grog, presumably stronger; then "slings" of rum-and-water half-and-half; then straight rum; eventually even the strongest Jamaica was too light, and to get the kick he craved he had to add a tablespoonful of ground pepper, and "soon after died a martyr to his intemperance."

Sometimes that powerful imagination of Rush's was constructive, as when he invented the modern technique of conditioned association between alcohol and nausea: He tricked an alcoholic Negro patient into sneaking a shot of rum into which had been mixed a strong emetic, which "puked him to such a degree [that] he could not bear the sight or smell of spirits for two years afterwards." He was sound in advising alcoholics not to try tapering off. Instead they should stop spirits *"suddenly* and *entirely,"* and to bolster resolution for so drastic a step, take an oath of abstinence before a magistrate. But Rush also made the error of allowing such suddenly deprived topers plenty of beer and wine. This is disconcerting. If his experience with alcoholics really was as wide as he implied, he should have known that such indulgence would only bring many such cases back to spirits and destruction. In Rush's time, however, most anti-Demon agitators had only hard liquor in their sights.

He leaned heavily on Benezet in advocating banishment of Rum from harvest field and workshop, recommending instead water mixed with buttermilk, cider, beer, vinegar or brown sugar. But after making such good sense he soared into one of his most disconcerting notions, warning that no laborer should ever drink such mixtures while heated from work without first wetting his hands, firmly grasping the cup and waiting at least a full minute—which would draw off the excess body heat as contact with metal draws off electricity from a charged body. Yet by 1787, in spite of such absurdities, the movement to suppress the jug in the fence corner was spreading well in Pennsylvania and New Jersey. Two years later some 200 landowners and master craftsmen round Litchfield, Connecticut, agreed to keep Rum from their help to increase output and reduce rowdiness.

The *Inquiry* was republished in Boston in 1790. Within a generation it had seen at least six more editions. Thanks partly to Rush's habit of handing it out in the right places, it was widely read among firm-mouthed men with gold headed canes: doctors—some of divinity, others of medicine—judges, merchants, passing it from hand to hand in the principal towns and often on into upcountry settlements. In 1808 a copy thus reached a certain Dr. Billy James Clark in the village of Moreau, New York, in the rapidly developing region between Saratoga and Glens Falls. In spite of his Southern-sounding name, Dr. Clark was a Yankee born and reared. His father had combined farming with tavern-keeping at Pownal, Vermont, so his son had long known about the evils of drink in country places, and since Moreau was in apple country, no doubt had seen plenty more of it in his practice thereabouts.

One dark, cloudy evening in the spring of 1808 the Rev. Dr. Lebbeus Armstrong, pastor of the Congregational Church at Moreau, opened to an unexpected knock and admitted Dr. Clark, well spattered from riding three miles over deep clay roads. "Doctor Armstrong," he said, "I have come to see you on important business." Taking a proffered chair, he lifted his hands like Elijah before the priests of Baal and spake of how hotly he had caught fire from reading Rush's strictures on the Demon Rum. "We shall all become a community of drunkards in this town," he said, "unless something is done to arrest the progress of intemperance."

At least that, weather and all, is what Armstrong wrote of the visit many years later. According to an old-timer interviewed in 1918 whose parents had lived in Moreau, the actual occasion of Dr. Clark's alarm had been a drunken evening at the local tavern involving himself, Armstrong and a neighbor named Mott who drank so much that he had had a narrow squeak with death. There is nothing inherently too unlikely about the minister's having got drunk with the doctor at the local Sickle and Sheaf. Firsthand evidence is far preferable, however, so take it that Rush's *Inquiry* really was the immediate cause of the consequent meeting—at that same village tavern, by the way—that founded the Union Temperate Society of Moreau and Northumberland, its members pledged to drink no spirits, and wine at public dinners only.

Historians generally consider this the first permanent stone in the soon vast structure of American Temperance, for it lasted for generations in various forms and set many other communities going and doing likewise. The same impulse had already founded not dissimilar organizations elsewhere. In 1800, a Methodist named Micajah Pendleton persuaded some of his neighbors in the Shenandoah Valley to pledge abstention. In 1805, a schoolmaster named Benjamin Ely banded his friends in Simsbury, Connecticut, into an "Aquatic Society" that had nothing to do with boating but much with swearing off hard liquor. That same year Mrs. Maria Frelinghuysen Cornell, wife of that Presbyterian minister at Allentown, New Jersey, whose installation dinner saw so much good drinking, founded a "sober Society" pledging members against drinking at home.

All these sporadic candidates for first Temperance society soon petered out, however. Their significance lies mainly in the flavor of Reform-in-general that clings to them: Ely tried to get his fellow members to vote against local politicians known to be guilty of gambling or adultery, and to promise to read the Bible, go to church and stop swearing. Mrs. Cornell was also a pioneer in the Sunday school movement, and her much younger brother, whom she reared after their mother died, was Theodore Frelinghuysen, who became a sort of Pooh-Bah of righteous good causes as well as United States Senator and a candidate for Vice-President. The very strong-mindedness that led Mrs. Cornell to take the lead in a scheme involving both men and women was prophetic of much in Temperance history. But the significance of the

Moreau society lies in its founding principle. It seems never to have occurred to either Armstrong or Clark that for all the harsh things Rush's *Inquiry* said about hard liquor, it took no such sweeping position as that Clark hurled at Armstrong. Wrongheaded as Rush could be, he never assumed any such universal susceptibility to alcoholism. That the population of Moreau was headed for a collective drunkard's grave unless it swore off hard stuff was Clark's own frantic conclusion. And that statistical error, that terrified overstating of odds, created what was eventually not only Temperance but Prohibition.

The reformer . . . frequently so indiscriminate in his choice of causes, taking on all comers. . . .
—A. M. Schlesinger, *The American as Reformer*

Dr. Rush had busy ideas on not only drink and hospitals but also on tobacco (bad); Sunday schools and Bible reading (good); exercise (good); Negro slavery (bad); capital punishment (bad) and contemporary mistreatment of jailbirds as well as the insane (both bad). The most engaging thing I know about this amazing man is that in summer he sent watermelons to all inmates of Philadelphia jails as well as good Christmas dinners in winter, both at his own expense.

Benezet's range of interests was almost as wide and often coincided with Rush's. In this zeal to "reform," both the frenetic physician and the solicitous schoolmaster were very much leaders of their time and typical of it. For as the latter half of the eighteenth century took shape certain sanguine and conscientious men—and women—came deeply to believe in *doing something* about things. That habit of mind was specially lively in the English-speaking world. It had secular roots in new, social-minded philosophies in Britain and France; and religious roots in hope of protecting one's soul by saving one's brother's. It was felt that when Richard Roe, Esq., brutalized John Doe, he harmed his own soul and John's too as well as often his body; and—this was the nub of it—a third party failing to do everything possible to redeem the pair of them was also imperiling *his* by neglecting a plain Christian duty. That obliged one to take any and all means to change Richard's brutal shortcomings and John's ignorance and perversity.

Hence George III's England bubbled with attacks on one or another set of things-as-they-were-and-long-had-been. Callous treatment of debtors, criminals, women, seamen, chimney sweeps, factory hands, the insane, animals, children; slavery; the curse of drink; the related curses of pauperism, illiteracy, profanity and fornication; lack of public sanitation; heathenism among neglected slum dwellers at home as well as among overseas pagans; tight lacing for women. . . . Within a few decades all those and dozens of related matters were dragged squirming into the public eye as prelude to Reform of them with overt motives well summed up by Dr. John Jewett, an important early Temperance organizer. He called it "part of the duties of . . . every Christian, to wage a constant and uncompromising war on every demoralizing and destructive habit, custom or institution of [his] community. . . . We share the guilt of every wicked system existing within the sphere of our influence . . . which we do not study and perseveringly labor to annihilate." The principle is markedly Puritan but not ignoble. But, like other worthy principles, it is readily run into the ground.

Against each such iniquity there had to be created what E. S. Turner calls "the sense of urgency without which a reform can never reach the statute book." To work up the necessary public heat and light, British Reformers soon developed—indeed invented—a whole arsenal of public relations and lobbying techniques of a sort still indispensable to modern crusading movements. Abolition of the British slave trade was the first cause to employ the full orchestra: local committees and associations; special periodicals full of *ad hoc* propaganda; itinerant lecturers; women's auxiliaries; fund-raising festivals. . . . In the young United States imitative associations were soon distributing Bibles and trying to redeem "the lower orders" from pauperism and to reduce illiteracy, British style. In Temperance alone were the States ahead of Britain. What usually happened was that the mother country zeroed in on some crying need, then American Reformers, sniffing the new battle from afar and easily finding similar conditions at home, transplanted the new crusade. Whereas, when Temperance finally got under way in Britain, it was as an avowed and admiring imitation of the American movement. And lively though it was and remains, British Temperance never "took" as well, never succeeded in imposing even local-option style Prohibition on its public, let alone anything like the Eighteenth Amendment.

The reason may be that in England, Reform generally and Temperance particularly were liveliest among the "dissenting" religious sects—Quakers, Methodists, Congregationalists, Baptists, certain Presbyterians—with correspondingly meager support from the Church of England, which pretty much monopolized social prestige. Any "dissent" was low, smelling of factory hands, self-made cotton magnates and ironmasters with absurd accents, and gaunt hypocrites like Dickens's Mr. Stiggins. The only usable bridge, and it was narrow, was the "Evangelical" faction of the Church of England that hankered after Methodist emphasis on the Christian's need to further the salvation of others on pain of his own perdition. Where Dissent-sponsored Reform dealt with small special groups, often of low social standing themselves—prison-warders; or Jews stubbornly rejecting the New Testament; or overseas slave traders—it sometimes made progress in spite of the Establishment's contempt or hostility. But Temperance took the whole population, Tory squire as well as Mr. Gradgrind, for its province, which made the going much harder for prestige-poor minorities hoping to persuade John Bull that his punch or gin-and-water were both socially bad and morally evil.

In the States the shoe was distinctly on the other foot: Some of the same sects that the British Establishment looked down on dominated much of the American scene. Congregationalism was the semi-established, tax-supported core of New England and strong in upper New York State. Quakers and immigrant German sects dominated eastern Pennsylvania; Presbyterians were rife in the interior hills. Baptists and Methodists were gaining numbers all over the new nation. It is no accident that Temperance first took hold in Pennsylvania, thence all over the Northeast. The ministers of that area differed savagely on other points of doctrine but not on the high advisability of minding one's brother's moral business for one's own good in the next world as well as his, and among them their denominations represented power and prestige as no British Dissenters possibly could. Hence Temperance flourished to the point of saddling Prohibition on us. Sweet, in England anyway, were the uses of snobbery.

. . . not only have Reforms a sympathetic even if ill-understood relationship, but the *enemies* of Reforms are united by a free-masonry equally potent and comprehensive.
—HORACE GREELEY, *Recollections*

The problems of slavery, tight lacing and chimney sweeps are now pretty much defunct. Some of Reform's other targets have been greatly alleviated. The problem of drink has not. But it usefully exemplifies the cross-connections that so often tempt Reformers to espouse multiple good causes. The Demon Rum has been all too closely tied in with crime, slaving, whoring, bankruptcy (hence miserable debtors), unemployability (hence paupers), moral numbness (hence domestic heathenism). To reduce the Demon's scope would obviously reduce these other ills. Indeed, to sanguine minds it sometimes seemed that to get rid of the Demon altogether would wipe out the bulk of sin and misery. So those concerned with other vices would do well to lend a hand to Temperance. Thus, for instance, the American Tract Society, a pioneer in several fields of organized Reform, handed out many, many copies of Rush's *Inquiry,* and the Rev. Dr. Justin Edwards' *A Well-Conducted Farm,* a famous tract preaching that rum and agriculture don't mix.

Relations among good causes espoused by an individual or organization are not always necessarily logical. Reformers are temperamentally prone to deplore the present but yearn for The Good Time Coming when, once the Right People do enough of the Right Things, mankind will no longer torture and pollute one another in this life and damn themselves in the next. A gnawing need of reassurance about the essential worth of the world and its human tenants often involves such temperaments in glaringly unrelated crusades, just as an electric spark will jump to any of a wide range of metals. Otherwise why does the same Reformer so often go in for both Utopian economics and vegetarianism? And the bent of the Puritan mind encouraged this versatility. Heavenly sanctions for given reforms, a small part of our thinking now, were indispensable then. Our forebears' aim in setting up Sunday schools to teach the poor to read and write (their original purpose) was not to make more complete or abler persons of them but to enable them to read the Bible and the tracts that would steer them to salvation. The great points against slavery were that it often kept the slave from Christianity and usually hardened the hearts, hence imperiled the souls, of the masters.

Such habits of mind help to explain the apparent inconsistency of the early Reformers' embracing what now seem to us repressive as well as "liberal" causes. The Tappan brothers, silk merchants and eminent Reformers of New York City, gamely supported Abolitionism through thick and thin and fired any of their employees known to enter a theatre or barroom. Their British opposite numbers gave money and lent their names to the London Missionary Society to force floppy clothing on Tahitian women—and to Elizabeth Fry to promote decent treatment of women prisoners. The obscure connection, puzzling now but plain then, was the belief that both humaneness in jails and the discouragement of nakedness made the climate of this world more favorable to salvation. Only by realizing that that was a valid point a hundred years ago can we realize why Wendell Phillips, eminent Abolitionist and advocate of labor's and women's rights, was as hot for Temperance-*cum*-Prohibition as for any of those other causes.

Other kinds of cross-connection still lurk beneath modern espousals of causes, whether among the ADA or self-styled "Conservatives," for people still think—anyway get ideas—in clusters. Chances are good, for instance, that anybody attack-

ing the graduated income tax also thinks that MacArthur
should have been allowed to cross the Yalu; right-to-work
laws are a good thing; the South could have solved her Negro
problem if left alone; and there was something, exact nature
unstated, to be said for Trujillo. Chances are just as high that
anybody once convinced that the Chinese Communists were
simple agrarians still shrinks automatically from crossing
picket lines, whatever the merits of the dispute; and still considers slum clearance the sovereign remedy for juvenile de-
linquency. Flaws in these formulae are always refreshing and
sometimes identify persons at least trying to do their own
thinking. But in most cases the whole cluster will prove up,
like a disease unfolding symptom by symptom till it can be
clearly distinguished from other ailments—what doctors call a
"syndrome."

The Syndrome of Reform has always shown inner con-
sistency. That impulse to *do something* regardless is almost
omnipresent. So is the fallacy of *post hoc,* sometimes in the
form of guilt-by-association. But since Benezet's and Dr.
Rush's time the idea-content has shifted to match changes in
moral fashions, in the religio-socio-emotional assumptions
beneath the surface. The Temperance movement is now too
impossibly corny and naive for the liberal to stomach. But
from 1800 to 1860, say, when Temperance was making
straight the way for Prohibition, it shared the top rank of
good causes with Abolitionism and prison reform, well above
Women's Rights (including dress reform); diet reform (usually vegetarian in drift); the Peace Movement; hydropathy
(use of cold water as panacea); phrenology (deducing the
basic personality from the shape of the skull); spiritualism;
the rehabilitation of unmarried mothers and of prostitutes;
anti-tobaccoism. . . . Loosely marginal were strict Sunday
observance and cheap transatlantic postage.

Some stuck pretty much to one cause at a time, merely ap-
plauding others as they paraded by. Theodore Weld, for instance, began as an outstanding Temperance speaker and en-
thusiast about diet reform and the "manual labor" cult in
schools; but once Abolitionism came over him, he gave it all
his time and energy, keeping Graham crackers and teetotalism for his private life. Others kept extensive harems of

causes without apparent fear of spreading themselves too thin: Senator Frelinghuysen was simultaneously some kind of high officer in the American Tract Society, the American Bible Society, the American Temperance Union, the Sunday School Union, the Home Missionary Society and the Congressional Temperance Society. William Lloyd Garrison, now remembered only for his screamingly militant Abolitionism, was also distractingly active in spiritualism, anti-tobaccoism, Women's Rights and hydropathy. Gerrit Smith, greatest American landowner of his time, embraced practically everything except—so far as I can find—phrenology. With such widely involved men of affairs as Frelinghuysen and Smith the result was often what critics of the corporate system call "interlocking directorates." A given Reform society was almost sure to have at least one of the several Tappan brothers on its steering committee. Without the resulting innocent collusion the crusaders would have got in one another's way much more than they did.

Across-the-board acceptance of the whole Syndrome was not insisted on. A ratio of seven or eight out of ten available crusades was tolerated. Thus Horace Greeley, conspicuous editor of the great New York *Tribune,* swallowed most of it, cracked wheat included, but opposed votes-for-women. "Dr." Dio Lewis (of whom much more later) stopped short at Temperance, resisting the blandishments of Prohibition. Most Temperance stalwarts made up sizable bouquets from the above lists, however, and felt invaluably supported by the general conviction among Reformers that the war on the Demon was a prime Good Cause, as civilized as the best.

[Spirits are] anti-federal . . . companions of all those vices that are calculated to dishonor and enslave our country.
—Benjamin Rush, M.D. (1788)

The illiberal flavor of some of Temperance's sister-causes is less surprising when one learns that Reform in the new

United States began with goldheaded-cane overtones. To make the "lower orders" thriftier, more pious and less dissolute, well-placed men in Philadelphia, New York City and soon Boston organized and financed Societies for the Prevention of Pauperism, founded savings banks—originally aimed largely at the workingman—and fostered Home Missions, Sunday schools and Bible reading. And nothing did more to get Temperance airborne than the glib findings of early sociology—only the word did not yet exist—that the bulk of pauperism, prostitution, crime and so on could be blamed on drunkenness. Characteristically the Massachusetts Society for the Suppression of Intemperance of 1813 vowed war not only on Rum but also on the "kindred vices, profaneness and gambling" and urged members to "discourage . . . by . . . example and influence, every kind of . . . immorality."

The cause of Temperance in Connecticut very closely identified with the Federalist Party. John A. Krout, the definitive historian of early Temperance, points out that three members of the Society for the Suppression of Intemperance represented Massachusetts at the hot Federalist Hartford Convention that seriously considered New England's seceding from the Union in 1814–15. Later that same association in terms of Whigs/Democrats and then Republicans/Democrats hampered anti-Demon activities in New England and elsewhere. In the Federalist view, drunkenness tied in all too closely with the lower orders' dissolute recklessness in voting Federalists out of office, agitating for manhood suffrage, generally flouting their elders and betters, many with D.D. after their names, whom God had chosen to lead them in appropriate garments of broadcloth. Such political viciousness, it was felt, herded not only with drunkenness but also with irreligiousness; fecklessness on the job; lack of thrift; sexual immorality. When the Democrats took the lead in disestablishing the Congregational churches of Connecticut, Lyman Beecher described the elements responsible for that outrage as representing either jealous "minor sects" (meaning other than Congregational) or "Sabbath-breakers, rum-selling, tippling folk, infidels and ruff-scuff generally." It was the same tone he would use later in violent Catholic-baiting.

At first New England had somewhat lagged behind the Middle States in decrying the Demon. True, the Rev. Ebenezer Sparhawk (magnificent name!) of Templeton, Massachusetts, had preached against abuse of spirits in 1776. But not until 1800 did the Rev. Dr. Timothy Dwight, president of Yale—and another ardent Federalist—take up in his pulpit where Sparhawk had left off. Not until 1809 did Beecher, then a young minister in the Yankee-settled eastern end of Long Island, thunderously rehash Rush's *Inquiry* for his congregation. The yeast of local Temperance societies emulating Moreau's had already been working two years in New York State when the *Panoplist,* a conspicuous Boston religious paper, spoke out sharply against Rum.

Once the Yankee stream began to run, however, it was forceful. Hear the Rev. Dr. Nathaniel Prime of Long Island in 1811: "No better fuel can you afford the lusts of the flesh than ardent spirits—drunkenness and lewdness go hand in hand . . . few who have drunk a gill of ardent spirits can be exposed to . . . small temptation without becoming adulterers in the sight of God. . . ." And next year the Rev. Dr. Heman Humphrey, virtual founder of Amherst College and early patron of John Brown of Harpers Ferry: "Intemperate drinking is the highway to perdition . . . a fiery stream which empties into the bottomless pit. All who . . . embark on this flood, are in danger of hell fire." But since these reverend gentlemen failed to rule out spirits altogether, merely warned with rising vehemence against the hazards that they presented, they still left too much latitude for the overpliable conscience. It was another twelve years until Beecher, moved by the alcoholic death of a neighbor, warmed over his Long Island sermons, set them in a rich theological commentary on drunkenness, and launched his fateful *Six Sermons . . . on Intemperance* delivered in Litchfield in 1826.

They were fateful because they put his great authority behind "total abstinence" ("from spirits" is understood), the idea on which Temperance based its national appeal; and because he improved on Rush by calling any use whatever of spirits un-Christian: ". . . no man can use [spirits] prudently," he said, "or without mocking God can pray when using [them], 'lead us not into temptation.' There is no necessity for using [spirits] at all, and it is presumptuous to do so." None of this was exactly new. A pamphlet of 1819 had not only warned the public of New York against spirits but also ruled out wine as too dangerous to palter with. But this was Lyman Beecher! famous and redoubtable theologian, as conspicuous in his day as Harry Emerson Fosdick in ours. Thenceforward God was firmly aligned with the physician and the welfare worker (who existed long before acquiring his or her modern name) against the distilled form of the Demon.

An immediate result was the founding of an American Society for the Promotion of Temperance—the first interstate organization, though it remained largely a New England affair dominated by ministers sharing Beecher's raucous righteousness and mistrust of ruff-scuff, closely interlocked with foreign missions and tract and Bible societies. Note "Temperance" conspicuous in the title. The word unwarped still means prudent, non-extreme, "moderate as regards indulgence of appetite or passion."* The temperate man, properly so-called, can and usually does drink spirits moderately in civilized fashion. But Beecher, the roughshod spokesman for God, had proclaimed that no man can use spirits prudently, no Christian can do so without mocking God. In that case Temperance had to mean "total abstinence" from spirits, or so it seemed to those eager to retain the old connotations of the word as used in the old pleas for temperance in drinking. Presently this casuistry became official as the American Society for the Promotion of Temperance set it down:

"Temperance . . . is the moderate and proper use of things beneficial; and abstinence from things hurtful. Ardent spirits being . . . a poison . . . one of the things hurtful, and . . . the grand means of intoxication . . . abstain from the drinking, and . . . furnishing of [spirits], and . . . endeavor . . . to induce the whole community to do the same." Thenceforward, as the Society's pamphlets and lecturers

---

* *American College Dictionary.*

fanned out across the nation, as Yankee migrants filled up York State and the upper Old Northwest, as preachers took to regular sermons against the Demon, "Temperance" was more and more widely understood to mean "total abstinence from ardent spirits," which was represented as a positive virtue as well as a hypercautious piece of hygiene. A dubious dodge but excellent propaganda: It is simpler and easier to put across: "Don't do this at all, it's a sin *per se*," than to have to say: "Use the discretion God gave you in doing it; it's a sin if it gets too important to you."

The Rev. Dr. Justin Edwards, staff captain of the Society, described its purpose as to keep the temperate safely so while letting the already intemperate die off and rid the world of "an amazing evil." That cold-blooded approach, plus Dr. Clark's fear lest all Moreau go alcoholic, sums up the weaknesses of early Temperance's ideas. They assumed, as Krout points out, the naïve eighteenth-century doctrine of "the perfectibility of man," which relied on "intellectual appeals . . . to correct conduct and to elevate moral standards." Hence Temperance had only to impress on reasonable people "the effects of intemperance and the practicability of abstinence as a remedy . . . since sin was due to ignorance, knowledge would turn men from vice to virtue." And those too stupid or vicious to see the light could drink themselves to death and be damned to them—literally, for did not Scripture say that the drunkard could not enter into the Kingdom of Heaven?

The other wrong assumption was that, given unlimited access to spirits, almost anybody who liked booze at all was very likely to become a chronic drunkard. This was daily contradicted by the existing social picture, where, among those best able to afford unlimited spirits, alcoholics were a small minority. But it appealed strongly to chronic viewers-with-alarm, like Dr. Clark and Beecher's associates, and on the tactical side, it did much to foster a sense of urgency. It may have had ties to the Calvinist doctrine that the vast majority, evil by reason of original sin and not among those chosen by God's grace, are chronically wicked and so relatively helpless if exposed to temptations as great as the Demon unquestionably can exert.

That may also help to explain Temperance's early pessimism about alcoholics, taking it that few if any could ever be
reclaimed, and, supposing they could, their Demon-seared
souls would be so numb and withered it was hardly worth the
trouble. Souls, as strict Calvinism saw them, were either inevitably saved or inevitably damned and, though no man
could be sure which was which, God knew and always had
known. Similarly, women were either virtuous or lost; and
Temperance came to draw a rigid line between the total ab-
stainer and the person paltering with spirits; he was already a
little bit pregnant, as Temperance saw him, and the swelling
consequences would grow ever more scandalous:

"Mark that carbuncled, slavering, doubtful remnant of a
man," cried Dr. Humphrey, ". . . loathing his breakfast . . .
[drunk] before ten—quarreling by dinnertime, and snoring
drunk before supper. See him next morning at his retching
. . . and as the day advances, becoming noisy, cross, drivel-
ing, and intoxicated . . . dragging out months and years of
torture, till the earth refuses any longer to bear such a wretch
upon its surface." Drs. Humphrey, Edwards, Beecher and
Company preferred to write the existing drunks off and wage
what was essentially a preventive campaign.

The devices used to bully or cajole people into safeguard-
ing their souls and bodies by renouncing spirits were mostly
the same as those borrowed from Britain by other good
causes: traveling lectureres, usually parsons borrowing meetinghouses; so-called newspapers; local branch societies . . .
all parallel with Abolitionist and missionary activities. In
1833 a genuinely national convention in Philadelphia combined all local, state and regional Temperance organizations
into a United States Temperance Union, a name soon
changed to "American Temperance Union" to allow admission of Canadian societies. It could soon claim 5,000-odd local
societies in twenty-one out of twenty-three then existing
states, with more than a million members and, in spite of Dr.
Edwards, some 5,000 drunkards reformed. By 1835 it claimed
8,000 societies, 1,500,000 members and 4,000 distilleries put
out of business.

For better or worse, Temperance also had a tool that most

other Reforms lacked—the individual pledge. That had personal impact. Adherents to foreign missions, say, had only to hand over a few dollars a year, part of which brought them one of the cause's "newspapers," and attend meetings where speakers said the same things over and over about the need for clothing cannibals. Only a small, overzealous minority was personally involved in the good work in steamy, fever-ridden Borrioboola Gha. The signer of a Temperance pledge, however, had to renounce that hot flip on a cold night; pass up the tavern as he started home from town after selling his load of corn; or, if he went in, stick to cider, of which he got plenty at home. No doubt this was easier for the parson, who led a life apart anyway, and for most women, who stayed home more than their menfolk. But in view of how deeply the Demon was imbedded in American life when Temperance came along, it speaks well for the moral courage of our forebears that so many pledges were obtained and, though backslidings and hypocrisies were naturally rife, faithfully kept in so many instances. Where the newly pledged owned small distilleries or sold spirits in general stores, signing meant real economic sacrifice. It deprived everybody of an important feature of weddings, funerals and other occasions that meant a very great deal in your great-grandfather's relatively isolated life. Many an early signer was probably an ascetic-minded self-glorifier like young William Lloyd Garrison. But the same ranks making and keeping the same solemn promise also included young Abraham Lincoln.

"There is some sneaking Temperance Society movement about this business!"
—*Moby Dick*, LXXII

As the Anti-Saloon League's power grew after 1900 many politicians were justly accused of embracing the cause if not the practice of Temperance to curry favor with the voters back home in Buncombe County. In the early 1830's, when Temperance still smelled strongly of anti-Jeffersonism, to espouse Temperance might repel more voters than it attracted. Yet in 1831, the Rev. Dr. Edwards, Federalist record and all, was invited to address a Democrat-dominated Congress on the curse of Rum. Soon afterward the Rev. John Marsh, Yankee traveling "agent" (that is, organizer-propagandist) of the Baltimore Temperance Society, had generous Congressional support in getting up a great Temperance powwow in Washington. Lewis Cass, Secretary of War and a chronic teetotaler, presided. Among the speakers were Senators Frelinghuysen and Grundy aforesaid; and Daniel Webster, who offered an endorsing resolution. Ex-President John Quincy Adams (elected to the House after his defeat in 1828) attended and afterwards personally thanked Representative Bates of Massachusetts for the elegance of his speech. It was all bipartisan and intersectional: maybe a few more Whigs than Democrats but plenty of both; maybe a slight preponderance of New England and the Middle Atlantic States but not far off balance—average age forty-six, meaning men reared and come of age by 1806, well before Temperance was well organized. It is clear that, even after proper discount for politicians' love of speechifying, these men's main purpose was to stand up and be counted on a matter vital to the public good.

Next year much the same cast founded a permanent Congressional Temperance Society, its purpose "By example and kind moral influence to discountenance the use of ardent spirits and the traffic in it," with, please note, no hint of projected legislation. The first meeting heard a momentous lecture by Dr. Thomas Sewall, Professor of Anatomy and Physiology at the Columbian College, Washington, D.C., built around gaudy drawings of the human organs in various stages of damage due to drink. These were startling enough when reproduced in Temperance tracts with the feeble coloring then available to printers. The originals, allegedly based on Dr. William Beaumont's famous studies of what went on inside a patient with a never-healing hole in his stomach, must have sent the assembled statesmen away with whole larderfuls of food for thought. Dr. Sewall seems to have begun with how the network of blood vessels in the stomach lining distends when stimulated by alcohol; he went on to show the lining of the chronic drunkard's stomach with blood vessels so distended that "the most minute vessels [were] visible to the eye, like rum blossoms on the drinker's face [and] maintain their unnatural size even after death"; and ended by displaying (and lengthily describing) the stomach of a man dying of DTs as containing a lot of "dark fluid resembling coffee grounds" with the lining mahogany red in some areas, in others "quite black, as if in a state of incipient mortification."

Thus to alarm the statesmen present was advisable, many felt, because politicians of that day, as of ours, often kept their drinking well abreast of that of their constituents. Representative Henry A. Wise, eventually governor of Virginia and an able Confederate general, warned the Maryland State Temperance Society that certain highly placed federal executives were "Habitually affected by ardent spirits, drunk at least once a week," and that the houses of Congress so seldom resumed sittings after dinner because "too many members were unfit for public duty." Two years before, Wise had been one of three young Representatives—the others were E. C. Hannegan, eventual alcoholic murderer of his brother-in-law; and Franklin Pierce, eventual President of the United States—drunk in a box in a Washington theatre and thrown out when Hannegan drew a pistol on an Army officer whom he disliked. Nobody denied that the General Conference of the Methodist Church had good reason to say that "a large portion . . . of the most important and responsible business of the nation is often transacted under . . . a greater or lesser degree of alcoholic excitement." And as late as 1850 young Benjamin Harrison, son of a President and fated to be one himself, who had certainly been in a position to observe politicians from infancy, cited it in a college debate as taken for granted that "most of our public men drink, many to excess."

Surges of Temperance-mindedness among Congressmen inevitably splashed other federal institutions involving the Demon, notably the armed services. Thanks to the old notions about strength and disease prevention, Army and Navy

were still issuing daily spirit-rations, usually rum in the
Navy, whiskey in the Army, in two- to four-ounce tots depending on current regulations, in the morning when it was
worse for the men's viscera as well as for their efficiency later
in the day. By the late 1820's, Temperance ideas influenced
the War Department to look into whether this slight daily
fuddling was as advisable as had always been assumed. Reports from thoughtful officers, some medical, some in the line,
suggested that a grave proportion of the desertions always
plaguing Uncle Sam's small but indispensable Army came of
drink, for the Demon not only prompted privates to mis-
behave but also made sergeants unbearable. Certainly few
modern company officers would care to see four ounces of
whiskey poured into each man as a daily preliminary to duty.
In 1830, John Eaton, Jackson's Secretary of War, abolished
the Army ration, giving each man a few cents cash daily as
compensation. In 1832, Lewis Cass, his teetotaling successor,
substituted generous issues of coffee and sugar for the compensation. The "fatigue ration" to alleviate the results of
special exposure or the strains of combat was not affected.

Some officers had already tried to prepare the men for losing the ration by persuading them that they were better off
without it, setting up voluntary Temperance societies pledging them against drink even at their own ill-paid expense.
One such well-meaning zealot in epaulets reported to the
American Temperance Society that three-fourths of the garrison at his post had signed up; in the first six weeks no member had seen the inside of the guardhouse and only two non-
members had; whereas the outfit's previous rate of such epi-
sodes had been three a day. The men read aloud Temperance
tracts and their own essays on Temperance at fortnightly
meetings . . . It doesn't sound much like what one hears of
the Old Army. But maybe exactly the right C.O. could make
it stick for a while and certainly, tracts or not, the men were
better off without that morning jolt.

At much the same time the Navy allowed men refusing the
daily grog ration six cents a day compensation, and a number
of their officers did their best to encourage them to do so. To

genuine Temperance sentiment they often added a suspicion that without grog the hands would not need so many of the floggings that disgraced the discipline of the day. Thus the commander of U.S.S. *North Carolina* reported in 1839 that little punishment and not a single court-martial had occurred during her long cruise in the Pacific, largely, he thought, because 400-odd of the ship's company had commuted the grog ration throughout. Commodores James Biddle, Charles Wilkes and Thomas ap Catesby Jones were historically distinguished officers publicly deploring the grog tub. Commander Andrew H. Foote, later to show what gunboats could do on the western waters in the Civil War, encouraged pledge-signing in his ships. The Brooklyn Navy Yard was notable for hundreds of bluejackets signing the pledge before shipping out. A feature of Boston's great Temperance parade of 1845 was the band and complete complement of U.S.S. *Ohio,* receiving ship of the Charlestown Navy Yard. When the crack U.S.S. *Brandywine* visited India in 1844, so many of her men were pledged teetotalers that the British port officers said she should change her name. . . .

Even earlier Temperance had boarded merchant vessels, where grog rations were also traditional, often as part of the effort to get Mercantile Jack a better break afloat as well as ashore. John Nathaniel Barbour, teetotal Boston shipowner, forbade all alcoholic drink on board even as cargo, yet prospered and apparently had no trouble getting crews. By 1830, the American Temperance Society boasted of over 400 Boston ships at sea with no spirits aboard; and of 168 whalers out of 186 registered from New Bedford, Massachusetts, equally dry. Presently New York underwriters reduced premiums 5 per cent on vessels whose officers swore, on making home port, that none on board had had ardent spirits during the voyage. Melville seems to have been well within the probabilities when he had Aunt Charity ordering the steward of the *Pequod* to substitute ginger-and-water for rum for exhausted harpooners.

The queerest note was a report to the American Temperance Union in 1844 that Temperance pledge-campaigns among Erie Canal boatmen had petered out, "for none are left to sign." On the Erie Canal, rowdiest and frowsiest of waterborne worlds! That is as hard to believe as, say, that the Salvation Army had pledged everybody on San Francisco's Barbary Coast to vows of poverty and chastity.

3

THE CRIME OF
MODERATION

Many will not allow men and women to dance together, because it is a provocation to lust; they may as well forbid the
drinking of wine, for that it makes some men drunk.
—ROBERT BURTON, *Anatomy of Melancholy*

Dr. Rush sometimes sounded like an inexperienced convivialist: His *Inquiry* laid it down that fermented drinks contain so little alcohol that few can absorb them to the point of intoxication without "exciting a disrelish to their taste, or pain from their distending the stomach. They are, moreover," he went on, deviating into sense, "when taken in moderate quantity, generally innocent, and often have a friendly influence upon life and health." Obviously he took too little account of the way his gentle-manly contemporaries got falling-down drunk on port or Madeira, even on wines as low in alcoholic content as red Bordeaux. In thus belittling the virgin products of fermentation he forgot that Noah and Lot knew not distilling but got scandalously drunk all the same; that Bacchus, god of inebriety, knew only wine; that Flemish paintings often show boors staggeringly full of beer; and that the chronic cider-drunk was a principal nuisance in rural New England.

This doctrine that fermented drinks are the innocent sheep and spirits the noxious goats arose early as the sober-minded saw how spirits made men behave and concluded that wine, beer and so on were not only more familiar but probably safer. English Methodism's denunciations of spirits—beer and wine implicitly exempted for a while—had begun in 1749 though with small effect in the Colonies till after the Revolution. Seventeen years earlier those founding the new colony of Georgia had, as previously noted, banned spirits to "prevent the pernicious effects of drinking Rum" among settlers whose past careers had often exhibited those very effects. (Dr. Stephen Hales, one of the Georgia trustees and author of *A Friendly Admonition to the Drinkers of Brandy,* sought to interest English landowners in anti-spirits legislation because hard drinkers of hard stuff lost their appetites, hence consumed less farm produce.) But Savannah was soon full of illegal tippling shops, and in no time the ancestors of Tyrus Raymond Cobb and Scarlett O'Hara were praying for leave to legalize spirits on the usual grounds that the water was intolerable straight and on the original plea that Georgian traders among the Indians were losing out to South Carolinian traders allowed to deal in Rum. The trustees soon gave in, but their effort at partial prohibition had shown how some minds were already running.

Commonsense mistrust of spirits was bolstered by the snobbery that committed Colonial as well as metropolitan gentry to wine because distilled stuff was cheap and popular among the masses. The cultural newness of spirits may also have played a part: In Rush's time they had been in common use hardly a century; whereas wine, beer and so on had millennia of tradition behind them. Indeed some held that spirits, which require artificial processing, were less "natural," hence less wholesome than fermented drinks. In the nineteenth century this doctrine of naturalness acquired a "scientific" basis: It was maintained that alcohol, by then known to be the dangerous ingredient, was actually created by the process of distilling; whereas merely its "elements," not yet fused into actual alcohol, were present in wine and beer. Better methods of extracting alcohol from solution spoiled that comforting theory, but meanwhile it supported the delusion that Rush did so much to foster. True, he once casually advised "simple water" for those working hard in warm weather; but was soon lamenting that the United States still lacked grape culture serious enough to supply native wines as drunk among the "sober and healthy French peasantry"—he had never visited France—and suggested improving cider by boiling apple juice to half its bulk before fermentation and keeping it two years or so in cask. The end-product, quite contrary to his purpose, must have been fairly powerful.

These misconceptions—that drunkenness is no great problem in wine-committed countries; that it is difficult to get seriously drunk on anything but spirits; that the alcohol in spirits is somehow more sinister than that in undistilled tipples—still survive to hamper those recommending moderation in all drinking, whether of beer, Burgundy or brandy. Consider the light-wines-and-beer laws of such states as Virginia, the once punch- and toddy-minded Old Dominion herself, which allows nothing stronger than wine to be drunk in public even in the laboriously restored taverns of Williamsburg. Actually, of course, such efforts to take the spirits drinker into winebibbing tend to develop the "wino" type of alcoholic—and the wine type of hangover, once ably described as feeling like rheumatism in every hair of your head.

Five generations ago this casting of spirits as exclusive villain had another result: As its unsoundness became glaringly evident it led Temperance to despair of all efforts at moderation and to damn fermented and distilled drinks alike—which created the higher, also unrealistic and most immoderate position of flat Teetotalism.* No doubt temperamental aversion to all conviviality encouraged such raising of the movement's sights. But as Temperance learned more about the Demon many of the less ascetic-minded, who had once considered the budding American wine industry a good influence, joined the hue and cry after alcohol in any form, in any dilution. By 1789, John Wesley had enlarged his taboo to cover wine. During the 1820's the "new pledge" renouncing any and all drinks containing alcohol came into use in local Temperance societies among specially zealous or shaky members. In 1831 the Pennsylvania Society for Discouraging the Use of Ardent Spirits banned fermented drinks as well. Over the next four years the state Temperance organizations of Mississippi, Vermont, Kentucky and New York did the same. In 1836, a national meeting settling this and other

---

* The word has rival derivations: in 1818 a Temperance society in Hector, N.Y., began to urge pledgees to abstain from all fermented as well as distilled drinks to supplement previous pledges applying only to spirits; the secretary set "T" for total beside the names of members taking the new form. *Or:* In 1833 a stammering member of a Temperance meeting in Preston, England, was insisting that the pledge cover fermented drinks: ". . . we can't keep 'em sober unless we have the pledge total; yes, Mr. Chairman, tee-tee-total." (*Cf.*, Gough, *Platform Echoes*, p. 550; and *Standard Encyclopedia of the Alcohol Problem*, "Teetotal.")

loose-end issues created the American Temperance Union—
a new broom sweeping clean as successor to the United States
Temperance Union—which cautiously but definitely raised
the uncompromising New Pledge to the status of nationwide
policy.

That was momentous. First Temperance had been a virtue, as Christianity and sober pagans too had recommended
it; a dignified, individual self-control that excluded neither
common sense nor frequent enjoyment of alcoholic drinks.
Then they applied the word to the content of the Old Pledge
—total abstinence from ardent spirits. At that point "Temperance" ceased to mean a virtue and was incorrectly applied
to a taboo. Then the taboo was extended to cover fermented
drinks too, the name "Temperance" remaining in an even
more misleading fashion. From the propagandist's point of
view the zealots did well to keep it: "Temperance" maintained a borrowed flavor of virtue around a rigid, apprehensive, categorical, responsibility-avoiding denial. It usually
means something important when a word thus expands its
areas of impact without a matching change in itself. Thus
presently the noisome connotations already smeared over the
Demon Rum rubbed off on his pre-distilling ancestors. Dr.
Oliver Wendell Holmes was understandably testy when a fellow boarder asking "Whether I went in for rum as a steady
thing?" had in mind hock and Hermitage as well as the raw,
hard stuff that Medford, Massachusetts, distilled for West Africa.

That use of "rum" as abusive blanket term for everything
from lager beer to ouzou was well established when Holmes
wrote.* It came from the prevalence of rum among hard
liquors of the Colonial period when Temperance was born
and the primacy of spirits (generically Rum) in the Temperance mind during the movement's adolescence. (In Britain,
gin had much the same history though not so sweepingly.)
By the time Temperance went teetotal, whiskey was actually
the nation's dominant spirits and eventually almost com-

---

* *A Dictionary of Americanisms* quotes the New York *Tribune* in 1855:
"The legislature is heavily Democratic and Rum" three years before Holmes.
The usage is certainly much older: consider Danforth, *An Alarm to the
Citizens of Washington* in 1830: "[the drunkard] would walk before an ex-
ploding canon . . . rather than not obtain Rum."

pletely monopolized shirtsleeve drinkers. Toward the end of the century, George Ade observed, gin was confined largely to cocktails, which were called for only in fancy places, and rum was "merely a guaranteed remedy for bronchitis." "Rum" is, however, a fine, short, disreputable-sounding syllable, admirable for rhetorical uses: "Hail, mighty Rum!" sang Samuel Smith, a Temperance bard who obviously admired Byron,

> . . . and by this general name
> I call each species—whiskey, gin or brandy:
> (The kinds are various—but th'effect's the same,
> And so I choose a name that's short and handy;
> For, reader, know, it takes a deal of time
> To make a crooked word lie smooth in rhyme. . . .
> Hail, mighty Rum! to thee the wretched fly,
> And find a sweet oblivion of their woes;
> Lock'd in thy arms, as in the grave, they lie—
> Forget their kindred—and forget their foes.
> And Lethe's stream (so much extolled by some
> In ancient times) I shrewdly guess was Rum. . . .

Whatever spirits actually filled the shotglass, the Demon Rum, horrendously taking shape out of the bottle to personify the underlying evil of drink, was handy for Temperance orators to evoke, apostrophize and defy. Since it was invaluable, the word stuck. In Temperance lore the saloonkeeper, though dealing largely in beer and whiskey, remained a "rumseller"; the splotch on the tosspot's nose was popularly a "rum blossom"; and when, during Prohibition, the ships hove to to discharge their whiskey and gin, their anchorage was "Rum Row," their crews "rumrunners."

Cider is the devil's kindling-wood.
—HENRY A. REYNOLDS, M.D.

The new teetotal Temperance wrought a minor cultural revolution. Thenceforth the kind of people who read Tem-

perance papers and valued Temperance hymns and sermons
had to regard a single sip of Grandma's elderberry wine as a
trafficking with the devil as heinous as if it were moonshine
whiskey; and the last rag of respectability was stripped from
cider. Indeed, what made Dr. Charles Jewett of Rhode Island
into a crusading teetotaler of formidable talents was seeing
how wild a local farmer got on a barrel of cider sold him by
the doctor. Its content of malic acid was alleged to have dis-
abled another cider-addicted farmer with partial palsy. A
family in Northampton, Massachusetts, drank some fifty barrels of cider over the winter; by May the lady of the house
had died of fits, so had the youngest son; the eldest son had
them bad but lived; the old man was seeing snakes regularly
and had developed a disconcerting habit of getting up in the
middle of the night and running round the house hollering
"Fire!" Harrison's rowdy hard-cider presidential campaign of
1840 was blamed for leaving many new alcoholics in its wake.
A man who killed a girl in Rochester, New York, confessed
that it had taken swilling hard cider in the cellar to nerve
him to it. . . .

Since apple juice insisted on fermenting to the sneaky delight of sinners and the enticement of the unwary, the Sons of
Temperance outlawed even the cider press because it was so
difficult to determine when "fermentation has progressed far
enough to be a dangerous beverage." A rival Temperance
lodge, the Good Templars, took the more moderate stand
that the brothers could make cider if it was used strictly for
vinegar and apple butter. But the Temperance ladies of
Chester County, Pennsylvania, made it clear in 1848 that
"whoever . . . drinks even the sweet cider weakens his own
moral strength, becomes a tempter to the weak, and casts
away the pure influence of an unsullied example."

No more heady odors down-cellar as the clustered barrels
sighed forth recollections of autumn; no more tingle of CO_2
as the cool stuff slipped down the throat. Though some farmers tried to fatten cattle on the apples that no longer went to
the cider press—which must have afflicted many unhappy
cows with colic—the family orchard's economic standing was
badly shaken. One New Hampshire farmer of strong Tem-

perance principles took the ax to his apple trees to spare others the temptation that their windfalls represented, and the Old Oaken Bucket stood primly victorious on the music rack of the parlor melodeon.

O, water for me! bright water for me,
And wine for the tremulous debauchee. . . .
McGuffey's New Eclectic Speaker (1858)

Beer would soon begin a flourishing second career in America in the form of German lager brewed by immigrants whose Teutonic names still dominate our brewing. Round Cincinnati, relying on other Germans from the wine districts of the Vaterland, philanthropic Nicholas Longworth, hoping to woo Americans away from hard stuff, was founding the first considerable American wine industry. European visitors called his "Sparkling Catawba" equal to many champagnes, and local Germans actually paid more for his hock than for the genuine imported because they liked it better. Temperance deplored both beer and wine, however. Horace Greeley likened any moderating trend toward beer or wine instead of spirits to "the casting out of big devils by . . . little ones." The Rev. John Jewett prayed: "May God . . . send blasting and mildew on the products of every acre of American soil . . . devoted to the production of intoxicating wines. . . ." And Lucius Manlius Sargent, the cultivated Bostonian classicist who wrote some of Temperance's best early propaganda, advised schools and colleges to cut all references to wine drinking out of their Greek and Latin texts, just as they had already bowdlerized Catullus and Lucretius lest the young gentlemen get lewd ideas in their heads.

Now that alcohol in whatever dilution was all horns and tail, the new Satan needed a St. Michael as foil. Temperance found one: Water—the colorless, weakening stuff of which Grandfather had fought as shy as if anticipating W. C. Fields. The presses clanked and the lecturers spouted with pumped-up praises of water rather more extravagant than any Bacchantes' praise of wine. Gushing fountains infested the illustrations of Temperance books. Local or state periodicals of the pledge-seeking organizations of the 1840's were called the New York *Crystal Foundation,* the White Mountain *Torrent,* the Taunton, Mass., *Weekly Cataract,* the Worcester, Mass., *Waterfall,* the Fitchburg, Mass., *Cold Water Cup*—anything associated with fresh water. Even Nathaniel Hawthorne committed a drippy Temperance-slanted panegyric of water in a magazine piece, "Rills from the Town Pump." Inaugural ceremonies for the sanitary water systems that were built in the 1840's usually involved Temperance powwows, partly from association and partly because, as the head of New York City's Water Commission pointed out, the new facilities would spoil the poor man's "apology for mixing brandy and rum with water—that of making it drinkable." Pallidly the guests at such occasions and at Temperance dinners toasted one another in water and trolled out some such song as:

> All hail! ye friends of temperance,
>   Who're gathered here tonight, sirs,
> To celebrate the praises of
>   Cold water, pure and bright, sirs . . .
> For great reforms are going on,
>   'Mong every rank and station,
> And better days are dawning on
>   The rising generation.
> Though Alcohol has had his day
>   And great has been his slaughter,
> He's now retreating in dismay,
>   And victory crowns cold water. . . .

All this emphasis on *cold* water is curious. Apparently it was assumed that to take the chill off would damage its mystic virgin virtue; which, come to think of it, may have tied in with the concurrent popularity of that already mentioned cult of "hydropathy" that cured most mortal ills by such sopping tortures as wrapping the patient in sheets wrung out in cold water and playing a cold-water hose on him.

Most Temperance speeches and sermons came to include

both the most severe Scriptural strictures on wine and a florid tribute to Water often borrowed wholly or partly from a rhapsody attributed to a Methodist missionary, Paul Denton, holding forth at a place called Double Spring Grove in Texas. He had advertised the occasion as "a good barbecue, better liquors and the best Gospel." Taking the bait, a local rowdy asked where the liquor was. Denton pointed toward the springs that gave the grove its name and let him have both barrels:

"There! There is the liquor which God the Eternal brews for all His children! Not in the simmering still over smoking fires, choked with poisonous gases and surrounded with the stench of sickening odors and rank corruption doth your Heavenly Father prepare the precious essence of life, pure cold water; but in the green glade and grassy dell where the red deer wanders and the child loves to play. . . . No poison bubbles on its brink; its foam brings not madness and murder; no blood stains its liquid glass; pale widows and starving orphans weep not burning tears into its clear depths; no drunkard's shrieking ghost from the grave curses it in words of despair . . . would you exchange it for the demon's drink, alcohol?" And "a shout like the roar of the tempest answered, 'No! No!' "

Those old enough to recall such gems of old-time spellbinding as Senator Vest's celebrated eulogy of the dog will be able to believe that many of our forebears found that sort of thing impressive. The young must just take my word for it that in the old folks' ears it did not sound as ridiculous back then.

Come! fill a fresh bumper,—for why should we go
     logwood
While the ~~nectar~~ still reddens our cups as they flow!
     decoction
Pour out the ~~rich juices~~ still bright with the sun,
       dye-stuff
Till o'er the brimmed crystal the ~~rubies~~ shall run.

half-ripened apples
The ~~purple-globed clusters~~ their life-dews have bled;
taste   sugar of lead
How sweet is the ~~breath~~ of the ~~fragrance they shed!~~
rank poisons   wines ! ! !
For summer's ~~last roses~~ lie hid in the ~~wines~~
stable-boys smoking long-nines.
That were garnered by ~~maidens who laughed through the vines~~
scowl   howl·   scoff   sneer
Then a ~~smile,~~ and a ~~glass,~~ and a ~~toast,~~ and a ~~cheer,~~
strychnine and whiskey, and ratsbane and beer
For all the ~~good wine, and we've some of it here~~

In cellar, in pantry, in attic, in hall,
Down, down, with the tyrant that masters us all!
~~Long live the gay servant that laughs for us all!~~

—OLIVER WENDELL HOLMES,
The Autocrat of the Breakfast Table

Those were the "slight alterations," Dr. Holmes told his readers, made in verses that he had written for a banquet unaware that it was to be a teetotal occasion. In 1857 they were a good if elaborate joke; now they are significant history. For Temperance dwelt on *pure* (as well as *cold*) water in the belief that besides being unwholesome at best, most fermented drinks were polluted or dangerously spurious. Those revisions of Holmes' bacchanale were no exaggeration of what the Demon's enemies had long been saying about wines. And there seems to have been something in their pious outcry impugning the ancestry and purity of what passed for wine in a good many places.

In the 1850's the New York *Tribune* averred that of 13,000 bottles of "wine" annually sold in a certain New York sporting house, fewer than 1,000 had any grape in them. Captain Marryat, the astringent British author-sailor who admired few things American, thought "Jersey champagne" made of turnips, brandy and honey was "a very good imitation" but hardly genuine. John B. Gough, Temperance lecturer supreme, who liked to dwell on "champagne" made of carbonated hard cider and sold in fake French hampers with forged customs markings, had a daunting tale of a man accidentally stepping into the slush coming from a factory producing the stuff "and . . . his boots were burnt." Horace Greeley gravely listed poisons used to doctor or fake wines:

sugar of lead, opium, henbane, vitriol, arsenic. . . . To clarify spurious port "a preparation of fish and sulphuric acid" was used, said the *Temperance Advocate and Family Visitor*. And a retired Philadelphia wine merchant had assured a parson friend of Dr. Armstrong, of Moreau Temperance Society fame, that the Madeira he sold got its prized "nutty" flavor from having cockroaches dissolved in it.

Obviously much of that was just irresponsible slander in the good cause. But Temperance could show awkwardly numerous trade manuals telling vintners how to use logwood (a red vegetable dye), cayenne pepper, caramel and odd herbs to make several bottles of sherry grow where only one had landed from Spain; even how to get a fair imitation of sherry from neutral grain spirits, water and no grape products at all. There were no food-and-drug acts then, and customers who really knew wine were probably as scarce as now, so no doubt such frauds were common. The art of faking familiar alcoholic drinks was well known long before the bootlegger of the 1920's needed it—at least since Addison had written in 1709 of the London vintners who made Bordeaux from sloes and champagne from apples with "great injury not only to her Majesty's customs but to the bodies of many of her good subjects." Actually, supposing sound alcohol used, the faked wines that Temperance so scorned *in terrorem* probably did no special harm. Neutral spirits colored with caramel, flavored with herbs and diluted to 20 percent with water is probably a slightly more wholesome drink than genuine sherry. In 1850, however, neither Temperance zealots nor winebibbers knew that, so neither can be blamed for considering authenticity healthier.

A second club to beat the wine Demon with was ready at hand in the American preference for highly alcoholic "fortified wines"—champagne, sherry, Madeira—and neglect of the much milder table wines sold without being spiked with added alcohol. The American drinker sometimes tried to excuse that by saying that unfortified wines did not "travel well" across the Atlantic. That made little sense even in those days of long and rough westward voyages. André Simon of the Wine & Food Society assures me that French table wines, if shipped "young," would not only have stood it well but arrived nicely "aged." The best American hotels consistently listed both Bordeaux and Rhine wines, and Britons who took wine seriously, such as Thackeray and "Bull Run" Russell, were delighted with some of the Bordeaux they met in the States in the mid-century. So the high popularity of fortified wines running 19 percent alcohol over those of excellent quality running from 7 percent to 14 percent meant just what Temperance thought: the American winebibber was drinking not for subtleties of bouquet and body but for kick combined with the prestige of ordering something imported and expensive.

Nor did Temperance miss the opportunity to deplore the process of "fortifying" with added brandy as subtly unwholesome "adulteration." Consider the verses in which Henry Wadsworth Longfellow decried imported wines in order to praise Ohio's Sparkling Catawba:

> Drugged is their juice for foreign use
>   When shipped o'er the reeling Atlantic,
> To rack in brains with the fever pains
>   That have driven the Old World frantic.
>
> To the sewers and sinks with all such drinks
>   And after them tumble the mixes;
> For a poison malign is all such wine,
>   Or at best but a Devil's Elixir. . . .

The best way to account for such doggerel from a professional poet of high skill in prosody is to assume that when he wrote it he was already well into the second bottle of the case sent him by Nicholas Longworth.

> Some love strong beer, and the maniac's cheer,
>   And the bacchanalian's glee;
> But the gurgling rill, from the rock-bound hill,
>   And a peaceful home for me!
>   —*The Temperance Musician.*

Beer was soon under heavier attack than either cider or wine. Already in 1826 Lyman Beecher was saying that its only virtue lay in giving its victims "more of the good-natured stupidity of the idiot and less of the demoniac frenzy of the madman." Dr. Henry A. Reynolds, founder of the Red Ribbon pledge-cult of the 1870's, averred, with the authority of a genuine medical graduate of Harvard, that lager beer, "the great evil of the West," killed more quickly than bad spirits. At best, said Temperance consistently, beer too often cajoled the drinker into upgrading himself to hard stuff like a marijuana smoker moving on into a heroin habit. And there was much quotation of august physicians, such as London's Sir Astley Cooper, who considered beer itself the highroad to death on the gallows or in bed, one of the two almost inevitable. Beer drinkers stricken with disease had abnormally small chance to recover, he said. And though spirits drinkers often murdered in drunken passion, the beer drinker was your cold-blooded killer seeking gain, often disproportionately small. The beer drinker's children too were particularly prone to hereditary handicaps partly because beer has a certain "animalizing tendency," partly because (in England anyway) women also often drink beer, which doubled the genetic hazard. Such talk helps to explain the Temperance song, "Plow Up Your Hops!" that urged Yankees to abandon that minor but convenient cash-crop because to supply the brewer's needs was to play the Devil's game.

Wine was often a fraud, Temperance further taught, but beer! It was loaded with stupefying drugs to supplement its low alcoholic content. Elaborating on that, the Rev. George B. Cheever, entering on a lifetime of intemperate Temperance propaganda, produced "Deacon Jones' Brewery," a satire on brewers including a parody of *Macbeth*'s witches:

> Round about the cauldron go,
> In the poisoned entrails throw.
> Drugs that in the coldest veins
> Shoot incessant fiery pains;
> Herbs that, brought from Hell's back door,
> Do its business slow and sure . . .
> Dropsies, agues, fierce catarrhs,
> Pestilential inward wars,
> Fevers, gouts, convulsive starts,

Racking spasms in vital parts,
And men shall call the liquor good,
The more with death it thicks the blood. . . .

Even if undrugged, Temperance shouted, beer was usually
filthy because brewers used water polluted with stable-drain-
age to richen the flavor. Proof of such charges was occasionally tenuous, often lacking. But they began to sound all too
well based when Dr. Edward Cornelius Delavan of Albany,
New York, published in a local newspaper in 1835 charges
that local maltsters used water from a pond thick with refuse
from a slaughterhouse and glue-works—and the local brewers,
important in Albany's economy, had the bad judgment to sue
for libel. The defense proved to the hilt the noisome truth of
the allegations; indeed its witnesses added many previously
unmentioned details about dead hogs, privy-drainings and
the local custom of drowning superfluous cats in the waters
whence the maltsters' tank wagons supplied the malting tubs.
The verdict for the defendant must have made Albany topers
look thoughtfully at malt beverages for some months to
come. Temperance was often willingly gullible, sometimes
casuistically dishonest; but throughout its long war with the
Demon and his allies its leaders were seldom such consistent
fools as their opponents.

Delavan was already a hero of Temperance. He was not yet
forty when, in 1830, he retired from business with a fortune
made in Albany real estate, hardware and wines, and devoted
it and himself for forty years to battling the Demon. He paid
the bills for New York State's conspicuous Temperance publications; for thousands of copies of Dr. Sewall's famous colored plates of the drinker's stomach; for his own trips abroad,
armed with other thousands of copies of Edwards' Temperance writings, spreading the good word in Britain and on the
Continent, where he bedeviled, among others, Louis-Phi-
lippe and Lord Acton with his insistence that the Demon was
the root of all evil; and he teamed up with Gerrit Smith
to finance the post–Civil War Anti-Dramshop party that
blended into the Prohibition Party. It was not lost on his admirers that at least some of the resources so widely and often

effectively lavished had come from the sale of the very wines he was denouncing. Wherever the Demon's enemies gathered, there was Delavan's smooth round face above an under-chin goatee Uncle Sam style, and there were his ready pen and even readier purse doing more than any man of his time to keep New York State the pivot and hotbed of pre–Civil War Temperance.

Temperate drinking is the downhill road to intemperance.
—Motto of *The National Philanthropist* (1826)

With ruthless logic, taking all this outcry against fermented drinks as fair, L. M. Sargent carried Beecher's ferocious hint a step further and advised putting wine and cider drinkers on hard liquor because that would kill them off sooner—though no more surely—and take the burden of their support off the hands of family or society. The effectiveness of it all is clear in the case of P. T. Barnum: The great showman had long considered himself temperate because he never drank spirits and took wine (champagne usually) only at dinner after the back of his business day was broken. Then he happened to hear a parson friend preach a powerful sermon against any and all alcoholic indulgence. Barnum went home to Bridgeport, personally smashed every bottle of wine he owned and never touched alcohol again. That pleased his wife and mother-in-law, who had been getting uneasy over what the daily bottle of fizz did to his disposition. It also gave him a new trophy to show visitors, a smugly displayed heap of broken glass; and the reward of his virtue returned to him after not too many days when he put on *The Drunkard* at his Philadelphia and New York theatres and saw that already well-seasoned Temperance melodrama become the first modern-scale "hit" of the American theatre.

By Barnum's time the lines were drawn: Temperance was out to show either that moderation could not exist; or suppose it sometimes did, was nevertheless intolerably dangerous to society. To seek moderation by taking a jolt or two and then stopping had long been denounced by the Old Pledge as wicked trifling with evil. To seek it by confining oneself to fermented drinks, however judiciously, was denounced by the New Pledge as leading to much the same thing, only more slowly. The resulting teetotalism excommunicated any tactless enough to be moderate drinkers of any class of tipple. This was the period when Leverett Saltonstall, a Boston Brahmin of Brahmins, admitted that when drinking a tumbler of water in a public place like a hotel, he always made sure that everybody nearby could see it was nothing stronger than water.

Keep it in mind that the moderate drinker was specially unpopular because he made Temperance propaganda look bad. The spewing drunk in the gutter was a fine Exhibit A, but not the well-tailored gentleman having a cool sherry cobbler at the bar on a warm afternoon and going his urbane way certainly none the worse for it, probably rather the better. So Temperance almost openly hoped he would hurry up and go alcoholic, obvious and disgusting, and not stand there putting ideas into others' heads. Several years before the New Pledge became national policy, the Rev. Eli Meech (another marvelous name!) of Rhode Island concluded that the respectable, moderate drinker did far more than anybody else "to perpetuate the evil of intemperance." Fifty years later in Urbana, Ohio, Brand Whitlock recalled, a Moderate Drinker was considered worse than a sot because he "showed that a man might use liquor and yet not beat his wife, wreck his home, defraud his creditors, destroy himself body and soul, and fill a drunkard's grave." While ornamenting the U.S. House of Representatives as a member from New York State, Gerrit Smith cried: "I would that no person were able to drink intoxicating liquors without immediately becoming a drunkard. For who, then, would . . . drink the poison that always kills, or jump into the fire that always burns?" It couldn't have been more clearly put.

The decent drinker thus cast as the morally infectious villain of the Temperance melodrama could not, however, call the case against him absurd. Given Temperance's terms, it had force: Nobody can know in advance whether drinking may not eventually betray him into self-destroying excess. Therefore any ingestion of alcohol, however diluted, is as immoral a paltering with danger as an adolescent's experiments with dope. And though certain lucky ones may have temperaments so stable and systems so insusceptible that they can drink moderately for life, they are nevertheless wrong to do so, for that encourages those less fortunately endowed to try it—and come to ruin. Therefore, moderate drinkers who really can take it or leave it alone must abstain for others' sake. If they hesitate to swear off because they suspect it will be irksome, they are obviously already in danger of having their established habit turn into alcoholism, and for their own sakes had better go on the wagon at once while there is yet time.

It was seldom so soberly stated, of course: Thomas A. Grimké, intellectual of Charleston, South Carolina, told a Temperance gathering there early in the war against moderation that "all the victims of intemperance were once as safe as [the moderate drinker] believes himself to be . . . this is the master-habit of the human constitution . . . the very Vulture of Prometheus, devouring its enchained and agonizing victim. . . . Why should all this ruin be the lot of any community . . . because the self-confident . . . and the lover of his own pleasure . . . have resolved to sacrifice all this vast amount of public and private good? . . . TEMPERATE DRINKERS ARE THE PARENTS OF ALL THE DRUNKARDS WHO DISHONOR AND AFFLICT OUR COUNTRY."

Never mind the classical allusions and upper-case type, the position that far is tenable: Those taking alcohol undeniably run certain social, emotional and physical risks ranging from grave to negligible depending on the individual's temperament and circumstances. The same is true of being born. That is not voluntary, however, whereas drinking is. Other things being equal, human beings may well be foolish gratuitously to add this hazard to the many others already inevitable in life. If the protection of potential alcoholics were a principal concern of society—as the protection of children actually is—and if five first-drinkers in ten eventually went alcholic, society could conceivably ask us all to give up alcohol in the interests of those whom free access to it will destroy. Moreover, certain religious ideas (to be discussed later) led many of our forebears to consider drinking a sort of slow spiritual suicide for anybody who sets any store by it at all.

But Temperance did not let those arguments for teetotalism stand on their own to attract and maybe benefit the timidly ascetic and the hyperconscientious. Like its sister good causes then and now, Temperance could never shut up and leave well enough alone. It had flagrantly to falsify the odds of alcoholism in the drinking population to alarm the weak-minded: "I never knew a man who was in the habit of drinking regularly that did not become a drunkard," James B. Finley, early Methodist circuit rider told a bibulous elder. T. S. Arthur, author of *Ten Nights in a Bar-Room,* so often called "the Uncle Tom's Cabin of Temperance," shamelessly assured readers that "for every [moderate drinker] who restrains himself, ten will rush on to ruin," which is almost as much of a lie to the same purpose. Occasional tippling, wrote a Blue Ribbon pledge-signer of the 1870's, is like going out in a boat just above Niagara Falls and saying, as the brink comes nearer, "I am not in danger! I am only taking a row on the river! I shall not go over!" But "not more surely will that little boat with its living freight go down to a dreadful death than will the moderate drinker become eventually a drunkard. . . ." Those are extremes, true; but even more conscientious Temperance propagandists tended to imply that the bet was something like even money.

Then the threat to female virtue: A National Temperance Society tract anticipated Ogden Nash with the semi-demi-truth that moderate drinking "is a mighty strengthener of lawless desire in man, and a great weakener of the resisting power of women. . . . [Adulterers] in high life and low . . . are mainly either moderate or temperate drinkers." O. S. Fowler, the great popularizer of phrenology, took it unchivalrously further: "A man or woman, be they ever so moral or virtuous, when under the influence of intoxicating drinks, *is of easy virtue.* Before the *first* advantage can be taken of a virtuous woman, she must be partly *intoxicated,* and the advantage can be taken of almost any woman thus stimulated." One wonders in just what sort of circles Fowler moved.

As for the moderate drinker's belief that a drink often did him good and seldom harm, it was all self-delusion. Consider the Baltimore businessman who got into his forties with a "youthful step . . . the hue of health" and a consistent habit of brandy-and-water with his dinner and a champagne nightcap. People pointed him out as an example of how moderate drinking was safe. But when he died of diarrhea in his early fifties, autopsy showed his whole alimentary tract to be "a mass of disease," and the hereditary effects of his steady, mild tippling on his offspring were: one daughter dead of scrofula (lymphatic tuberculosis) at fifteen; another in the madhouse; the third and fourth "faded into heaven, we trust, in their sweetest teens; another is tottering on the verge of the grave; and only one [son] is left with all senses, and each of them is as weak as water."

For such horrors, taboo was obviously the only remedy. The "taste-not, touch-not, handle-not" attitude managed complete loss of common sense when Temperance took out after use of wine and spirits in cooking, for even the limited science of the time recognized that the heat involved usually drove off all the alcohol before the mince pie or sherry-flavored soup was eaten. The Rev. John Marsh advised shunning wine custards and such "as the viper's tooth." The Rev. Dr. Theodore L. Cuyler had an appetizing tale of a little apprentice who, dining at his master's table, tasted brandy in the pudding and spat it out on his plate, saying: "I belong to the Band of Hope and I won't touch it." In view of such august authority no wonder that nearer our own time poor charging that the wines in the sauces and the brandy in the old ignorant, crazy Carry Nation made a spectacle of herself puddings served in the Yale dining halls were stupefying and corrupting the undergraduates.

Still more fantastically the taboo carried on past alcohol into dim suspicions that other luxuries consumed for pleasure in public places had a sinister aspect. Describing a high-toned establishment of the 1850's on Broadway, all gilt and mirrors and blazing gas jets and men escorting gaily dressed women, Greeley's New York *Tribune* noted: "'Tis here that mothers suffer younger daughters to come at this untimely midnight hour to . . . eat ice cream drugged with passion-exciting vanilla." Fifty years later the same instinct set a Conference of the Methodist Church South denouncing Coca Cola as "enemy of our young men" because its caffein would "keep an average boy awake till two o'clock . . . stimulate his whole nervous system, and turn him loose in a . . . city full of temptations . . . his destruction is almost sure to follow. Mothers all over this land are bewailing the fact that their boys do not come home at night . . . 'coca-cola' is one of the causes of this nocturnal revel."

And there was Asa G. Candler of Georgia, founder and chief beneficiary of Coca-Cola, a pillar of the Methodist Church!

4

AWAY THE BOWL!

Our youthful hearts with temp'rance burn,
From dramshops all our steps we turn,
   Away the bowl! away the bowl! away, away the bowl!
Farewell to rum and all its harms,
Farewell the wine-cup's boasted charms. . . .
                    —*The Temperance Musician* (1854)

We have also settled the principle that it is possible to reform a drunkard.

    —CHARLES JEWETT, M.D., in *The National Temperance Offering* (Sons of Temperance) (1850)

THE Rev. Dr. Edwards' plan—let drunkards drink themselves to death, keep others from replacing them—worked so badly that even he came to mistrust it. The day-by-day facts were glaring: No matter how many Temperance "agents" inveigled their fellow men into pledges of growing stringency, a fresh crop of drunkards succeeded those whom the Demon eliminated. Like the poor they were always there; indeed, alcoholic and pauper were often significantly identical, chicken-into-egg or vice versa. So presently Edwards' widely circulated *Temperance Manual* was praising a group of Yankee workingmen who, once out-and-out drunkards, had managed, in spite of the toploftical pessimism of their betters, to reform and organize to help one another stay reformed.

"FRIENDS," said their manifesto, "you are miserable and wretched, in body, in soul, and circumstances. You have no peace here, and can have no peace hereafter . . . we were once drunkards . . . We are now happy; our wives are comfortable; our children are provided for; we are in better health . . . we now drink . . . no kind of intoxicating liquor. There is no safety for you nor for us, but in giving it up entirely. Come then, ye drunkards, attend our meetings, be resolved to cast off the fetters of intemperance, and for ever determine to be free."

Here were "the lower orders" striking out for themselves; whereas until then, of course, Temperance had been child of the traditional oligarchy of parson, doctor and sometimes

87

judge or plutocrat. These workingmen had organized without reference to local grandees. Further, they knew from experience what the oligarchs usually denied: that some among even desperately hard cases could be salvaged—a new and more humane notion. Their purpose was mutual support in teetotaling. The phrase "no peace hereafter" implied certain religious values already strong in Temperance. Anybody reminded of Alcoholics Anonymous is right. Once Temperance got away from the firm-mouthed gentlemen with gold-headed canes it developed several such anticipations of our own time.

In the mid-1830's, workingmen thus got together sporadically in New York City, Baltimore and Philadelphia. Temperance was not properly given over to the people until 1840, however, when a group of skilled workmen frequenting a tavern on Baltimore's Liberty Street took it into their heads to send two of their number to hear a well-known Temperance-lecturing parson, the Rev. Matthew Hale Smith. It was at best a laborious joke; next night it proved to be no joke at all. Smith had been disturbingly effective. The emissaries came back retailing his arguments to uncomfortable purpose. For several evenings the boys scoffed and argued, and listened and argued, until at last six of the hardest drinkers among them, each with what we now call a definite "alcohol problem"—a tailor, a carpenter, two blacksmiths, a silversmith and a coachmaker—formed a society pledging them "as gentlemen" to abstain from "spiritous or malt liquors, wine or cider." (Curious that this and the Moreau society, the cornerstones of organized Temperance, were born in taverns.) Why they took the name "Washington Temperance Society" remains unexplained. The Father of Their Country liked Madeira as well as most Virginia gentlemen, and when wines grew scarce during the Revolution, willingly drank lowdown rum-and-water.* Nevertheless it was

* The only Washington I can find who deserved having a Temperance-teetotal movement named after him was a Dr. B. Washington, U.S. Navy surgeon, who intemperately and by no means scientifically denounced alcoholic beverages in the late 1830's (Hopkins, *Correspondence*, p. 53). The dates fit well enough to make it possible, though highly improbable, that what the original Washingtonians had in mind was the teachings of the surgeon, not the anomalous example of the national hero.

as "the Washingtonian Movement" that they became immortal in the annals of the war on the Demon.

To their first meeting, in a carpenter's shop, each brought another problem drinker. Their way of bolstering up one another was to get on their feet and tell frankly how deeply the Demon's claws had sunk into the speaker, what a struggle it was to get away, how good it was to be able to live with oneself again after self-rescue. An admirer of the movement summarized the pitch thus: "I was a drunkard. As I *was* so may you become. I was industrious as you; I went to the almshouse. I loved my wife and children as much as you do. I beat my wife and abused my children. . . ." Or: "I looked and felt as bad as you do. . . . Look at me now . . . healthy, happy and respectable . . . good clothes . . . money in my pocket. All comfortable and happy at home; no more rags and starvation *there,* to buy silk shawls and bonnets for the tavern-keepers' wives and daughters. . . . Come and sign the pledge, *as I did,* and you'll be a happy man. Keep the pledge and all will come right again!"

That rash but sincere promise reflected the Puritan's belief that righteousness and prosperity went hand in hand, a principle pervading Temperance propaganda right down to our own time. These citings of personal experience were like the "testimony" that those "getting religion" at camp meeting were supposed to give at subsequent "experience meetings," though Washingtonianism did not rely heavily on religious appeals. It soon outgrew the carpenter's shop, numbering almost 700 members by the year's end. The six founding fathers became able speakers and turned into catch-as-catch-can missionaries. And two months after birth the movement gained its keenest tool—John Henry Willis Hawkins, hatter.

Like printing, the hatter's trade was associated with hard drinking. In spite of pious rearing, a pious youth and two successive pious wives supporting his occasional attempts to pull himself together, Hawkins had been going on frantic sprees at shortening intervals. As the Washingtonian showpiece he told over and over how his adolescent daughter Hannah shook him into self-rescue: He was in bed that morning with a hideous hangover. Hannah, well aware what his usual cure was, said piteously: "Father, don't send me after whiskey today!" and was ordered out of the room. Actually he had hidden a pint in the cupboard and had only to totter out of bed to get at the hair-of-the-dog that he craved. But somehow the girl's voice kept him from it. He called her back and said: "Hannah, I'm not angry with you—and I shan't drink any more!" and burst into tears, and so did she. He knew of the Washingtonians, sought them out, and found the comradely support that made the difference this time. Hannah became a sort of Temperance saint, with pamphlets written about her and pictures of her stamping on the hydra of Intemperance painted on Washingtonian banners, for her ruggedly handsome father was the first great Temperance spellbinder, an eloquent brand snatched from the burning.

The next spring, Temperance men in New York City invited Hawkins and others to come up and show how Washingtonianism worked. Standing on rum kegs in City Hall Park and elsewhere, they enlisted 1,800 members in a week's campaign that firmly established the movement thereabouts. Then Boston invited them. Things went so well there that, on invitation from local admirers, Hawkins moved his family to New England and turned paid organizer, traveling, speaking, founding Washingtonian branches. Up and down the Atlantic Coast, fanning out into the new states beyond the mountains, went more such zealous lecturers, often two by two, spreading the word of hope for drunkards. It was all too loose and sudden for careful records. But even the *Standard Encyclopedia of the Alcohol Problem,* compiled by Drys at the height of their triumph in the 1920's, sniffy about the movement because it rejected Prohibition, estimated that it made teetotalers of 250,000 drunkards and reclaimed 750,000 "common tipplers . . . at least temporarily."

It also revived the lapsed Congressional society under leadership of Representative (later Governor) George N. Briggs of Massachusetts and Representative Thomas F. Marshall of Kentucky, renowned as much for sprees as for oratory. His platform prowess was welcome and he worked devotedly for the cause as a conspicuous lecturer. But on the whole he proved a mixed blessing: His addiction to tobacco, of which

Temperance disapproved, was almost as marked as his thirst for whiskey. Brought to New York City to address a national Temperance convention, he outraged his prim sponsors by fighting a duel with James Watson Webb, swashbuckling editor of the New York *Courier & Enquirer*. And he showed insufficient talent for teetotaling. Even on Temperance lecture tours the Demon sometimes caught up with him. The Rev. John Marsh saw him so drunk on the platform that he fell over the edge, only to pick himself up, climb back and, apparently sobered by the crash, take up the thread of his interrupted spellbinding and go on even more impressively than before. Yet this very shortcoming may have increased Marshall's value to the cause: The brilliant but unstable man martyred by drink can be the most telling kind of Temperance exhibit. The spectacle of his struggles and recurring falls may have done more to reform his political colleagues than any of his soaring denunciations of the Demon before preselected audiences.

Oratorical success is in the ear of the listener, of course, inevitably qualified by the forensic fashions of the day. Surviving examples of Marshall are Temperance eloquence with its best foot forward:

"Sir!" the poor windy devil cried, addressing the president of the Congressional Total Abstinence Society, "the pledge I have taken renders me secure forever from a fate . . . more terrible than death. That pledge I would not exchange for all earth holds of brightest and best. . . . Sir, I would not exchange the physical sensations, the mere sense of animal being, which belongs to a man who totally refrains from all that can intoxicate his brain or derange his nervous structure—the elasticity with which he bounds from his couch in the morning—the sweet repose it yields him at night—the feeling with which he drinks in through his clear eyes the beauty and grandeur of surrounding nature—the bounding vivacity with which the life-blood courses its exulting way through every fiber of my frame . . . the splendors of the morning, the softness of the evening sky—the bloom, the beauty, the verdure of earth, the music of the air and the waters . . . not for the brightest and noblest wreath that ever encircled a statesman's

brow . . . would I cast from me this precious pledge of a lib-
erated mind, this talisman against temptation; and plunge
again into the dangers and temptation that once beset my
path!"

ҨӬ

". . . if we take habitual drunkards as a class, their heads
and hearts will bear an advantageous comparison with those
of any other. . . . The demon of intemperance seems ever
to have delighted in sucking the blood of genius and of generosity."
                    —ABRAHAM LINCOLN, address before the Spring-
                    field (Ill.) Washingtonian Society

Washingtonianism was exuberantly splendid while it
lasted. It had a weekly newspaper; a ladies' auxiliary, the
Martha Washington Society, of course, to rehabilitate the
families of reformed drunkards; a juvenile auxiliary too; it
infiltrated the rowdy volunteer fire companies of the large
cities, a good way to reach local roughs; pounded steadily
away with two-man teams of lecturers, meetings, pamphlets,
processions.

In 1842, Charles Dickens admired celebrant Washingtonians parading by his hotel in Cincinnati several thousand
strong, "marshalled by officers on horseback . . . with scarves
and ribbons of bright colors fluttering out behind them gayly
. . . bands of music . . . banners out of number . . . very
well painted [with] the smiting of the rock and the gushing
forth of the waters . . . a temperate man . . . aiming a
deadly blow at a serpent which was apparently about to
spring upon him from the top of a barrel of spirits . . .
[and] a huge allegorical device, borne among the ship-car-
penters, on one side whereof the steamboat 'Alcohol' was represented bursting her boiler . . . while upon the other, the
good ship 'Temperance' sailed away with a fair wind."

Indeed, Washingtonian processions must have been great
sights: The one celebrating the Massachusetts convention of
the movement in 1842 had banners showing the woman of

Samaria giving Christ water; another a cluster of grapes and a sheaf of grain, motto: "Food, if eaten; poison, if drunk"; another with a well, motto: "Drink from the bubbling fountain —drink it free;/'Twas good for Samson, and 'tis good for me." . . . In New London, Connecticut, the largest procession the town had ever seen escorted three wagons lighted by torches and full of barrels of rum to a conspicuous site and set fire to the lot.

"Dr." Dio Lewis, a doughty veteran of the wars against the Demon, said that because Washingtonianism "threw the arms of love around the rum-drinker" it was uniquely effective in promoting Temperance. He meant that whereas previous Temperance effort had looked down on rummies and stuck pretty much to preselected audiences already Temperance-minded, the Washingtonians went rummaging where those needing help were numerous. To the extent that its pledges stuck—and many seem to have done so—it kept hundreds of thousands from annihilating themselves with drink, a genuine achievement. Today its equalitarianism is specially appealing: As a lukewarm witness wrote, it ignored "distinctions created by wealth or superior education. . . . A man without a penny . . . who could neither read nor write, if he had once been a hard case and was now sober, was . . . just as much honored as a reformed judge . . . [and] heard in the meetings with just as much attention." That was good tactics on the far side of the tracks. And, also like AA members, the hard-core Washingtonians had the emotional bracer of frequent active casework, bucking up the fainthearted and fishing for new prospects—all a great help in staying on the wagon oneself.

As is usual in institutions based on emotion, however, the current of Washingtonianism ran briskest and clearest at the beginning. William K. Mitchell, leader of the founding six, opposed letting religion be called in to bolster the new convert's backbone. The original Washingtonians had needed no such help, had relied solely on comradely support from the others, and that was the way Mitchell wanted it to stay so earnestly that he banned opening meetings with prayer. He also refused to denounce rumsellers and rumselling, maintaining that the decent approach was not to abuse them but to fade them out of the picture by persuading all their customers to go teetotal. Indeed he sometimes went so far as to buy one of his unregenerate friends a drink at a bar, though abstaining himself—if the fellow as yet saw no reason not to drink, that was his business and why be stuffy about it? He even opposed any and all restrictions on rumselling, from mere early closing to outright Prohibition, because in his view such appeals to law blurred the central importance of the individual in the problem.

Tom Marshall again outraged the righteous by sweepingly backing this purist attitude. Otherwise it was so alien to Temperance's previous and subsequent trends toward smugness and billingsgate that most Washingtonian branches defied Mitchell and encouraged prayer and religious values. That was good tactics in view of the importance of appeals to a Higher Power in modern rehabilitation of alcoholics. John Hawkins went even further, presently becoming an ordained Methodist minister, endorsing the principle of Prohibition, advocating "moral suasion for the unfortunate drunkard, and legal suasion for the drunkard-MAKER," and ranting shrilly against the trade: ". . . you might as well talk about a pious devil, a virtuous prostitute, or an honest thief as to talk of a rum-seller . . . having 'a good moral character.' "

Such schisms cost the movement needed support. Ministers not infrequently denied Washingtonian apostles use of their pulpits and well after the Civil War, veteran Temperance men were still blaming the Washingtonian take-over for having slowed Temperance's progress toward Prohibition. By slackly enrolling any who signed the pledge and came to meetings, even though not yet thrall to the Demon, the movement gained great numbers, including Abraham Lincoln. But such neophytes, who had never known the drunkard's private hell, necessarily diluted the zeal and drive of those who had. A little more of that come-one-come-all attitude and Washingtonianism would have been just another pledge-waving Temperance society. Worse, the detailed candor encouraged in the personal case histories given at meetings began to give the movement a bad name. Speakers sought to outdo one another in boasting of the peculiarly loathsome depths of their previous degradation.

What with this and that, Washingtonianism soon petered out. But Lyman Abbott, who grew up in its great period, justly considered forty years later that it had been an extremely useful "crying in the night of Fire! Fire!" If nothing else, it had made Temperance equalitarian and convinced the world that many abject drunkards could be rescued. And it had enlisted in the cause and done much to develop the greatest Temperance propagandists of the mid-century, Timothy Shay Arthur and John Bartholomew Gough.

Believing . . . alcoholic liquors . . . the prolific source (directly or indirectly) of nearly all the ills that afflict the human family. . . .
—Organizing manifesto of the Sons of Temperance (1842)

In strict chronology the notion of a *secret* fraternal order centering around Temperance arose first in England in the Independent Order of Rechabites, named after the teetotaling, tent-dwelling and traditionally ascetic clan of Jonadab, son of Rechab, a splinter-group among the ancient Israelites.* Their first American "Tent," founded in early August, 1842, seven weeks before the Sons of Temperance, introduced to the States the idea of combining organization for Temperance with sickness- and death-benefits. But though the Rechabites flourished mildly, the size of their roster never came close to that of the Sons or of some of their competitors and successors.

* *Jeremiah,* 35:5–6: "And I set before the sons of the house of Rechab pots of wine. . . . But they said, We will drink no wine, for Jonadab the son of Rechab our father commanded us saying, Ye shall drink no wine, neither ye nor your sons forever." In 1867, Jonadab was thus honored by an evanescent Temperance order gloriously entitled the United Order of the Golden Cross and Sons of Jonadab.

For as Washingtonian zeal waned a group of the faithful in New York City headed by the brothers Oliver who printed a Washingtonian paper, the *Organ,* saw sadly that pledges were fragile bonds. They determined to enlist stauncher Washingtonians in "an organization of a more permanent character" binding them to teetotaling and intended to "elevate their characters as men, and afford mutual assistance in adversity or distress." Discussion of religion and politics was barred from meetings but "the religion of the Bible is the stay of the Order," boasted one of its state chaplains, and "The [lodge hall] is often the direct way to the Church." Again the founders, sixteen in all, were mostly skilled craftsmen: printer, diesinker, bookbinder, paper hanger, house painter. . . . They called it the Order of the Sons of Temperance. Its immense success was due both to that hifalutin style of organization and to the mutual-assistance feature which, being interpreted, meant not only the Washingtonian kind of comradely support but emergency insurance features producing hard cash when most needed.

Maybe they had got wind of the Rechabites and stolen their thunder. It does not necessarily follow, however, for that was the heyday of "fraternal orders" imitating Masonry but borrowing from the British workingmen's "friendly societies" arrangements for sick-benefits and funeral expenses: The Independent Order of Odd Fellows, the United Ancient Order of Druids, the Ancient Order of Foresters, the Improved Order of Redmen, had already come into being to familiarize Americans with the alliance of improved economic security with grips, passwords, signs of distress, door guards, elaborate "regalia" and adjective-studded officers. Before it dwindled, this fad of the esoteric had tinged with pseudo-Masonry the Prophet Joseph Smith's new Mormon religion; certain early labor unions; and the farmers' first national protective movement, the Patrons of Husbandry, alias "The Grange." Some of the founding Sons are said to have formed a taste for ritualized fellowship in the Masons or Odd Fellows, which is likely enough. Anyway they now rejoiced in an ample rig-out with a password changed quarterly, state organizations called Grand Divisions, a Most Worthy Patriarch as national chief, and great embroidered horse collars to wear at meetings and parades.

These trappings put off some Temperance leaders. Dr. Jewett joined the Sons because he thought them effective but said he'd gladly pay quadruple dues rather than to have to "hang on my neck, for a single evening, the very brilliant decorations which . . . many excellent men wear with apparent pleasure . . . which probably cost them not less than twenty-five dollars"—a considerable sum in those days. The Rev. John Marsh reproached the Sons with ignoring drunks too broke to pay even small dues and initiation fees—which was unfair; only by such payments could the insurance benefits be covered. The Sons excused their oath of secrecy as protection for the privacy of backsliding members, and their password as safeguard against impostors. Those features nevertheless alienated many who shared the contemporary hostility to secret orders that produced the ephemeral but politically pregnant Anti-Masonic Party.

The rigmarole and the delight of being called Most Worthy Brother probably attracted more men than they alienated, however. The usual ladies' and juvenile auxiliaries appeared—the former most stormily, as we shall see later. Concentrating first on the likeliest Washingtonians, the Sons snowballed to the level of 200,000 members by 1850. The surest token of their success was the crowd of imitating rivals: The Order of Templars of Honor and Temperance; the National Temple of Honor; the Society of Good Samaritans; the Independent Order of Good Templars—some born of schism in already existing orders, some spontaneous, all carrying the double appeal of ritual and benefits. The Good Templars flourished most of all, spreading into Europe as well as the British Empire and outnumbering the Sons themselves in the States. As Temperance resumed stride after the Civil War both these orders had momentous offspring: The guns were hardly cold when a Temperance convention at Saratoga dominated by the Sons set up the National Temperance Society and Publication House, the outfit that revived and stoked the fires that melted the metal from which the Anti-

Saloon League was cast. And in 1869 the Good Templars fathered the Prohibition Party.

Rum, Romanism, and Rebellion. . . .
—THE REV. SAMUEL D. BURCHARD

The packetship *Ashburton* hove to in the Narrows on July 1, 1849. A bosun's chair was rigged, an elderly friar of the Capuchin order was lowered into a boat, set ashore on Staten Island and solicitously received in the house of a wealthy resident for a rest on dry land very welcome after the tossings of a westbound Atlantic passage under sail. It was his last peaceful day for a long time to come. Next morning the whole municipal council of New York City came down the bay on a steamer to escort him to an uproarious welcome in Castle Garden, the converted fortress at the Battery which served as municipal auditorium. The Irving House, where they put him up in a four-room suite furnished in solid rosewood, had decorated the lobby with mottoes painted on white satin, and a portrait of him had been placed over the bar. The mottoes, being Biblical, fitted well enough, but the location of the portrait did not. For this was Father Theobald Mathew come hot from Ireland to the New World to promote total abstinence, particularly among the masses of Irish-born already accumulated in the States, and to express his people's gratitude for relief supplies that U. S. naval vessels had brought during the cataclysmic potato famine of 1846–7.

The portrait probably gave Father Mathew no stronger reaction than an easy chuckle, for he was no man to be troubled by anomalies. His uncertain use of hand and leg showed that he had not yet completely recovered from a stroke suffered the previous spring, and he was otherwise not a well man at the age of fifty-nine. Yet he was setting out on—and completed—a twenty-eight-month tour of the States that would have daunted Theodore Roosevelt at his fittest. Even more anomalously he was Irish; Catholic; in holy orders, though he never wore the Capuchin beard and gown—each datum an occasion for deep suspicion and hostility in those days of best sellers about orgies in convents and papal conspiracies to take over the Ohio valley, believed in by men as august as Lyman Beecher. Yet the President of the United States gave a banquet for him, and the United States Senate voted him the privileges of the floor, an honor given only once before, to the Marquis de Lafayette on his triumphal tour of 1824–5. The reasons for this hero's welcome were that the Washingtonians had so resoundingly dramatized the efficacy of teetotalism in reforming drunkards; and that Father Mathew, practically single-handed, had imposed the teetotal pledge on the majority of the population of the drunkenest nation in Christendom.

His striking achievement also had Quaker roots. Middle-aged Father Mathew, sweet-tempered, intensely earnest founder of schools for the illiterate poor of Cork, served on the governing board of the Cork House of Correction (workhouse) along with several prominent local Dissenters including an old Quaker named William Martin. The cause of teetotalism was Friend William's hobby pursued with un-Quakerish rambunctiousness. Liking his Catholic colleague and sensing his latent abilities, the old man took every opportunity to urge the younger to take up the Temperance cause for the good of the miserable lower orders of Cork, the disastrous effects of whose drinking were daily, shockingly evident in the workhouse. Eventually his persistence conquered. In 1838, Father Mathew founded a local total-abstinence society that swept Ireland even more furiously than the Washingtonians did the States a few years later. Attendance at his meetings always ran to rapt thousands; his eventual number of pledges secured ran well over four million. He was so nearly irresistible that even the black Protestants of Ulster welcomed him about as readily as his coreligionists.

A fair number of distillers and brewers, whose business his crusade half ruined, actually signed his pledge and contributed to his war chest. Great noblemen like the Duke of Leinster and the Marquis of Lansdowne lent public support. Daniel O'Connell, the political hero of Catholic Ireland, endorsed Father Mathew. Maria Edgeworth, shrewd and eminent bluestocking novelist, described his campaigns with openmouthed approval and delight. But the basic appeal and the greatest good lay among the bitterly poor lower classes for whom drink had been the only amenity of their barefoot, empty-bellied, leaky-roofed existence. For them Father Mathew was a sort of white-neckclothed Pied Piper, blessing, cajoling, edifying them into sobriety and a generalized glimpse of better things. Along with blessing and pledge came a medal with the good man's image on it for which the prosperous paid with contributions and the poor often got for nothing. Indeed Father Mathew so assiduously handed them out free along with his own meager cash and anybody else's that came to him that, far from making a small fortune out of medals as the ill-natured claimed, he proved to be £7,000 in debt within a few years.

Soon people, impressed by his outgoing benevolence and energetic compassion, were flocking to him for faith healing as well as the pledge. Shrewd enough to recognize that this was dangerous ground, he sought to discourage it, consistently denying that he had any healing or miraculous powers. But when the seekers pleaded hard it just wasn't in him not to cordially bless them and pray for any recovery that might suit God's purposes—and in the usual number of cases they got well or felt better. Even after his death the caretakers of the graveyard where they laid him occasionally found a pair of crutches propped against the tomb where some crippled believer had prayed and risen, able to step out freely again.

Certain hypersensitized American Protestants muttered that this was a Roman Trojan horse exploiting American Temperance in the Pope's sinister interests. But all things considered, such nonsense was gratifyingly scarce, maybe partly because the goldheaded-cane gentlemen were grateful for anything that promised to cut down drinking among the Irish who had been arriving in such immense numbers after the famine. Father Mathew's Stateside troubles came from quite another quarter—the Abolitionists and their Southern enemies. When Father Mathew reached Boston, William Lloyd Garrison, then chief of the militant minority of the antislavery forces, invited him to attend—and by implication endorse—an upcoming meeting to celebrate the anniversary of the Emancipation of Negro slaves in the West Indies. The letter of invitation reminded him that in 1842 O'Connell and he, among thousands of others, had signed an address from the Irish urging their cousins in America to abandon race prejudice and support antislaveryism. And next day here were Garrison and friends in person to follow up. As sister Reform causes, peers in the great American Syndrome, Temperance and antislavery were logical running mates. But warned by either his own shrewdness or advice from his Boston host, Archbishop Hughes, who may have been aware that Garrison's group were unpopular even in most antislavery circles, Father Mathew declined with nimble, polite logic:

"I have as much as I can do to save men from the slavery of intemperance, without attempting to overthrow any other kind of slavery. . . . I am a Catholic priest; but, being here to promote the cause of Temperance, I should not be justified in turning aside from my mission, for the purpose of subserving the cause of Catholicism." Fair enough but it infuriated the Garrisonians, of course, who made the whole affair as public as press and platform could manage, eager to have the recusant sound like a callous time server.

Matters grew more awkward when Governor Thomas H. Lumpkin of Georgia, who had headed an invitation to Father Mathew to include that state in his projected tour, picked up the fact of the address of 1842 and informed him that unless he could deny all connection with any such document, it would be useless for him to visit Georgia; and when no such denial was possible, withdrew the invitation. The catalytic Irishman was damned if he did and damned if he didn't. In the Senate's debate on the resolution to honor him, Jefferson Davis of Mississippi was one of those speaking emphatically against it; and though the other senator from Mississippi, Henry S. Foote, Davis' sworn enemy, joined Seward and Clay in injecting some common sense into the debate, eighteen votes out of fifty-one went in the No column, and by no means all from Southerners either.

After this minor mess, more discreditable to zealots for and against slavery than to its nominal target, Father Mathew pluckily went South anyway and scored great successes, not least in Savannah, Georgia, and Vicksburg, Mississippi. Circling as far west as Arkansas, he returned through the Ohio valley and on up and around for over two years of trouping. His prestige stayed high throughout, his courage fought off his persistent ailments, his meetings were triumphs. When he sailed home late in 1851 he left behind many thousands better off for teetotaling. It was the end of his career. After some years of cumulative physical miseries he died in 1856.

The Catholic Total Abstinence movement, founded in his name before he arrived and deriving great impetus from his presence, kept alive through the Civil War and had a great rebirth under Archbishop John Ireland of St. Paul. As pledge-getter Father Mathew knew no peer in any Temperance movement, and personally he sounds more appealing than any of his Protestant opposite numbers. But there was usually a split between Catholic Temperance and the dominant forces in the war on the Demon. Though there were sporadic exceptions to the rule, Catholic clergy and laymen exercised about the menace of drunkenness jibbed at Prohibition, which accounts for the curious delusion among the emancipated youth of the 1920's that the Church was basically liberal. More importantly at the time—from the 1860's, say, to 1919—it encouraged the nativist, White-Protestant-Old-Americans-know-best feelings that stiffened the Prohibitionist movement as it picked up momentum from the 1880's on. It was the more Bible-thumping Protestant sects that furnished the militant lady members of the WCTU and the money for the Anti-Saloon League and Prohibition Party. Thanks to their cultural origins such bodies made great play with the contrast between the Catholic-Irish-German/big-city/hod-carrier/barkeeping/anti-Prohibition group and the whitecollar-or-farmer/Protestant/pro-Prohibition group that had a monopoly on self-respect. The resulting cheap and corrosive emotions had much to do with putting national Prohibition across.

I prefer Temperance hotels—altho' they sell worse liquor. . . .
—ARTEMUS WARD (1866)

Though the Washingtonian turnout in Cincinnati delighted Dickens, he had no personal leaning toward teetotalism. His books often distressed the righteous by deriding the smugness of Temperance. He was outraged when, traveling by stage from Cincinnati to Columbus, he had to dine at a "Temperance hotel" that could supply no brandy when he found the coffee, tea and water all intolerable. This was "not at all uncommon" in America, he noted, and accused Temperance landlords of charging more for inferior food and lodging to make up for lack of bar profits. The "plainest course for persons of such tender conscience," he said sourly, "would be a total abstinence from tavern-keeping."

It would hardly have sweetened his temper had he known that such squeamish hostelries were of British origin, early fruit of Temperance in the Dissent-heavy North of England, where the first example appeared at Preston in 1832. It was a logical growth: Once the Demon was taboo, his mere vicinity, not to mention sight and smell, became unbearable. A home-keeping teetotaler could manage fairly well to avoid the neighborhood of booze. But when traveling, forced to use the same inns as others, he was all too often elbow-to-elbow with those washing down their meals with one or another dilute poison; and in less pretentious establishments he had to pay his bill and otherwise deal with management at the bar itself where certain lewd fellows of the baser sort were absorbing gin slings to help them face the day. As Temperance grew, somebody was bound to think of specially catering to its fastidiousness.

Within six months the notion had jumped the ocean, founding Boston's Marlboro Hotel (attached to Marlborough

Chapel, traditional hall for Reformist meetings) on Temperance principles so strict that tobacco too was banned. At its grand opening on July 4, 1833, 200 gentlemen sat down to a banquet lacking both decanters and cigars. Imitation spread fast through the Northern states. The Croton Hotel in New York City was named after the new Croton Reservoir and waterworks. Soon Massachusetts enemies of the Demon were boasting of at least one Temperance house in every sizable town in the state. Landlords converted to Washingtonianism showed the courage of their new convictions—and risked insolvency—by closing their hotel bars. The Temperance House in New Haven, Connecticut, advertised as "formerly the notorious grog shop first door below Engine House No. 3." Nearby, Mrs. C. Hill's Washingtonian House offered "a quiet home . . . with no fear of being annoyed by the fumes of alcohol or . . . noise and vulgarity." Even the San Francisco of Gold Rush times had a few Temperance boardinghouses.

The idea inevitably spread into transportation: Dickens was lucky not to fall foul of a Temperance steamboat on the Long Island Sound run or the Temperance packet boats said to have been operated on the Erie Canal by General Ashbel Wells Riley—who, Temperance stalwart though he was, finally abandoned the scheme because it lost too much money. So did most of those Demon-proofed hotels. Though the first growth was vigorous, Temperance Houses gradually succumbed to lack of moisture round the roots. Even able men of large resources, like Dr. Delavan of brewery-libel fame, never got into the black with his great Delavan House in which he invested $200,000 in Albany; not till he sold it to less scrupulous owners did it make money as a haunt of high-ticket politicians and magnates of a stripe distinctly liking their toddy. (It burned down in 1894; the present fortresslike New York Central Station arose on the site.) And of all the fiascos in which Gerrit Smith, Dr. Delavan's wealthy New York State ally in Temperance, involved his well-meaning self, maybe the saddest was what happened when he tried to bring the blessings of a Temperance hotel to Peterboro, New York, his birthplace and the capital of his great landed empire.

We have already met this tall, paunchy, curly-bearded philanthropist as the complete Syndromist, taking up practically the whole spectrum of good causes. Naturally he was often disappointed, but only broke out in fresh places, making more speeches, writing more pamphlets—and more checks—in behalf of something else. He backed the "Colonizationist" movement to resettle freed Negroes in Africa, only to see it abandoned by the stauncher antislavery men; so Smith too abandoned it. He backed the Millerite (later Adventist) cult that, in 1844, predicted the immediate end of the world so confidently that its adherents, Smith and wife eminent among them, prepared white robes to go to heaven in—only to live thirty years longer with the end of the world apparently no nearer than ever. He backed Women's Rights—his wife was Elizabeth Cady Stanton's sister but he probably would have done so anyway—only to see the movement split and discredited after the Civil War by indiscreet acceptance of cranks and lady blackmailers. He got elected to the Federal House of Representatives and cut a wide swathe in Washington by lavish entertaining (cold water, of course), only to resign disillusioned before his term was up. He took fervent part in the small private conspiracy that created John Brown's amateur raid on Harpers Ferry—and when it blew up in his benevolent face, panicked into an insane asylum in a probably genuine psychotic episode. . . . Yet for all his quixoticisms he shrewdly manipulated the great fortune in land left him by his highly eccentric father.

The Osgood House of Peterboro stood at the other end of the village from Smith's classical revival mansion, but the lively business in its bar naturally dismayed the zealous teetotaler who also happened to be to Peterboro what Henry Ford was to Dearborn. For righteous competition with the Osgood House, Smith built a fine new hotel near his own dwelling with all necessary barns, carriage sheds, privies and so on and a Bible for each bedroom. "Temperance and the Bible" was painted up as house motto. The traveling public neglected to approve, however, and so did local bachelors needing board and room. Within two years the lessee-manager, who had dutifully run bone-dry, gave it up as economically hopeless. His successor, a local man in whom Smith had confidence, seems to have been allowed to buy in on the merely implied assumption that Temperance would be his policy. Anyway, to the squire of Peterboro's horror and the delight of the ungodly he also bought the decrepit old Osgood House, moved its stock and good will into the new hotel, and started selling booze as well as board and lodging right under Smith's nose. The only thing to do—and Smith did it—was to buy the traitor out at a fancy price and put in another manager to exorcise the Demon. The public promptly stayed away in droves, preferring the damper taverns in nearby towns. Smith had the hotel torn down and landscaped the site into the grounds of his mansion. After a while, in a sanguine fit, he set up another Temperance house rent-free to the lessee on that one condition. Even though it was the only public accommodation in the village and the new man sold a little booze on the side, this project too failed.

Such fatal lack of patronage must have come partly at least from the dismal reputation that Temperance houses soon acquired. Their owners advertised in Temperance papers; earnest Temperance lecturers sometimes recommended them in the letters they wrote to the press and scolded the faithful for not patronizing them: "[Temperance men] have a propensity to run their heads into the first rum-hole they come to," snorted John Hawkins while lecturing in Gerrit Smith's country. But honesty compelled other zealots to concede that lack of the cup that cheers was not the only reason. Dr. John Marsh, L. M. Sargent, the Rev. Dr. Edward Everett Hale—all great Temperance names—bemoaned their shortcomings: canvas on the floor instead of carpet, no newspapers, burned coffee. John B. Gough denounced Temperance houses as vehemently as if they had been dives: tablecloths so spotted with grease they looked like a map; butter obviously last cut with a dirty knife; sugar stained with coffee from wet spoons; and the patron paying "as much for dirt and discomfort as . . . in any other place for cleanliness and comfort." All the righteousness in the world could not counteract the economic fact that a hotel with a bar could afford to make a guest more comfortable than could one lacking that built-in subsidy for operating costs. The godly might try to boycott rumselling hostelries. Temperance editors might sneer at those regretting "the absence of that show and extravagance . . . at . . . 'fashionable hotels,' supported . . . by money which is the price of the health and reputation of the drunkard, of his wife's tears and his children's bread." But one way or another, Smith's experience was repeated again and again. Fifty years after the Marlboro House opened with the gentlemen toasting one another so propitiously in pure cold water, Boston, once boasting four or five Temperance hotels, had none at all.

There was money in Temperance—for lecturers; theatrical producers; manufacturers of hymnbooks, grape juice and white ribbon; but not for mine host at the sign of the Old Oaken Bucket.

5

FATHER,
DEAR FATHER...

I saw a woman weep,
    As if her heart would break;
They said her husband drank too much
    Of what he should not take.
I saw an unfrequented mound,
    Where weeds and brambles wave,
They said no tear had fallen there,
    It was the drunkard's grave. . . .
        —MRS. LYDIA HUNTLEY SIGOURNEY,
        "The Reason Why"

FERTILE Dr. Rush owed much of his renown as teacher to his face-to-face skills in the lecture hall. He seems to have administered ideas as freely as he did calomel, often with equally explosive results. The same rhetorical tricks, entertaining as well as convincing readers of his lectures-in-print, left heavy marks on the Temperance propagandists of the nineteenth century. From erudite Eliphalet Nott, D.D., in 1836 to ignorant Billy Sunday in 1916, all followed in paths first cut and trodden by Rush's *Inquiry.*

"Spirits," warned the physician turned sage, "impair the memory, debilitate the understanding, and pervert the moral faculties . . . produce not only falsehood, but fraud, theft, uncleanliness, and murder. . . . How deep the anguish which rends the bosom of the [drunkard's] wife . . . the shame and aversion which she excites in her husband! Is he the father of children? See their averted looks . . . their blushing looks at each other! Is he a magistrate? . . . What humiliating fears of corruption in the administration of the laws . . . in the countenance of all who see him!" As to economics: "Behold [drunkards'] houses stripped gradually of their furniture . . . to pay tavern debts . . . houses with shattered windows . . . barns with leaky roofs, gardens over-run with weeds . . . fields with broken fences . . . children filthy and half clad, without manners, principles, or morals. . . ." Addiction to spirits, Rush said, soundly enough, amounts to slow suicide. But the moral he drew was uncharitably murky and windy: "Yes—thou poor degraded creature, who art daily lifting the poisoned bowl to thy lips—cease to avoid the unhallowed ground in which the self-murderer is interred, and wonder

no longer that the sun should shine and the rain fall and the
grass look green upon his grave . . . his condemnation will
be less than yours at the day of judgment."

Such shaky syntax smells of the spoken word in a large hall
with an audience already confident that the speaker is qualified to pronounce the Almighty's dooms for Him. It would
suit the pulpit of 1850 or the Chautauqua tent of 1900 better
than the printed page of the 1780's, and successive generations of Temperance lecturers prospered by borrowing his
tone, elaborating his content and exaggerating certain of his
rhetorical tricks.

For instance, Rush introduced the corny-comic Temperance anecdote: There was a farmer whose pet goat followed
him to the tavern where the patrons so plied Billy with
liquor that beast as well as man went home the worse for
wear. Next time the farmer could not prevail on Billy to enter the premises where he had been so afflicted, and "his master was so much affected by a sense of shame, in observing the
conduct of his goat to be so much more rational than his own,
that he ceased from that time to drink spirituous liquors."
Thenceforward Temperance humor was of about that quality: The drunk falls into a sty, the hogs grunt in alarm, and he
says: "Hold your tongues, I'm as good as any of you." . . .
The drunk stumbles into an old-style pump, draws back,
squares off and says: "Lay down that stick and I'll lick you in
about three minutes." . . . Those were favorites with John
B. Gough, king of the mid-century Temperance platform.
Here is one from Dr. Charles A. Story, a medical lecturer
endorsed by the National Temperance Society: A man sees
his small daughter dipping a doll dress in a cup and asks why.
"I'm coloring my doll's dress red, Pa." He asks what with?
"With beer, Pa." "You can't color red with beer." "Yes, I can
. . . Ma said it was beer that colored your nose so red."

Rush also told of a certain Philadelphian who, despairing
of breaking his wife of drink—it's a Balzac kind of plot—tried
to use her weakness to get rid of her. He planted a tapped
cask of rum in an unused room and as if accidentally, left the
key in the door to tempt her to drink herself to death. The
lady divined his scheme and refused the opportunity; just to

spite him, in fact, she never touched another drop. Rush understood the uses of The Little Ones too: There was another farmer accustomed to come home drunk from market who, one Saturday before he had got in his weekly drinking, saw signs of rain and hurried home to save the hay drying in his field. His small son saw him drive up and ran into the house shouting: "Oh Mother! Father is come home and he isn't drunk." In this special world of Temperance propaganda Father was moved not to clout him but to vow never to go tippling again. And sonnyboy's piping voice was to echo down the generations with a smug insipidity that would have made William Blake lend Herod an eager hand.

That Out-of-the-Mouths-of-Babes-and-Sucklings motif was a principal resource of the movement along with The Drunkard's Wife, Over-the-Hill-to-the-Poorhouse and Delirium Tremens. The last three, being logical results of overdoing alcohol, would have been justifiable exhibits for the prosecution if kept in perspective and used with responsible restraint. Temperance was incapable of any such thing, however. Nor could it conceivably keep the posturings of Babes and Sucklings plausible: Here is a "confirmed inebriate who [has] squandered a large property in his intemperate career" entering "his cheerless home" too shamefaced even to look at his wife and child of six years (female), for both sexes among the limber-lipped children of Temperance-land often devastated Papa with their prattle. Wife tells child it's time for bed, she says her usual prayer, then asking leave to say one more, "lifted up her hands toward heaven, closed her eyes, and prayed . . . 'O Thou who hearest prayer, O spare my dear father! save him, I pray Thee, from the curse of intemperance!' That prayer was wafted with electric rapidity to the throne of God. . . . 'Amen' burst from the father's lips. . . . Wife and child were both clasped to his bosom and in penitence he exclaimed, 'My child, you have saved your father from a drunkard's grave!' "

The idiom is, of course, that of the early nineteenth century's admonitory tales for children by Hannah More, Maria Edgeworth, Mrs. Barbauld, *et al.*, on many different topics—thrift, obedience, honesty—but all aimed at training the young to do what they should by setting them rational, cause-and-effect examples. Those ladies happened to be writers of style though unsound pediatric psychologists. Their transatlantic imitators were even worse writers than psychologists and, fittingly, never more watery than when dealing with

I WAS ONCE WORTH $40.000.
I WAS ONCE RESPECTED AND RESPECTABLE.
I ONCE MOVED IN GOOD SOCIETY
SUCH THINGS AS I AM NOW ARE MADE
OUT OF SUCH MEN AS I ONCE WAS.

Temperance. Even in paraphrased summary they retain a tepid soapiness. A little boy of seven signs the pledge; presently an elder brother offers him brandy drops, but one taste tells the worst: "Don't you know I am a Temperance boy?" he says. "I won't eat them." When elder brother objects that they are only candy, our little hero says: "I think that brandy is brandy whether you take it out of a bottle or out of candy." Sometimes the intent is facetious: "Daddy, why is neighbor Smith's liquor shop like a counterfeit quarter? . . . Because you can't pass it." (POW!) Yet it was not always as false as it was sickly. Little Hannah Hawkins really did exist.

Note the hint of Over-the-Hill and the looming presence of The Drunkard's Wife in the bit about the little girl's prayer: Temperance was clever at blending minor themes in with the major one, and Over-the-Hill was a handy frame for whatever outrage the Demon had in hand at the time. The Rev. Dr. Heman Humphrey was soon right behind Rush in deploring the numerous families "literally reduced to beggary by intemperance. Business neglected, shops deserted, windows patched and stuffed with rags . . . long court dockets, crowded prisons, children crying for bread, and shivering with cold." In the next generation the Rev. Dr. Henry Ward Beecher, most conspicuous of old Lyman's many minister-sons, picked up the same theme describing a rum-ridden "town of lazy-men" that had "drunken, illegal, boisterous and brutal elections . . . doors hingeless and all a-creak . . . gates hung with ropes or lying flat in the mud . . . the school-house empty; the jail full; the church silent. . . . Good men [are] obliged to keep dark, and bad men . . . swear, fight, and rule the town." His hearers, the godly youth of Indianapolis, surely recognized that as a faithful portrait of the early Middle West's precociously run-down settlements of feckless trash. ". . . in a town of industrious people," Beecher went on, "grog-sellers would fail . . . elections [be] as orderly as weddings or funerals . . . fences in repair; school-houses swarming with rosy-faced children . . ." and so on, all outward and visible signs of freedom from vices of which the Demon was chief and of the Puritan theory that virtue and prosperity were chicken-and-egg.

Nevertheless, young Beecher could not be considered kiver-to-kiver sound on Temperance. He drank wine off and on throughout his unctuous career as minister of Brooklyn's famous Plymouth Church, and in this early lecture in Indianapolis he verged on the heresy that drunkenness is a symptom of instability, not vice versa. Down the generations that would occur to other, less cautious people greatly to the detriment of orthodox Temperance theory. Old Lyman's epoch-making *Six Sermons* had shown no such protopsychiat-

ric leanings. In his view the intimacy between Lady Poverty
and the Demon came of a subversive plot to saddle the shift-
less on the prosperous: ". . . the vicious portion of our community . . . drink up their daily earnings and bless God for
the poorhouse . . . as, of right, the drunkard's home . . . until the nation is bankrupt, the drunkard and his family must
have a home. . . . Every intemperate and idle man . . . regards your houses and lands as pledged to take care of him,
annually puts his hands deep in your pockets, and eats his
bread in the sweat of your brows, instead of his own." Keeping up the good work, the comic tippler of *Ten Nights in a
Bar-Room* would presently be telling audiences how he'd
never vote against Rum because Temperance men kept saying their success would abolish almshouses, which he might
need himself eventually, for: "I never knew a man to go to
the almshouse that he hadn't rum to blame for his poverty."
The Rev. T. L. Cuyler based a roguish tract on the economic
motif: Honest barkeeps, he said, should put up signs on their
premises thus:

> BANK FOR LOSINGS. Open at all hours. Nothing taken in
> but good money. Nothing paid out but disgrace and disease,
> and degradation and death . . . extra dividend of *delirium
> tremens* to old depositors. A free pass to *Perdition* . . . also
> tickets . . . to a *Drunkard's Grave*. All the children of de-
> positors sent without charge to the orphan-asylum or the
> alms-house.

The goldheaded-cane type of Temperance man liked to
rub his fellow taxpayer's nose in the cost of poorhouses full of
those whom the Demon had impoverished; of madhouses full
of those whom the Demon had sent out of their minds; of
jails and penitentiaries full of those he had tempted into mis-
behaving. Numerous superintendents of such places glibly assured the world that a high proportion of their inmates, ranging from a third to nine-tenths depending on the zeal of the
witness, were there through drink. Mankind's chronic taste
for *post hoc* logic and the simple-minded psychology of the
day kept such statistics impressive even under hardheaded
discount. They weighed heavily with men of substance, many

of whom came to consider contributions to the Temperance cause a property-protecting investment as well as a moral duty.

There was something in it, too: alcohol then was and still is an expensive luxury for society as a whole. Many persons, particularly the unstable and the dimwitted, of both of which groups we have too many, would be better off without access to it. The Sons of Temperance were probably justified in telling youngsters that joining up would help them get jobs. Whatever an employer's own dealings with Rum, he might well understand that the Sons' pledge led to punctuality and a clear head on Monday; and might further keep a boy out of mischief in the Sons' lodge rooms, "pleasant places of resort and social intercourse in which young men . . . may be lured from the bar-room and other scenes of dissipation"—the first hint, Krout says, of later effort to supply "substitutes for the saloon." But again Temperance overdid it, exaggerating the associated status symbols. In Temperance-land practically all bleary wrecks had squandered large properties. The Washingtonian exhorter was too glibly proud of how his toes had stuck out of his boots and his coat had been frayed and filthy, and now he was reformed, just look at his fine white shirt and flowered vest and beaver hat as good as the governor's! A tract about Little Hannah Hawkins contains some symptomatic verses about a drink-ruined family:

> I was a gay and happy girl,
>   And once I lived in wealth and pride;
> My father was a noble man,
>   With smiling children by his side.
> But now our marble house is changed
>   Into a hut with crumbling walls;
> The splendid pictures all are sold,
>   That once adorned our Grecian halls. . . .

In T. S. Arthur's *Woman to the Rescue* what most embitters the Rum-shattered hero is the local rumseller's bid to gain title to his victim's former house: ". . . the thought of seeing [his wife] go out from her beautiful home . . . into one comparatively poor and humble, while the coarse saloonkeeper's wife, who had more than once done service as menial in his house, passed up in her vulgar triumph and took proud possession of all that she had lost, almost maddened him." Decent housing and clean, conventional clothes as token of renewed self-respect and earning power were one thing; but this is worse than the Puritan doctrine that the wages of righteousness is prosperity—it is crude, shiny snobbery.

༄

> After supper pap took the jug, and said he had enough whiskey there for two drunks and one delirium tremens.
> —*Huckleberry Finn*

A very drunken citizen was jailed in Jefferson County, New York, in the early 1830's. Like many another chronic alcoholic denied drink after a heavy spree, he developed DTs—in the phrase of his time "the man with the poker was after him." His screams disturbed the jailer's family, whose living quarters were actually in the jail old-time, small-town style; and his leapings hither and yon in the cell as he tried to evade hallucinatory monsters were so violent that the jailer enlisted three other prisoners (also in for drunkenness) to help hold him down. It was all they could manage among them; I readily believe it because I was once one of three sizable persons trying to control a small man in alcoholic convulsions. And all night, as the jailer tried to sleep on the other side of the partition, he could hear these three horrified derelicts shakily promising one another they'd never touch the stuff again if this is what it did to you.

Whether or not that pledge was kept they illustrated—as did Jack Lemmon recently in *The Days of Wine and Roses*—that delirium tremens is magnificent Temperance propaganda. Telling wavering candidates for the water wagon about drunken murders and the drunkard's hell—necessarily speculative description—was all very well. But for lurid perorations that brought them twitching down the aisles the Temperance lecturer usually relied on the man-with-the-poker laid on as thick as he would stick. It is astonishing that Dr. Rush neglected the fascinations of DTs; he certainly must have seen cases. Anyway it was soon made up for. There were shrieking platform recitations in verse of which this must be a more than adequate sample:

> See how that rug those reptiles soil!
>   They're crawling o'er me in my bed!
> I feel their clammy, snaky coil
>   On every limb—around my head—
> With forked tongue I see them play;
> I hear them hiss—tear them away! . . .

In prose, the autobiography of a Temperance lecturer named Dutcher has five pages of by-one-who-knows description, close print. His serpents, fire-breathing demons, gigantic spiders, falls into bottomless pits, delusions of drowning, being burned alive and so on probably represent pretty much what he had given his audiences with the advantage of all the lung power and body-English he could apply. As snakes and imps palled, tipplers were warned of the victim of DTs who, imagining a rat had run down his throat, tried to haul it back up with tongs and fatally injured himself; or of a certain Abel Bishop of New Haven, accustomed to a quart of rum daily, who had the illusion that men were hacking off his flesh with saws and hanging his skin on wires to dry. . . .

Thus giving name and place was unusual. Most such instances were anonymous and, to judge from internal evidence, apocryphal. A certain Midwestern lawyer, they said, drank to the point of psychosis, yet still handled complicated cases well, though while speaking he "could see toads squatting in the corners of the courtroom . . . serpents . . . coiling all round before his eyes and hissing in his ears . . . imps dancing about in the air, spouting their blue breath in his face." The actual, unexaggerated horrors of DTs sound quite enough like the works of Hieronymus Bosch to need no such tall tales. This inability to play it honestly naturally led to listener's fatigue, travesty, and the imbedding of DTs in American folklore after the manner of *Peck's Bad Boy*. General Horace Porter, the George Jessel of the 1880's, told how the Puritans "generally began drinking on account of the bite of a snake, and usually had to quit on account of attacks from the same reptiles." The modern joke has the barkeep look up, see a row of little green men patiently waiting against the far wall, and say: "He ain't come in yet." Gadget stores sell cocktail aprons sporting pink elephants.

But before they ran it into the ground, Temperance got good service from DTs, even maintaining that this fulminating neuropsychiatric disaster is not confined to heavy drinkers. ". . . you are not as safe as you imagine," the American Temperance Society told the occasional imbiber. "Some of the worst cases of (DTs) . . . have been of persons who had rarely or never been known to be intoxicated . . . and were regarded by their neighbors as temperate men." The authority was a certain Dr. Hale. Temperance could always find well-meaning doctors eager to lie in the good cause.

The meanest men on the face of the earth are among the liquor-sellers in this country.

—JOHN B. GOUGH

As alcohol withdrew from the American dinner table as well as from the breakfast table, the barroom became what geometry would call the "locus" of the Demon Rum. Simultaneously, for associated reasons to be dealt with later, decent women pretty much abandoned public drinking places. The bar's customers were all men. Their drinks became shorter and stronger. The handiness of bars and the lubricant effect of alcohol on business deals led to tippling pretty much throughout the day in commercial centers. A drink was the next step after shaking hands on meeting a friend or closing a bargain. The drinks involved were no leisurely absorbed ale or cider or flip but rough-edged slings, cocktails or snorts of straight whiskey—and drunk the more quickly because sipping was thought unmanly or worse, penurious spinning-out to avoid having to order another. Drinking alone was so frowned on that a man who happened to be the only customer was obligated to ask the bartender to join him. And treating—the system of next-round-is-mine-boys—was so rigidly required that a man stopping in for one drink at a bar where he encountered six acquaintances would have to have seven before he left. Captain Marryat saw most of this already well developed on the eastern seaboard in the 1830's:

"If you meet, you drink; if you part, you drink. If you make acquaintance, you drink . . . it is a cause of serious offense to refuse . . . at times I drank much more than I wished . . . yet still I gave most serious offense, especially in the West, because I would not drink early in the morning. . . . I was introduced to at least twenty every forenoon; and had I drunk with them all, I should have been in the same state as many . . . not really sober for three or four weeks at a time." Such customs prevailed, as Ostrander notes about California, "among the social groups least able to afford it, down to . . . the Eighteenth Amendment."

These folkways meant good business for the rumseller all right. But in the long run they wrecked him because they focused the gaze of Temperance on the bar, soon called The Saloon, as the place where hard drinking most flourished; and of Dry-minded women on The Saloon as the place where, they suspected, their menfolks went to get away from them. So Temperance's pelting abuse of the Demon began to shift to the bartender and saloonkeeper. Drys were always far

harsher on the drink-supplier than on the drinker. It sought
to shame and frighten both into mending their ways. But
once jarred into pledge-taking, the reformed sot was presently getting pity and sometimes even help from the militantly righteous. The overt purpose of calling the rumseller a
grasping, cold-blooded villain deliberately making money
from the ruin of his fellow man was to make him quit the
business. But the shrillness of tone makes it clear that the
underlying motive was the need of every zealous cause for
something personal to hate. The rumseller was to Temperance what the silk-hatted capitalist is to Communism, what
Simon Legree was to Abolitionism.

Hard language for the man with towel and bung-starter
had old and deep roots. "Poisoners-general" was John Wesley's word for "all who sell liquor in the common way. . . .
They murder his Majesty's subjects by wholesale . . . drive
them to hell like sheep." Lyman Beecher, a man gifted in
holy hate, defied "any man who understands the nature of
ardent spirit, and yet for the sake of gain, continues to be
engaged in the traffic, to show that he is not involved in the
crime of murder." The Rev. Thomas P. Hunt, the Southern
Temperance stalwart who founded those Cold Water Armies
for children, said crisply that rumsellers deserved nothing
but a halter on earth and a hell hereafter. Presently a parson
named Beegle suggested rumsellers would do better to dose
each arriving customer with arsenic, "which would lay them
dead in a few hours and save their families so much sorrow."
(Again the presumption that at least a majority of those who
patronized the Demon were doomed to very grave trouble.)

Few such indignant parsons felt enough of the religion
they presumably exemplified to share the Rev. Dr. Nott's
opinion that thus to cry down the rumseller, "to injure his
business, to asperse his character, and to make him odious in
the community" might not be either kind or Christian. It
seems to have been principally the Washingtonians—basically
laymen and shy of religion—who hesitated to abuse barkeeps:
Speaking as a Washingtonian, Abraham Lincoln, for instance, questioned the wisdom of such denunciations. The
pulpit's prevalent tone was that of the Rev. John Marsh, who

accused barkeeps generally of hating reformed drunkards and sneaking alcohol into their soft drinks to trip them up.

Mrs. S. K. Leavitt, steely-eyed leader of Cincinnati's Women Crusaders, boasted of using sumptuary snobbery against the beleaguered rumseller: She accused a down-and-out married drunkard of loving the local saloonkeeper better than himself: ". . . he is a portly, nice-looking man and look at yourself. His house is a fine-looking house, and yours is in arrears for rent. . . . You love that saloon-keeper's little girl better than you do your own . . . [she] has a nice white dress and a blue sash and nice white shoes and look at your . . . little girl. And strangest of all I think you like his wife better than you do your own . . . as I was coming by, his wife was just going out to ride, and she . . . had on a nice silk dress and your wife has only a calico, and when she goes out she walks." Instead of throwing this sneering busybody out, the man signed the pledge and prayed, and three weeks later at Sunday school "a great tall man came down the aisle leading a little girl dressed in a white dress and a blue sash and little white shoes," and guess who it was! He had sworn off tobacco, too.

It got the rumseller nowhere to keep a decent place attracting only gentlemanly, solvent drinkers. If there had to be saloons Temperance wanted them to be dark, sordid, full of bums and seedy ward heelers to give drink a bad name and keep it worsening. Anything else they resented as they resented Whitlock's Moderate Drinker. Further, Temperance threatened the saloonkeeper with not only hell in the next world but a good chance of penury and a premature grave in this one. Zestfully they quoted dubious but startling statistics purporting to show expectancy of life abnormally low among bartenders. In Dr. Jewett's home village in Connecticut, back when a tavern-keeper's was still a respected calling, of four successive men trying it, he recalled, good, steady-going, genial types too, three died "the lamented victims of their own traffic" and the fourth saw drink ruin his family though not himself. Gerrit Smith averred that of twenty-nine rum-sellers operating at one time or another over twenty-two years in Peterboro, four died drunken and poor, twenty still lived drunken and poor, the five still in good circumstances had quit the business before succumbing to their own stock-in-trade. These dire predictions rounded out Temperance's secular case. Obviously the Demon benefited nobody but the brewer and the distiller—not even undertakers, for paupers' funerals hardly paid for the time and trouble involved, and yet added to the community tax load of which undertakers, like other local businessmen, had to pay their compulsory share.

> Farewell! farewell! a long farewell
>   To brandy, rum and toddy!
> Old Slade may buy, old Slade may sell,
>   And ruin soul and body.
> Of brandy tods I've had my fill,
>   Of whisky, rum and gin, sir;
> I leave them all with right good will,
>   And a temperance life begin, sirs. . . .
>   —Song to the tune of "Yankee Doodle" from
>   *Ten Nights in a Bar-Room*, V, iv

In 1943 the will of Samuel M. Schoonover of Stroudsburg, Pennsylvania, retired bachelor schoolteacher, left his life's savings to the local high school on condition that its library keep ten copies of *Ten Nights in a Bar-Room* always on its shelves available to students. But the library had only one copy and the book had been out of print for many years. Hoping to locate a few copies in local attics, the principal gave the story to the press. The wire services, always pleased with curious wills, sent it all over the country. One rewrite man put in his lead that, taking the bequest at the stated $25,000, copies of *Ten Nights* were worth $2,500 each in Stroudsburg. After that the deluge—almost 2,000 offers in letters and telephone calls from all over, many getting the principal or the school librarian out of bed late at night. Among the enthusiasts planning to get married or have an operation or go to Europe on the proceeds were enough offers free or at nominal price to enable the school to stockpile ninety-six copies with which to observe the conditions for the foreseeable future. Income from the bequest is regularly expended on school equipment that the budget fails to cover.

Even now, twenty years later, two or three offers of a copy at $2,500-or-make-me-an-offer trickle in annually as persons see the picture-story about it in an old copy of *Life*. Stroudsburg youth have not given those ten shelved copies the complete snubbing that might have been predicted; in token of some kind of interest five have been stolen so far. That should certainly gratify the shades of Mr. Schoonover and Timothy Shay Arthur; and of Dr. Rush, for essentially *Ten Nights,* though Arthur wrote it, is fictionized Rush supplemented with teetotalism.

Born in Newburgh, New York, reared in Baltimore, identified mostly with Philadelphia, allegedly delivering himself of *Ten Nights* while visiting in Allentown, Pennsylvania, Arthur is further evidence that the Middle Atlantic States set the tune for early Temperance. (Prohibition, it will be seen, was rather the child of New England and the Yankee-tinged upper Middle West.) His meager autobiography tells of his failing to profit by the way Baltimore schools taught arithmetic and quitting the classroom at the age of thirteen to become a watchmaker's apprentice. He nevertheless acquired fluency with the pen and a bookish bent, for he damaged his eyesight by reading in bad light after his day of eye-challenging work, left his trade for commercial jobs, and took to scribbling as a hobby. His joining an early Temperance society at the age of eighteen and then the Washingtonians (Baltimore-born, remember) in the early 1840's did not, he hastily assured his readers, betoken "experience in my own person of the evils of intemperance" but approval of Temperance's objectives. At the age of twenty-four he was editing a Baltimore paper. Among his contributors was Edgar Allan Poe, who called him incapable of work appealing to "a refined taste." In 1844 he shifted base to Philadelphia to become one of the hacks supplying publishers there and in New York City with their run-of-mine press-fodder. He also edited this or that magazine and eventually acquired one of his own.

Soon he was an old pro in a field requiring only mild ingenuity, frictionless conformity to the vocabulary, style and content that editors expected and readers put up with, and glib productivity. There he excelled—Frank Luther Mott, expert on American mass-literature, calls him one of our most prolific writers. His score or so of Temperance novels are only a minor fraction of his logorrheic output. The bulk of it was aimed at housewives, sometimes incidentally their menfolks, under titles eloquent of content and watery handling: *Tired of Housekeeping; The Mother; Retiring from Business; Rising in the World; The Way to Prosper; The Old Man's Bride.* . . .

Likely it was the Washingtonian connection that set him on the high and Dry road to immortality. He edited several of the elaborate Sons of Temperance yearbooks, working up fulsome biographies of the Order's leaders complete with steel-engraved portraits, gathering outside contributions in verse and prose from names more or less known, and filling the chinks with journeyman bits of his own. His first full-length Temperance book, *Six Nights With the Washingtonians*, sold encouragingly well. Many Temperance novels had preceded it and some, such as L. M. Sargent's *Temperance Tales*, which eventually ran to 130 editions, were far better written. But with the appearance of *Ten Nights in a Bar-Room* in 1854 Arthur became and remained chief of the guild of Temperance writers. Its special advantage was, on a guess, its all-out appeal to heightened public reprehension of the man behind the bar. That was the core round which he dangled Rush's standard clichés: The Drunkard's Wife, Babes-and-Sucklings and so on, basic as Jung's archetypes, cozily inevitable like the enchanted princess' long golden hair and the king's sons numbering three, no more, no less.

His gentlemanly narrator, respectable though inexplicably foot-loose, tells of his successive visits to Cedarville—location vague; Allentown claims that Arthur had in mind a nearby hamlet called Cetronia, but it could have been anywhere from Terre Haute to Troy. The first episode occurs soon after Simon Slade, local miller, has sold his mill and bought and spruced up the previously run-down and disreputable local tavern, the Sickle and Sheaf. He thinks of it as more profitable than milling with less work and higher prestige. Mrs. Slade has misgivings but loyally takes over the kitchen and housekeeping. Their adolescent son Frank proves a clever barkeep. In the hands of a man like Slade the Sickle and Sheaf attracts the custom of the local oligarch, Judge Hammond, his happy-go-lucky son Ned, and others who had formerly stayed away; it bids fair to prosper.

Another steady patron is one Joe Morgan, who once worked at the mill but is now nearing the bottom of the drunkard's downward path. Agonized pleas from his wife and small daughter Mary cannot keep him from spending every dime he lays hands on for more blue ruin at the tavern. Late every night Little Mary seeks him out there to beg him to come home. In his cups Morgan has a sulky way of reproaching Slade with being the community bloodsucker. One night he tries it once too often and Slade, tipsy himself, throws a heavy tumbler at him. It misses Morgan but fells Little Mary, just entering. She is taken home seriously injured. As her condition worsens, Morgan has a fit of DTs in her sickroom. During his ensuing remorse she tells him of a dream she has just had: She dreamed that in spite of his promise to stay, he left the house and she anxiously followed him to the tavern, only it was no longer that but a store filled with useful goods, with Morgan's name over the door, and there was himself "dressed so nice," she says, ". . . a new hat and a new coat; and your boots were new and polished just like Judge Hammond's. I said 'Oh Father—is this you?' And then you took me up in your arms and kissed me and said—'Yes Mary, I am your real father, not old Joe Morgan—but Mr. Morgan now.' Oh! I was so glad!" And she dies, exacting promises from him never to go to the tavern, never to take a drink again.

Slade scrapes clear of prosecution for manslaughter. Morgan, staying teetotal, gradually rises as Slade sinks. On each recurring visit the narrator finds Slade and his son drinking harder, the once trig Sickle and Sheaf dingier and nastier. A gambler whom Slade tolerates as a well-paying customer fleeces and then kills young Hammond and is in turn killed while trying to evade a lynch mob. Judge Hammond, whose boots were Little Mary's shining symbol of righteousness, goes to the poorhouse ruined by drink. His wife dies insane. Quarrels between Slade and Frank end in the boy's killing his father. . . .

Cedarville is understandably dismayed by these heaped-up catastrophes. *Mr.* Morgan strikes while the iron is hot: "As one who has himself been well-nigh lost," he tells his fellow citizens, ". . . who daily feels and trembles at the dangers that beset his path—I do conjure you to stay the fiery stream that is bearing everything good and beautiful among you to destruction. Fathers! for the sake of your young children, be up now and doing . . . resolve, this night, that the . . . traffic shall cease in Cedarville. Is there not a large majority . . . in favor of such a measure? And whose rights and interests can be affected by such a restriction? . . . Was [Slade] benefited by the liberty to work harm to his neighbor?" This might be merely a plea for local option. But a previous chat between the narrator and the hostler of the Sickle and Sheaf has endorsed the Maine Law type of statewide Prohibition, which was at the height of its glory at the time.

As Temperance picked up speed again after the Civil War, Arthur turned out several more anti-Demon novels: *The Bar-Rooms at Brantly; Three Years in a Man-Trap,* hammering it home that rumselling endangers seller as well as customer; *The Strike at Tivoli Mills,* depicting labor organization as based on the vicious influence of the saloon; *Danger,* best written of the lot, making fashionable parties responsible for entrapping reformed drunkards or creating new ones. . . . None approached the success of *Ten Nights* which had shared best-selling honors of its year with Bulfinch's *The Age of Fable;* Ingraham's *The Prince of the House of David* (a forerunner of the *Ben Hur* sort of thing); Reade's *The Cloister and the Hearth;* Thackeray's *The Newcomes;* and Whitman's *Leaves of Grass*—fast company indeed. And even so, says Professor Mott, it did not come into its own till, on expiration of its copyright in the 1890's, a rush of twenty-five-cent editions enabled Temperance societies and Sunday school libraries to distribute it really widely.

Comparison with *Uncle Tom's Cabin* of the same decade is

Kansas State Historical Society

Carry A. Nation in full smashing regalia but looking pleasant for the camera—an unusual expression.

The New York Times

At the age of sixty, Dr. Benjamin Rush, father of most of the ideas basic to Temperance, looked just as sot-in-his-ways as one would expect. [From drawing by William Haines]

John Bartholomew Gough, outstanding Temperance "lecturer" of the mid-nineteenth century. [From *Autobiography* (1867)]

Frances Elizabeth Willard, "Uncrowned Queen" of the Woman's Christian Temperance Union, at the height of her powers in the early 1890's. [From *The Review of Reviews;* clipping in the Picture Collection, New York Public Library]

A *Harper's Weekly* depiction of a typical big city doggery in 1874. Note the drunken woman, the boy stealing the customer's handkerchief and the scantily clothed child involved in the scene at the doorway.

The Delirium Tremens Room in a Philadelphia prison as depicted in T. S. Arthur's *Three Years in a Man-Trap* (1872). The gentleman taking the prisoner's plight so hard is his partner in a saloon.

COMMIT HIM FOR MANSLAUGHTER IN THE GREATEST DEGREE.

One of the numerous anti-Demon cartoons that *Harper's Weekly* ran in early 1874 as the Women's Crusade increased interest in Temperance. Note that both the turnkey and the broom-armed guard on the wall are women.

These Almanacs sent free, on application to R. H. McDonald & Co.,
cor. Washington and Chariton Streets, New York.

An enthusiastic response to the Women's Crusade of 1873–74. The ribbon across the lady's bosom reads TOTAL ABSTINENCE. Note the torch falling from the hand of the skeleton as a symbol of death.

Taste not the Cup.

Oh ! teach not the love of the tempting cup
   To the darling son at home ;
There are snares enough that beset the paths
   Amongst which his feet must roam.
Oh ! throw not around the alluring drink
   The sanction of thy use,
Lest the beautiful child in ruin sink,
   The victim of its abuse.

[From *The National Temperance Almanac,* 1878]

HARPER'S WEEKLY.

A JOURNAL OF CIVILIZATION

Vol. XVIII—No. 911.]   NEW YORK, SATURDAY, JUNE 13, 1874.   [WITH A SUPPLEMENT.
[PRICE TEN CENTS.

Entered according to Act of Congress, in the Year 1874, by Harper & Brothers, in the Office of the Librarian of Congress, at Washington.

Harper's Weekly (the artist the famous Thomas Nast) depicts as hogs the Cincinnati police who arrested Mrs. Leavitt's Women Crusaders. A hundred years ago Cincinnati was often called Porkopolis because so many hogs were butchered and processed there.

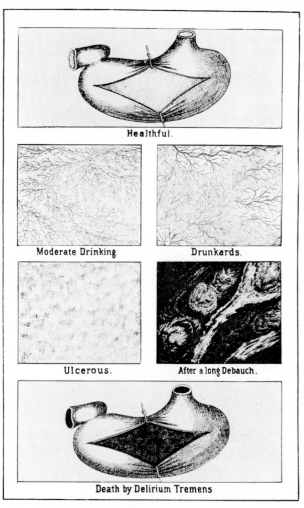

DIAGRAMS OF THE HUMAN STOMACH IN VARIOUS CONDITIONS
First published in 1842 by Dr. Thomas Sewall, Professor of Pathology
in the College of Columbia, D. C.

Engravings of the famous colored pictures of what alcohol does to one's stomach that played a crucial role in early Temperance propaganda; prepared by Dr. Thomas Sewell of Columbia Medical College. [From Delavan, *Temperance Essays*]

Timothy Shay Arthur, highly prolific author of *Ten Nights in a Bar-Room*. [From Arthur, *Orange Blossoms*, 1871]

The Reverend Theobald Mathew, who probably administered the Temperance pledge to more persons than any other Temperance crusader ever did. [From Maguire, *Father Mathew*]

General John P. St. John, Prohibition Party candidate for President in 1884, violated the rules for Presidential aspirants in the 1880's by not having a full beard. But he made up for it by the finest mustache since Vercingetorix.

Kansas State Historical Society

John Jacobus Flournoy of Georgia, eccentric who made the first effort to get Temperance into politics. [From Scomp, *King Alcohol in the Realm of King Cotton*]

General Neal Dow, most conspicuous leader in making and keeping the State of Maine the first in the Union to try statewide Prohibition. [From Clubb, *The Maine Liquor Law*]

A Women's Crusade "praying band" in Hillsboro, Ohio, beleaguering a saloon. [From Harper's Weekly, March 14, 1874]

inevitable: Both were shameless propaganda and immensely helped their respective causes, yet the Reformist organizations helped did not commission them directly. Both texts are pretty wordy and watery though in most literary respects *Ten Nights* is rather worse—yet Little Mary never quite reaches the heights of mawkishness to which Mrs. Stowe pushed Eva St. Clair. (Only relative to other hack fictions of the day does Arthur's book deserve Mott's goodhearted ascription of "extraordinary vitality . . . vivid scenes, sharp characterization, vigorous writing.") Of the two, *Ten Nights* has higher authenticity. Arthur obviously knew country taverns. Mrs. Stowe had never been near a slave auction, a cotton plantation or New Orleans.

Both novels became far more widely known in stage versions than they could have in print alone. *Ten Nights* was as well fitted for stage adaptation as if Arthur had kept that in mind, whereas *Uncle Tom* was clottily difficult to tailor to stage needs; yet over the generations *Uncle Tom* as play far outstripped *Ten Nights*. The latter's distinction was merely that of being the outstanding Temperance drama and a surefire item in the repertories of second-rate troupes. They made the Sickle and Sheaf almost as well known in tanktown America as the Palmer House in Chicago, and Little Mary's traditional interpolated number, "Father, Dear Father, Come Home with Me Now," was almost as deeply soaked into the national consciousness as Little Eva's death scene. As the Civil War made slavery an anachronism *Uncle Tom* lost its original point, so its stage versions degenerated into travesties of the already depressed Negro. But after 1865 the good cause that *Ten Nights* espoused took on new life and meanwhile book and play—particularly play—had done much to keep anti-Demon feeling warm against the great day coming of the Women's Crusade and the Prohibition Party. It was actually filmed with serious intent only thirty-five years ago, last of six known movie versions, and the stage version is still in print for amateurs to produce for laughs. One hopes that Arthur, wherever he is, is unaware of this perversion of his immortality.

At least he made a little talent go a very long way in a

direction in which far greater ones accomplished much less; for a peculiarity of the literature—if that is the word—of Temperance is the botches that reputable writers made when trying their hands at it: Walt Whitman, Hawthorne, Mrs. Stowe, Alice and Phoebe Cary, Edward Everett Hale, George W. Cable. Admirers of Whitman do well to neglect his Washingtonian-flavored Temperance novel, *Franklin Evans or, The Inebriate*. It shows the catalytic poet-prophet apologizing for Negro slavery; clumsily committing melodrama; and all in a cliché-ridden prose showing no hint of the originality of the author of *Leaves of Grass*. In mitigation consider that he was only twenty-three years old at the time and doubtless needed whatever he was paid for it. Mrs. Stowe's "Betty's Bright Idea" is both vulgar and flabby except when, maybe thinking of her own alcoholic son, she enters a plea for the drunkard as intermittently miserable himself. Cable—who flirted with Temperance though he did troupe with Mark Twain—was at nothing like his best in "Gregory's Island," which advises self-exile on an uninhabited Gulf sandbank as sole hope for an alcoholic.

≋

Mr. [Francis] Murphy has no use for temperance poetry, looking upon the subject as too severe for doggerel, and of too practical and common-sense a nature to be treated in rhyme.

—DANIELS, *The Temperance Reform*

Sickly as Temperance fictions were, however, the allied poetry was worse, as the reader may have guessed for himself from mottoes so far in this book. Verse writing was a disease of the time. Newspapers of all sizes and degrees of importance had "Poet's Corners" sometimes filled with stuff cribbed from other papers but all too often with the rhymed, diabetic verbal equivalents of silk embroidery produced by local bards, usually but by no means always female. The verse that Mark Twain attributed to Emmeline Grangerford in *Huckleberry Finn* hits the tone precisely. Young men with honorable in-

tentions sweat out verses for their sweethearts' albums. Any
given banquet, anniversary or reunion was usually occasion
for half-witted but at least nominally fresh-cut rhymes. "An-
nuals"—fancy-bound books full of steel engravings of bosky
dells and bits of fancy writing, were stuffed with dim verse.
And among the dimmest were always found those dealing
with the Demon Rum. Or if vigorous, they were as grotesque
as William H. Burleigh's "The Rum Fiend":

> Through the rusty gates of a prison-door,
> Handcuffed and chained to the granite floor,
> With granite walls around and o'er,
>   He saw on the damp straw lying
> A drunken father whose hands were red
> With the blood of his boy in madness shed,
> And he muttered, "Dead! ha! ha! he's dead!
>   'Tis a capital joke—his dying!"
> What a shriek he gave, for a child so small,
> When his thin skull crashed on the garden wall,
> And the brains gushed out with a crimson jet! . . .

That sort of thing could almost drive one back to the
works of Mrs. Lydia Huntley Sigourney, the chronic poetess
of Hartford, Connecticut, with whose occasional handlings of
Temperance the reader is already familiar—as familiar as he
cares to be, no doubt, so no more will be quoted. We cannot,
however, afford to ignore Ella Wheeler Wilcox's youthful
affair with Temperance. Her name persists in our time only
as creator of "Laugh and the world laughs with you" and the
Poems of Passion and *Poems of Pleasure* that caused such
shocked outcry in the press eighty years ago. Much earlier,
however, she had been precocious girl-author of *Drops of
Water,* a volume of hot anti-Demonizings that she had ex-
truded back home on the farm in Wisconsin in consequence
of much reading in the Temperance press. She got all of fifty
dollars for it, and presently had the pleasure of seeing the
National Temperance Society and Publication House take
up her book for nationwide distribution: Mark Sullivan as a
Pennsylvania schoolboy was one of many thousands made to
learn by heart "The Two Glasses," her rhymed debate be-

tween a glass of wine and a glass of water. Another of her
Drops precisely summarized the Temperance approach of her
day:

> I saw the youth lift a mug to his mouth,
> Drink the last drop of the fearful *first glass!*
> Oh! his veins thrill in a fierce scorching drought,
> He fills it again, again drinks it! Alas! . . .

That has curious overtones of Gerard Manley Hopkins,
though it is chronologically impossible that the pigtailed Ella
Wheeler of the 1870's could have had knowledge of his work.
It is more plausible that, among her several styles, she sometimes dabbled in pre-Raphaeliting:

> I saw a mother give wine to her boy,
>   The rainbows fall and fall,
> The pride of his parents, a household joy,
>   A mother's blessing, her all.

> I saw the cheek of the youth grow red,
>   The rain falls o'er the lea,
> The light of his eye shone like jewels, they said,
>   It spoke of ruin to me. . . .

In her sterner aspects she was often her own idiosyncratic
self, however, and pretty memorable:

> I saw the maiden sweet, loving, confiding,
> Smile when he whispered, "Mine!"
> Saw her lips meet his with no word of chiding
> Though his breath fumed with wine.
> I saw the lover and maid at the altar,
> Bound by the bands divine,
> Heard the responses, they fail not nor flutter,
> Saw the guests pledge in wine.
> Howl, howl, ominous Owl!
> Shriek of the terrible tempest's scowl! . . .

Others may prefer prose to the same purpose in the same
period, such as the numerous Temperance novels of Mrs.

Julia McNair Wright, *Nothing to Drink; Jug-or-Not*—at least they are better than Walt Whitman's.

> We do not think
> We'll ever drink
>   Whiskey or Gin,
>   Brandy or Rum,
>   Or anything
> That'll make drunk come.
>   —Pledge of the Cold Water Armies

At the age of seven or so they sent me to an elderly piano teacher across the street. He was a poor instructor; I was a bored pupil; nothing much came of it. But his practice materials included a book of songs that he claimed as his own compositions,* one of which sticks in my head, a waltz tune sounding as if written for a muted calliope, the lyric beginning:

> Touch not the wine in the days of thy youth!
>   Touch not the wine, touch not the wine!
> It brings only sorrow, it takes away truth—
>   Touch not the wine in thy youth!

Anybody marveling that so young a child received such premature warnings—I never so much as laid eyes on wine for a dozen years afterward—has not grasped the educational role that Temperance managed to arrogate to itself in the years up to World War I. Most Americans born before 1910 and reared in Protestant sects (except Episcopalian) have youthful memories of some such Temperance war chants. Long before Pavlov and Watson the Demon's foes had the hang of behaviorist conditioning. Hannah Hawkins was a mere toddler when the Rev. Thomas P. Hunt, who reared five daughters teetotal and hoped to effect the same clean sweep in all

---

* I always suspected the old gentleman of being a faker, so I was delighted to find in *The Temperance Musician* (1854) glaring evidence that he had plagiarized both air and lyric.

godly families, began to enlist his "Cold Water Armies" of boys and girls. Boys wore blue ribbons, girls white, to betoken commitment never to trifle with the Demon and to scorn any of their elders doing so: "Drunkards have no right to celebrate the Fourth of July," said the Cold Water Army catechism. "Benedict Arnold was a rumseller and a drunkard. Three of the most important defeats . . . during the Revolution were sustained by men who died drunkards. . . ."

Late in the 1850's the Band of Hope movement came from England to compete with indigenous organizations for the privilege of protecting youth from the Demon. Its pledges barred tobacco and profanity as well as alcohol, a common Syndromism already suggested by Dr. Rush, of course: "Smoking and chewing tobacco," he had written, "by rendering water and simple liquors insipid dispose very much to the stronger stimulus of ardent spirits." Several generations later a quondam hotel proprietor from Elmira, New York, turned Temperance lecturer, was telling audiences of children: ". . . when I see a little boy smoking or swearing, it is sufficient evidence to me that it is but a question of time when he will acquire greater vices . . . tobacco and blasphemy are linked together." I once knew a Methodist-reared boy who sometimes broke absently into a song that had evidently burned itself into his soul:

> We're marching, we're marching, our brave little band!
> On the right hand of Temp'rance we now take our stand.
> We don't use tobacco, because we do think
> That those who do use it are li'ble to drink.
> Down with King Alcohol! Ah-ah-ah-men!

(When I last heard of him he was successfully managing a brewery.)

The captive audiences afforded by Sunday schools were the favorite forcing beds for Cold Water Armies, Bands of Hope and so on. The results were visible at Temperance parades, picnics and conventions in straggling bodies of small fry squeaking out anti-Demon catchwords and Temperance adaptations of well-known hymns. Those objecting that to

pledge a child to lifelong abstinence before he could responsibly make such a decision was as immoral as to cause him to
sign a check to be honored later were told that it could never
be too soon to renounce sin; and that many children thus
alerted against the Demon at impressionable ages in tones
fraught with due horror would turn into indelibly Dry-
minded voters and parents. There was very clear warning in
the slogan of the Loyal Temperance Legion, juvenile wing of
the WCTU: "Tremble, King Alcohol," its members chirped
in unison, "we shall grow up!"

A special Temperance literature for children was distributed to Sunday school libraries by religious bodies such as the
American Tract Society as well as by Temperance agencies.
Its quality was ineffable: Please hold still for a couple of
samples from the easy-rhyming pen of Dr. Jewett:

> Now the poison hot and strong
> Trickles through the pipe along,
> Till it drops into the cask.
> Little reader, do you ask
> Why they turn molasses sweet
> That is given us to eat
>   Into rum? I'll tell you why:
> 'Tis that foolish men may buy
> And drink the poison stuff and die.

And now the versified tale of little Margaret Briggs,

> . . . a sweet little child,
> And always to good was inclined;
> She was honest, obedient, pleasant and mild
>   And her heart it was tender and kind.
>
> Her mother, when sober, was one of the best,
>   And loved little Margaret well;
> But she was a drunkard, and loved to taste
>   The poison which rum-sellers sell . . .

and when drunk, often whipped the child and sent her to bed
supperless; while the sight of her weeping bitterly on her way
to fetch booze for Mamma was all too familiar to the neigh-

borhood. One day a local storekeeper threw out a batch of
cherries that had been soaking in rum; a sow with a litter of
pigs ate them, got drunk and staggered along

>   . . . to where Margaret lived,
>   Then stumbling she fell on the ground,
> While the poor little pigs of her care now deprived,
>   Ran squeaking and squealing around.

> Such a sight as this could not fail to stir
>   The feelings of Margaret Briggs;
> So she ran to her mother and said unto her,
>   "How I pity those poor little pigs!"

> "You pity the pigs! and for what, I pray?"
>   "Oh ma, come and look in the street;—
> Their mother's got drunk and fell down by the way,
>   And the poor pigs have nothing to eat.

> "Oh how will they find their way back to the sty?
>   Or where through the night will they stay?"
> "I'm sure I can't tell," was the mother's reply,
>   As she turned from the window away.

> But the vision stuck by her—herself she had seen
>   In the beast that lay drunk at her door;
> So she called in her children and washed them up clean,
>   And never drank rum any more.

As generations passed, the content remained pretty much
what a certain Mrs. Stuckenberger fed a juvenile audience in
Brattle Hall, Cambridge, Massachusetts, in 1896 at a celebration of the tenth anniversary of the town's going dry: "I con-
gratulate you children that you do not know what it is to see
a saloon in your city. . . . When I was a little girl . . . my
schoolhouse was surrounded by saloons. . . . I used to hear
the screaming of the children because a drunken father was
whipping them . . . we . . . were often frightened by the
sight of bloody, fighting men . . . not only the common ignorant people but . . . men who were called gentlemen. . . .
On one side of my father's grounds lived a brewer. He had
two sons, nice, bright boys, but the oldest died young—of
drinking. . . . The other lives yet . . . ruined because he

cannot keep sober. . . . On the other side was a doctor. His oldest son was a man to be proud of, but his father began to keep a drugstore, where he sold drinks of liquor, and this promising son . . . died of drunkenness after making his wife and children very unhappy and also very poor. Another neighbor . . . a minister's son . . . also got drunk and at night he would frighten his wife and children so that they had to run away. . . . All the trouble . . . and not having enough to eat . . . drove his poor, lovely wife crazy; and she, the kindest, sweetest, happiest mother of my little schoolmates, died in the poorhouse, and her youngest boy, a drunkard, was buried at twenty-four."

The compact, classic form is best seen, however, in a tale vouched for by staunch Dr. Delavan of the "little golden-haired boy" whose elder adolescent brother was inveigled into a groggery, plied with drink, came home surly drunk, found little brother hoeing his little garden patch, took umbrage at a chance remark of the little fellow's, killed him with his own little hoe and was hanged for it. "Was this youth the only guilty person deserving punishment?" asked the final paragraph. "Let the children of District and Sunday schools decide this question." On reaching voting age many of them did decide it in just the indicated way. Not all, of course—in my childhood a tougher-minded minority of Sunday school pupils felt it in their bones that any idea that a preacher or a lady unrelated to you (like 'rs. Stuckenberger) presented was probably treacherous nonsense. But in the plastic majority, intellectual docility was strong.

The end-product sought was epitomized by Cincinnati's Mrs. Leavitt, of the Women's Crusade: She was walking downtown with her little boy. At a certain point his hand tightened in hers and he huddled close as if in fear. She asked: "Why, Willie, what's the matter?" There were volumes of meaning in the reproachful roll of his solemn blue eyes as he whispered: "Didn't Mama know that her little boy was a-passin' a saloon?" Frances Willard often borrowed that one to make the WCTU ladies' eyes moisten and throats swell inside their high-boned net collars. She also made great play with a certain Little Bessie, who came forward at a meeting when pledge-signers were sought: "I can see her yet in her white dress and blue ribbons and little white shoes," and was asked if she understood what the pledge implied. "I shall never forget," Miss Willard would go on, "how her little face lighted up with the words, 'I sign not for myself so much, but at home I have a little brother Artie, he is only four years old, and when he grows to be a man you said that folks would ask him to go into the saloon and drink, and I thought maybe if he knew I had signed the pledge it would help him, so I want to sign as an example.' Could a better reason have been given?"

Redding Ridge, Connecticut, was where this preternatural sisterliness allegedly occurred. Whenever I am in that neighborhood I think of Little Bessie.

9

TUNES FOR THE
ANGELS

. . . the "moral" drunken drama is hurtful in an indirect
and not easily explainable way.
—OLIVE LOGAN, *Women and Theatres* (1869)

TEN NIGHTS by no means founded the Temperance drama but was only the peak of a tradition already lively. As Washingtonianism crested in 1844, the management of the Boston Museum* sought to exploit it by hiring a local "gentleman of known and appreciated literary talents" to do a Temperance play. He may have been the Rev. John Pierpont, that prolific source of Temperance poesy. Whoever he was, his script proved not stagey enough, so W. H. Smith, actor-stagemanager of the Museum, fattened it up with the stage clichés of the time: The lawyer-villain stealing the will; the comic yokel always there in the nick of time and flirting with the comic spinster afflicted with Malapropism; and the mad girl talking poetical gibberish and strewing flowers à la Ophelia. For Temperance bait there was a Washingtonian rescuing the hero from drink, and what was probably the first DTs scene ever staged, played by Smith in person.

The plot was largely Over-the-Hill. When the rumseller taunts the down-and-out hero with: "Ha! ha! what has brought you to this beastly condition, young man?" the hero shouts: "You! Rum! Eternal curses on you! Had it not been for your infernal poison shop in our village, I had been still a man—the foul den, where you plunder the pockets of your fellows, where you deal forth rum in tumblers, from whence goes forth the blast of ruin over the land to mildew the

* The "museum" theatres of large American cities had usually begun as paid-admission shows of stuffed and other curiosities, gone on to exhibit live freaks of sideshow level, then offered "moral exhibitions" that were actually stage plays in the "lecture" or "concert" room—a subterfuge taking the curse off things theatrical, which enabled God-fearing folks to attend.

bright hopes of youth, to fill the widow's heart with agony, to curse the orphan, to steal the glorious mind of man, to cast them from their high estate of honest pride, to make them—such as I!" Mr. Smith wrote himself a fat part.

The Museum's management was so confident it had something that, defying tradition, it ran *The Drunkard* unsupported by musical acts and farce afterpieces at the same performance. It justified their faith, playing 140-odd times off and on that season and next—an unheard-of number—and was soon regularly billed by touring troupes. It is still done for laughs, like *Ten Nights*. Three of those in the Boston company were later among those staging *Uncle Tom* in Albany in 1853—a cross-relation between the drama of Temperance and that of antislaveryism which persisted. Thus in 1860, Cordelia Howard, the infant phenomenon who created the stage Little Eva, played both Little Mary in *Ten Nights* and Little Katy in *Hot Corn,* a stage version of Solon Robinson's lurid, Temperance-hot newspaper series about gutter life in New York City.

The Boston stage soon also saw *One Cup More* and *First and Last Pledge.* By 1847, American managers had available *The Bottle,* a tableau-studded melodrama cobbled up in London from the prints of a drink-doomed family engraved by George Cruikshank, the great English illustrator who was also a Temperance zealot. His series ended with the daughter a whore and the son a criminal. The dramatist showed them reformed by the shock of seeing father in the madhouse. *The Drunkard's Warning* came along in 1856.

Meanwhile *The Drunkard* itself, staged by P. T. Barnum in the "lecture-room" of his American Museum on Broadway, had racked up "the first run of modern dimensions" (says George C. D. Odell, historian of the New York stage), of some 150 *consecutive* performances. W. R. Goodall, who did the alcoholic hero for Barnum, is said to have died of drink within a few years. C. W. Clarke, who had staged it for Barnum, took over that role after a few weeks—was Goodall already living the part too eagerly?—and did it so well and played it so often here and there that he became known as "Drunkard" Clarke. In its time *The Drunkard* helped *Ten*

Nights keep the shrieks of DTs alive in the nation's consciousness. But with the 1880's it tended to drop out of standard repertory, possibly because the smaller casts and fewer changes of scene of the younger play made it cheaper to produce.

Owing so much to the stage, Temperance proved shockingly ungrateful. In 1843 the selectmen of Worcester, Massachusetts, citing a local ordinance against theatrical exhibitions, forbade some strolling Washingtonians to pollute the town with a "Moral Exhibition of the Reformed Drunkard." The American Temperance Union, approving, said that "the cause of God and humanity [Temperance] needs not the aid of buffoonery, mountebanks, and theatrical exhibitions." In the next generation, Frances Willard of the WCTU refused free seats for her ladies at a dramatization of Arthur's *Three Years in a Man-Trap* on the grounds that she and they needed all their time for "higher things." As a girl she had once attended a theatre—a performance by Lester Wallack that she found charming—but "in this age, with my purposes and its demoralization, the stage is not for me." Carry Nation made more sense booking her vaudeville act into low theatres on the theory that that would put her message across to boys and no-goods.

Much of Temperance's fear of the stage came of a prejudice already centuries old and still lively in pre-Civil War times. Originally it had reflected social actualities. In England, source of most of the actors and plays of the Colonies and the early States, the theatre had long been associated with not only the lust of the eye and a light-mindedness distasteful to the Puritan-Evangelican-Dissenting kind of Christianity, but also with social ostracism. By the time Temperance was in flower, actors were no longer proscribed vagabonds saved from the law only by special grace of some noble patron-sponsor. But many kept up the old raffish ways and values; few attained the respectable standing enjoyed by the Kembles, say, and Charlotte Cushman. In the 1870's the cultivated Rev. Dr. Edward Everett Hale praised a town for amateur theatricals so fine that "no strolling company of irresponsible blackguards" (his polite description of a professional troupe) ever found it worth while to play there. In big-city theatres the cheaper parts of the house long remained clearinghouses for pimps and prostitutes. Though ladies could and often did attend in the dress circle of the better ones, the strait-laced might prefer not to: Harriet Beecher Stowe had never been in a theatre until curiosity forced her to see a stage-version of *Uncle Tom*. For the Rev. Dr. T. L. Cuyler, eminent Temperance leader, it was immoral to encourage theatres by paying to get in "not merely because I shall see and hear what is ensnaring and polluting to myself, but because the whole garnished and glittering establishment, with its sensuous attractions, is to many of my fellow-men a chandeliered and ornamented hell—a yawning maelstrom of perdition—whose dark foundations rest on the murdered souls of hundreds."

Indeed, for Temperance relations between drink and the theatre were as hellishly close as those between drink and tobacco. Solon Robinson held that theatres were poorly ventilated on purpose so that their air "will breed a feverish thirst, which will tempt you to quench it in potations of poison" in the house's own bar or next door in the saloons usually clustering around a popular theatre. "I don't know of a theatre," said the Rev. Dwight L. Moody, king evangelist of the 1870's, ". . . that hasn't a bar connected with it, or near by. What is that bar there for? Fallen women go to the theatres, and for no good purpose." Another parson thought the stage a "most potent evil influence . . . in the maudlin sentiment which makes vice tolerable—the ribald jest which teaches the lad of sixteen to despise his inexperience in sin—the disgraceful levity upon sacred subjects—the sensual exhibitions which wear away the admiration of virtue. . . . Nor is the habitué exempt from danger. . . . The play fails to excite him, and he must therefore drink himself up to the enjoyment of it." Horace Greeley had it the other way round, calling Rum "the grand aliment of our public vices" without which horse-racing, gambling hells and lotteries as well as theatres would wither away. He also mentioned a minor but sore reason why Temperance hated theatres: because they were full of "scurrilous [anti-Temperance] jests, invidious flings, and mean insinuations." For it often happened, true, that the same house that saw *Ten Nights* this week would next week run an afterpiece full of gibes at the Demon's enemies.

Why should the devil have all the good tunes?
—SIR ROWLAND HILL

Though Temperance would never have admitted it, the crusade against the Demon was soon borrowing from the despised stage. Organized causes, good or bad, tend to talk largely to themselves, making fine speeches favoring Women's Rights to audiences already convinced that women are shamefully downtrodden; or writing cogent propaganda for organic gardening in papers that only organic gardeners read. This serves to keep up the aggressive tone of the faithful, but most of it is necessarily waste motion. One of the best ways to break outside the circle and attract potential converts is to enlist the more or less candid showmanship of the entertainer-with-a-message, working alone with a long but lively monologue called a lecture or in a group singing propaganda songs or performing *Ten Nights*. However inconsistently, Temperance went farther than most of her sister Reforms in using techniques similar to those of the Kickapoo chief selling snake-oil from the tail gate after his doe-eyed squaw, Little Owl Feather, had sung "From the Land of the Sky Blue Water."

The Hutchinson Family of good-cause singers first showed the Demon what propaganda disguised as entertainment could do. They were the thirteen children of a New Hampshire farm family in whom the genetic odds had concentrated a double dose of musical talent. All could sing well; several were real Yankee nightingales with no more training than came of being reared in a household that sang at its work all day. Reform-minded, pious Baptists, early infected by both Abolitionism and Temperance—it is likely significant that three of their mother's sisters' husbands went alcoholic—they

took to harmonizing standard antislavery and anti-Rum songs
at local gatherings. Informal singing trips by horse and
wagon to nearby towns spread their fame gradually all over
the state; then beyond its borders to eminent Temperance
leaders. Their core was a quartet, Judson, John and Asa,
"raven-haired and keen-eyed as a group of young Bohemians,
tall and stalwart youths surrounding their rosebud of a sister,
Abby," though on occasion eight or ten assorted Hutchinsons
would temporarily join these. Eventually two troupes developed in harmonious rivalry. But it was the basic quartet that
gained such tumultuous success at a Temperance anniversary
meeting in New York City in 1843—they had tried to beg off
because their singing was "fitted only for the country village"—and then at major Temperance and Abolitionist meetings in Boston in 1844. Thenceforth in various combinations
and generations the melodious progeny of Jesse and Mary
Hutchinson were household words all over the United States
till almost the end of the century.

Two of the boys could knock off lame but lively jingles.
When standard material palled or failed to suit special occasions, they cooked up and sang their own lyrics to existing
airs in what was, by all accounts, great purity of tone and
subtlety of harmony. None of the lyrics were subtle, however,
as the titles alone show: "Drink nothing, Boys, but Water";
"Father, Bring Home Your Money Tonight"; "Lament of
the Widowed Inebriate"; "Ridden by the Rum Power"—
which turned into "Ridden by the Slave Power" when they
demonstrated in song that they were, if possible, even hotter
antislavery than anti-Demon. As sound Syndromists, the family was also pro-Women's Rights, phrenology, the Peace
movement and spiritualism. It was a historic if giddy moment
when the spirit of Jesse H. Hutchinson, recently deceased,
patted the gleaming bald head of William Lloyd Garrison at
a seance held by the then famous, and presently notorious,
Fox Sisters.

As they got into the swing of it the Hutchinsons did more
than merely don their Sunday clothes and sit or stand in a
row singing like larks. The men took to romantically long
hair and huge turned-down collars of a vaguely Miltonian

cut. They developed patter songs and solo character numbers with rudimentary costume changes, gradually working up interlocking routines that, except that they never danced, were hardly distinguishable from vaudeville turns. Between passing the hat and selling their songbooks they prospered to a degree that would have been impossible on the bleak farm in Milford, New Hampshire, though livelihood was certainly second among their motives in so assiduously trouping the country when trouping was arduous business. Their point for our purposes is that when they sang in the meetinghouse or town hall in Centerville or Jonesburg the audience was, all unwittingly, witnessing what was essentially a theatrical entertainment. But it never occurred to them that these country-spoken, homespun folks just like themselves could have anything in common with the sinful stage. So they could laugh fit to kill at John Hutchinson's comical cuttings-up and go home with no sense of guilt, only a Hutchinson songbook to try out on the melodeon—and minds more set than ever against Rum and slavery, more inclined than ever to vote for local option next time around.

> Two years ago the loafing throng
>   That hung around the inn,
> Would say—"Come sing us now a song,
>   And you shall have some gin."
> And I the drunkard's catch would troll,
>   The lowest of the low,
> And then in drink would drown my soul,
>   But two short years ago.
>   —REV. JOHN PIERPONT,
>   Song written for John B. Gough

If the Hutchinsons exploited propaganda disguised as entertainment, John B. Gough, their contemporary, showed how entertainment could just as effectively pose as Temperance propaganda. His "lectures" were so stagey that even Frances Willard who, recall, had seen only one play in her life, detected it: "An actor rather than an orator . . . that sallow, bearded face, framed in a shock of gray hair, was of protean aspect, now personating the drunkard, then the hypocrite, anon the saint. Those restless, eager hands . . . always busy, flinging the hair forward in one character, back in another, or standing it straight up in a third; crushing the drink fiend, pointing to the angel in human nature. . . ." In other words, Gough combined propaganda anecdote and the exuberant oratory of the day with the skills of a vaudevillian. Indeed, an Englishman seeing him for the first time compared him to Charles Mathews, the greatest lightning-change monologist of the century.

His staginess was readily accounted for: as a young man he had done his level best to prosper as an actor. He had been born in England of humble, worthy parents who procured him a few years of elementary schooling, then apprenticed him to an English farmer migrating to the States. Failing to take to farming in upstate New York, young John got released from his indentures and tried his luck in New York City, where he began to learn the trade of bookbinding. When his wages reached three dollars a week his mother and sister crossed the ocean to join him, eking out a living with needlework.

The boy made friends among other young workmen and took avidly to their amusements, particularly the crude popular theatre of the day. At the age of sixteen he saw his first stage performance: Junius Brutus Booth, psychotic father of Edwin and John Wilkes, in *The Apostate* at the Old Bowery Theatre with the usual farce, and Dan Rice, originator of the stage-stereotype Negro, doing his "Jump Jim Crow" number between the acts. Thenceforth skinny, sawed-off, dark-haired John Gough was as stagestruck as any of his pals, who spent their spare cash for admissions to the gallery at the cheap blood-and-thunder houses; put on amateur productions imitating what they saw there; bloodied one another's noses over the relative charm of leading ladies; haunted stage doors to glimpse real live performers and, in Gough's case anyway, pestered managers for opportunity to perform. One momentous evening they let him try a comic song (ominously entitled "The Water Party") between acts at the Franklin Theatre. He got an encore but no professional offer.

As a member of one of the volunteer fire companies that were then the American city's schools of rowdyism and drinking, he was getting a better start as a booze-fighter. Presently his employer moved his business to Rhode Island and, though Gough could hardly have seemed a promising type by then, took him along. The new bindery failed. The youngster got jobs enough in Providence but always lost them because he scamped work for the privilege of playing what he later called "a low line of character" (presumably in farce) with a local theatrical troupe. When it collapsed without paying salaries, some member of it passed him on to the manager of a similar fly-by-night company trying to make a go of it at the Lion Theatre in Boston, which had been built for low "equestrian" shows. Gough's first role, at a theoretical five dollars a week, was in a knockabout farce, *Departed Spirits: or, The Temperance Hoax*—a really admirable coincidence, for it not only lampooned Temperance hotels but also Lyman Beecher and Deacon Moses Grant, to whom Gough later dedicated the first version of his autobiography. The piece was otherwise notable for a fire scene in which a real fire engine was rushed onstage to drench him with its hose as he climbed out of a window.

This troupe too collapsed without paying salaries. That shook his stage ambitions but also—understandably in a trouble-prone personality—set him drinking more heavily. Because he was seldom sober in the shop he lost successive bindery jobs and migrated to Newburyport, where he shipped out in a fishing vessel. That kept him straight while at sea but did not prevent disastrous sprees in port. His charm persisted nevertheless, it seems, for the skipper's daughter married him—a step that only made his growing alcoholism and consequent shiftlessness more serious. For eating-and-drinking money he occasionally made short tours of nearby towns with a couple of accordionists—the newly invented squeeze-box was a novelty attraction in the late 1830's—who groaned out marches and quicksteps while Gough

filled the gaps with ventriloquism, which he had picked up
somewhere; comic songs; recitations of "The Sailor Boy's
Dream" and "Alonzo and Imogene"; and a four-ply number
of a squabble among a Yankee, a Dutchman, a Frenchman
and an Irishman—admission twenty-five cents. Later he trav-
eled with a diorama of the Battle of Bunker Hill, filling in
with songs and turning the backstage crank actuating the
contraption. But he was often too drunk to crank steadily and
missed too many sound-effects cues. Getting fired in Worcester, Massachusetts, left him high though unfortunately not
Dry. It was all probably just as seedy and sour-breathed as it
sounds. But also it was unwitting preparation for his eventual
career. Dialect-monologues and platform hokum were the
long suits of his prosperity-to-be; and the more he drank, the
lower he sank, the better he was qualified to tell audiences
just what the Demon could do to you.

In Worcester he sent for his wife and tried to pull himself
together. Soon it was the familiar story: job obtained, job lost
for the old reason. He arranged with one binder to give him
no cash, merely pay his board and clothing bills, only to find
that singing in taverns would get him plenty of drinks without cash. His wife had the luck to die in childbirth. Gough
came near suicide once, had DTs twice, and was arrested for a
drunken prank that disturbed a meeting of the local Miller-
ites planning for the imminent end of the world. Late in
1842 Hawkins, the great Washingtonian, came to lecture in
Worcester. Gough's landlady well-meaningly asked him to
get the young sot to sign the pledge. Gough told him sneer-
ingly that he would do so only "if I can get $1,000 a year and
expenses as you do." Eventually John B. Gough, "the Demos-
thenes of total abstinence," world's most conspicuous reformed drunk, got ten or fifteen times that.

For further poetic justice: The person who brought to teetotalism this quondam actor in *Departed Spirits* was one Joel
Stratton, a waiter in Worcester's American House, a Temperance hotel. One Sunday morning this ardent Washingtonian spied Gough slouching along toward a badly needed pick-
me-up. Experienced in coaxing alcoholics to put up a fight
for themselves, Stratton got him to attend a Washingtonian

meeting, stand up and tell the worst of himself and sign the pledge. Withdrawal of alcohol uncushioned by drugs brought on Gough's third, and last, bout with DTs. Of his next few months he later wrote that his neighbors might well have said of him what the Italians said when encountering Dante: "That's the man that's been in hell." He was always a self-dramatizer, indeed founded his career on it; but no self-salvaged alcoholic of his day or ours has any reason to call those shuddering memories exaggerated.

Gough's repeated "testimonies" at Washingtonian meetings expanded into performances of growing dramatic power. Increasingly in demand at Temperance doings for thirty miles around Worcester, he began to command small fees, in lieu of traveling expenses at first, then growing to where a margin of profit remained. As it widened he found himself combining succor for his fellow man—a purpose always validly evident in his case—with Temperance lecturing as livelihood, the very thing he had sneered at Hawkins for. A series of appearances in western New York State brought ten dollars a lecture. By May, 1845, he had been a huge success in New York City and Baltimore and, arriving in Boston to speak at a great Temperance powwow, was met at the station by an open carriage and four white horses as befitted a Washingtonian hero. His second wife, a farm-reared Yankee schoolmarm, trouped with him during these formative days to look after him when he came off the platform (I had almost written "offstage") having so torn the Demon to tatters that "he dripped with perspiration; his clothes were wringing wet . . . he was in a state of collapse. Hours of attention were necessary to soothe him . . . with bath and food; nor did sleep come till long past midnight." Enter the exigent prima donna latent in most successful and many unsuccessful actors.

This business of lecturing—on European or Chinese customs; or the True and Beautiful; or the Future of Electricity; or how to keep the bowels open; or Woman; or whatever—was already becoming a principal branch of the amusement industry and Gough would grow and prosper with it along with Dr. Holmes, Mrs. Julia Ward Howe, Victoria Woodhull, the dashing feminist blackmailer, and eventually Mark

Twain and John L. Stoddard, the king of travel-lecturers. It is difficult to pass over Gough's prosperity. True, he was giving the cause everything he had in him; true also that the cause did not muzzle the ox treading out the corn. By 1860 he was grossing sixty dollars a lecture, equivalent to at least $300 today. After the Civil War he added to his repertory several lectures on non-Temperance topics—"Lights and Shadows of London Life," "Fact and Fiction," "Eloquence and Orators," etc.—and raised his average per appearance to $170. His bookings and publicity were handled by the same agent who booked the great Henry Ward Beecher. On twenty-six acres five miles from Worcester he built a gentlemanly country mansion and filled it with the presentation medals, silver tea sets, trays, ladles, plaques, autographed books and engrossed civic addresses that greeted him wherever he went in the States, Canada and Britain. It gratified him immensely to visit Britain, to be feted by do-gooder nobility and gentry in the old country that he had left as a skinny urchin with parents too poor to give him further schooling.

The inevitable sour notes included mutterings against prospering by doing good. His best answer was that much of what came in went in expenses and benevolences, so that his net worth wasn't really near the $100,000 figure often quoted. Scorners forgot that Temperance often promised worldly prosperity as a reward for casting out the Demon; hence there was nothing unbecoming about the conspicuous affluence of the most conspicuous reformed alcoholic. It was much more awkward that he backslid at least twice: once early in the Worcester period, which he confessed and was forgiven by his Washingtonian comrades; and later in New York City when he disappeared for several days and was found confusedly unconscious in a sporting house. His story was that a stranger claiming old acquaintance from book-binding days had treated him to a glass of drugged raspberry soda water. The uncharitable made much of this lapse. But the Mount Vernon Congregational Church of Boston, of which Gough was a newish member, accepted his account and cleared him of unworthy fleshpottering. The incoherence of his story does make it more plausible. Had he been lying he could readily have cobbled up a better one.

Though some orthodox Washingtonian editors were severe about this episode, it seems not to have damaged his career except indirectly by encouraging his actorish persecution feelings. What really made his pre-Civil War years turbulent was a conflict of ideas. He was sound on teetotalism for rummies but annoyed many kiver-to-kiver Temperance stalwarts by strongly implying that genuine moderation was possible for many: ". . . some men . . . can drink moderately . . . others . . . cannot. My father was a . . . Christian moderate drinker [but] his son could no more be a moderate drinker than he could blow up a powder magazine moderately . . . say you, 'You are a weak-minded man.' Very well . . . if I am so weak-minded that I cannot drink in moderation, thank God I am strong enough to let it alone altogether. . . . You cannot make a moderate drinker out of a drunkard. . . . It has been tried over and over again. Total abstinence is absolutely necessary to save a man who has once been a drunkard."

And those white horses were hardly unhitched from the barouche before the Mitchell-minded school of Washingtonians fell foul of Gough on the matter of religion. He had church-committed admirers among his closest backers; was welcomed to many pulpits, a privilege denied many Washingtonians because of their explicit exclusion of religion; and had come to conclude from his own experience as a newly affiliated Congregationalist that mere "moral suasion" and sympathetic comradeship, the basic Washingtonian formula, seldom salvaged drunks without help from prayer and a sense of God's support. Gough, said his biographer, "transferred Temperance from the schoolhouse to the churches"—which overstates it but does bring out his religious bent, doubtless a result of his humbly pious childhood. He was, like the Boston mechanics, anticipating Alcoholics Anonymous, but this position necessarily rubbed many staunch Washingtonians the wrong way. They had already been tactless about his rising lecture fees, for by their standards anything over five dollars smacked of money-changing in the Temple.

Then Neal Dow, stern and rock-bound chief of the Maine Law (statewide Prohibition) movement, planned a visit to England to hearten British Prohibitionists. Gough, writing to an English acquaintance, mentioned Dow's impending trip and went on to say that, between poor enforcement and recent public lassitude about Temperance, Maine's famous pioneer Prohibition statute was already "a dead letter." His friend published these pessimistic though by no means inaccurate words in the British Temperance press. That outraged the militant Prohibitionist segment of the British movement. What they had planned to hear from Dow was incontrovertible word that the Maine Law was doing marvelously well. On Gough's next trip to England the old-line Temperance men were cordial as ever but the Prohibitionists savagely attacked him as a jealous turncoat. One of them put it in writing that Gough had often been seen in public "intoxicated" by drugs if not alcohol. Gough sued, got a retraction in court and nominal damages of five guineas (say twenty-five dollars), and published the complete proceedings in the expanded new edition of his wide-selling autobiography. But the backbiting continued under cover. The whole affair was a depressing example of how the righteous are often as unscrupulous and irresponsible as the unregenerate.

Such deplorable squabbles need not detract from Gough as performer: the bright-eyed, vivacious though increasingly potbellied virtuoso, working up to a Longfellow-scale beard, who leapt and skittered, trembled and shrieked, bayed and intoned his vociferous way through 5,000-odd "lectures" in seventeen years. The contents were often taken down in shorthand and published, probably not too much changed from the originals. There was nothing subtle about these performances, but neither was there about the miserable degeneracy of the Demon's victims whom he sought to salvage. He relied heavily on the dialect comedy learned in his strolling days—Negro, Irishman, Cockney, German, Yankee rube, stuttering drunk, impish street urchin, sweet little girl. . . . The gags, as samples have already shown, would have embarrassed Thomas A. Jackson, the creator of *A Slow Train Through Arkansaw*. On the serious tack he said little directly about religion but went in heavily for extreme horror material, by no means only about DTs:

Now this man had been gambling and drinking all Saturday night in a room over a bar in New England. Sunday morning, as the boys were having a pick-me-up, they were startled by a drop of blood falling on the bar in their midst. Looking up, they saw a red stain spreading on the ceiling. As the drops fell thicker they went upstairs and found that the poor, desponding, whiskey-sodden gambler had cut his throat. Not only did the bar not close, Gough averred with relish, but that grisly stain on the ceiling attracted so much sensation-seeking custom that the cold-blooded owner hired an extra barkeep and went on rejoicing to do the best Sunday's business he had ever known. Or: Now this cooper in Albany, New York became a perfect sot and was always falling down on his way home from the tavern, so his despairing wife would have to go find and fetch him reeling home. One cold night she again went looking for him but could discern no trace of him anywhere along the way. Not until morning did he turn up, rather his bones did. He had stumbled into an outhouse in which hogs were penned. . . .

After softening up his audience with a few of those he would shake back his long, lank hair, glare over their heads, take a long, rasping breath and a long stride and "call upon the tomb to break forth! Ye mouldering victims! wipe the grave dust crumbling from your brows, stalk forth in your tattered shrouds and bony whiteness to testify against the drink! Come, come from the gallows, you spirits-maddened man-slayer! Crawl from the slimy ooze, ye drowned drunkards, and with suffocation's blue and lurid lips speak out against the drink! Unroll the records of the past, and let the Recording Angel read out the murder indictments written in the book of God's remembrance! aye, let the past be unfolded, and the shrieks of wailing victims be borne upon the night blast! Snap your burning chains, ye denizens of the pit, and come up sheeted in the fire, dripping with the flames of hell, and with your trumpet tongues testify against the deep damnation of the drink!" A reasonable acquaintance with the theatre of the period 1820–70 identifies the above as mere adaptation to the platform of the rhetoric typical of the big scenes of hifalutin melodrama of the day. It may be difficult now to understand how anybody could take it seriously. But it is also easy to believe that anybody delivering those lines with maximum noise and gesture would leave the platform sweat-soaked and exhausted.

Temperance had had highly effective speakers before Gough went on the wagon: Theodore Weld, a most impressive figure learning on the Temperance platform the fulminating skills with which he later denounced slavery; General Ashbell Wells Riley, who used to offer to pay men to come hear him, fifteen cents each for rank-and-file drinkers, twenty-five cents for rumsellers, provided they could look him in the eye afterward and claim dissatisfaction with what he had said. And Tom Marshall, that highflying spellbinder aforesaid, was also in the field ahead of Gough. After him came worthy others, maybe the most conspicuous being William Ross, also a British soldier's son (only his father was an officer) and reformed drunkard who declared war on the Demon because his sister was killed by a glass thrown at her by her drunken husband, much like Little Mary in *Ten Nights*. Ross reinforced his spellbinding with "science," bringing to the platform a small portable still in which he demonstrated the faking and adulteration of liquors. There was Festus G. Rand of Vermont: He first realized the evils of drink when the boss of the sawmill in which he worked got drunk, sat down on a moving sawlog and the saw did the rest; but Festus went on drinking till the night he fell drunk into a snowdrift and froze his hands and feet so badly that all four had to be amputated. There was Luther Benson of Indiana, who first got drunk at the age of six. His descriptions of DTs were the most detailed on record. Interspersing a successful career of platform-lecturing with periodical sprees, he ended up a permanent resident of the Indiana State Insane Asylum.

As Temperance gathered momentum again after the Civil War, scores and scores of such professionals, typically reformed drunkards exulting in making themselves pungent examples, told thousands on thousands of freshwater tent meetings and Sunday schools how low the Demon had brought them, how it felt having snakes in your boots, and how hopeless it was to try to drink moderately. Even though he did not despise moderation, spindly little John Bartholomew Gough was daddy of them all, however. And it seems never to have occurred to most of them, Gough included, that they were neglecting the first principle of the off-the-cuff Washingtonians: the audiences they drew, whether in the First Congregational Church or the Chautauqua tent, assayed not one drunkard in a hundred. The men that the Washingtonians went after were not buying lecture tickets but drinking in saloons and headed for Skid Row. Entertainment widened Temperance's audience, but unless it reached more heavy drinkers it was bound to turn into a mere device for drumming up votes to suppress the saloon.

7

AS MAINE GOES...

. . . until the liquor traffic is abolished . . . all efforts at moral reform must languish . . . The CURSE is upon us, and there is but one CURE: *Total Abstinence*, by the help of God, for the Individual, and *Prohibition* for the State.
—T. S. ARTHUR, *Grappling with the Monster*

THE Rev. Mr. Seeley was to preach in Boothbay, Maine, on a certain Sunday in the early 1850's. His way to church took him past the pierhead where several hundred mackerel fishermen were loafing away their day off; some, he noted approvingly, were reading Bibles. "Hadn't you better go to church, shipmates?" he said. After some discussion, numbers got to their feet and followed his suggestion, much to his wonder: "I could not help saying to the landlord of the hotel that he must have a curious class of fishermen in that quarter. 'Ah,' said he, 'if you had been here before the Maine Law passed, you would have seen, on such a day as this, those rocks all along covered with blood. No female dared venture out of the house at such a time.'"

The unwary might take that anecdote to mean that "the Maine Law" forbade assault and battery or maybe the molestation of females. Not at all—it was, as already identified, the first statewide statute outlawing sale of alcoholic beverages for any but medical or industrial uses. In short, the pilot plant for Prohibition.

"I ain't greedy for land," the old farmer said. "I only want what jines mine."

—Traditional

While Temperance hardened into intemperate Teetotalism it also flirted with the notion of enlisting law in the good cause. The "moral suasion" that led persons to renounce

Rum might profit from so-called "legal suasion" as eliminator of temptations. (A Galveston, Texas, bar of 1842, by the way, listed a drink called "Moral Suasion" along with the usual juleps, slings and so on.) Once Teetotalism creates a taboo, categorical, self-defining; once the pledge says *never* anything "that will make drunk come," law becomes a potential ally. Just what degree of what duties is imposed by the positive precept "Honor thy father and thy mother"? But there can be little courtroom shilly-shally about the negative "Thou shalt not commit adultery"—a straight issue of did they or didn't they? Or about "Thou shalt not ingest anything detectibly containing alcohol."

Dr. Rush—again the great idea-man—had recommended using law against the Demon, urging decent men to "besiege . . . governments with petitions to limit the number of taverns . . . impose heavy duties on ardent spirits . . . secure the property of habitual drunkards for . . . their families in the hands of trustees." The first suggestion was soonest taken up. Indeed in the many places where selectmen or chosen freeholders or municipal councils had licensing power, limitation of the number of taverns was already at least potentially in effect. But though alcohol keeps organic matter uncorrupted in laboratory jars, it usually corrupts human institutions, in the United States anyway. The situation usual in Rush's day and later was too many taverns in business, violating sales-limiting ordinances in order to stay afloat; and too many stores flagrantly selling by the drink where licensed only to sell to take out. John Adams once told Dr. Rush of his pre-Revolutionary bout with the problem: Disturbed by the number of "idlers, thieves, sots and consumptives" made by "taverns, retailers, dram-shops and tippling-houses," he applied to the courts for a Committee of Inspection and Inquiry and "reduced the number of license houses, etc., but I only acquired the reputation of a hypocrite and an ambitious demagogue. . . . The number of licensed houses was soon reinstated; drams, grog and sotting were not diminished and remain to this day as deplorable as ever."

As Temperance sentiment spread and the net results of "moral suasion" proved disappointing, bold minds took up rather beyond where these Founding Fathers had left off. Thomas S. Grimké had predicted in 1833 that "some who hear me may live to see the day when . . . traffic in ardent spirits shall be forever abolished." That same year the Rev. Dr. Francis Wayland, president of Brown University, an unusually intelligent Temperance partisan, called "prohibition of the traffic in ardent spirits . . . a fit subject for legislation" promising "the most happy results." And a Temperance tract of 1835 foresaw a time when "the manufacture of intoxicating liquor for common distribution will be classed with . . . counterfeiting. . . and forgery."

Many clear heads tried to hold organized Temperance to its early pledge "never to make any appeal to legislators . . . for the aid of authority in changing the habits of any class of their fellow citizens." They had a healthy dread of getting their all-important movement mixed up with politics. But short-range realism wanted any stick to beat the demon with and was soon launched on the bit-by-bit "no-license" movement that was the nursery of Prohibition. This assumed that the power to grant a license implies power to withhold it; and urged the states to empower townships to hold local referenda instructing local authorities to grant no license-to-sell at all. Where such a "no-license" cause won, legal sale of intoxicating drink stopped the next time licenses came up for renewal. The new United States Temperance Union endorsed the device in 1833; and though Daniel Webster and Rufus Choate handled the case against it, the U.S. Supreme Court upheld it. That implicitly allowed any regulation or prohibition of the liquor trade that any state might undertake. "Local option," another form of the same basic device, now survives in several states, as the dismayed motorist may find when unwittingly crossing the line of a "Dry" county.

"No-license" had an air of fairness. It did not meddle with the right to buy, possess or drink Rum, merely withheld opportunity legally to *sell* it where local anti-tippling sentiment had been responsibly expressed. It offered communities a democratic means to get rid of the noisome doggeries and youth-tempting taverns that distressed the well-meaning. Enforcement would be the difficulty. Prohibition taught us to assume that as matter of course. It was not so obvious when the no-license cry was new. Soon, however, local constables proved to lack time, inclination or both to keep doggeries from reopening on the sly without license, their stock-in-trade clandestinely imported from unregenerate communities over the township line.

That has always been one of Prohibition's principal miseries: It cannot tolerate "Wet" neighbors nor can its adherents keep local sinners in line. Too many—doubtless a minority in many cases—so liked or profited from bar-style drinking that they would go to great trouble, including free-wheeling law-breaking, to keep it up; whereas the law and the majority who had voted "no-license" proved either too easily corrupted or too lackadaisical to do enough about it. Newborn Georgia saw the same thing a hundred years earlier. Prohibition of spirits spawned in Savannah a plague of "private rum-shops" supplied from wet South Carolina and stubbornly surviving occasional raids.

Georgia gave up early but New England was stubborner. Temperance-minded Yankees argued plausibly that the remedy was to dry up the neighboring township; and the next; and the next; until sources of supply would be impractically distant. Or supposing that too cumbrous, why not look to the state for legislation prohibiting license-to-sell in all townships? That single stroke would force into line those inconvenient sin-minded communities persisting in voting Wet. Thus to enlist the state ignored any regard for local preferences, of course. Temperance hastily dropped local preference and embarked on a program of gradual encroachment that had probably been inevitable once law was invoked and enforcement found difficult. Dry townships needed insulation from Wet ones, so the state had to go Dry. Dry states needed insulation from Wet ones, so the nation had to go Dry. Then Rum Row showed how badly a Dry nation needed a Dry world. . . . Even after Prohibition had become a national absurdity, the Anti-Saloon League, the Methodist Board of Temperance, Prohibition and Public Morals and allied organizations were still confidently beating the drums for worldwide Prohibition.

Massachusetts, first with statewide uniformity in 1838, stopped short of downright prohibition but with elephantine ingenuity forbade sale of spirits in lots under fifteen gallons, to be taken from the premises at once. The purpose was to stop bar-type drinking—the prime target of militant Temperance—and to discourage the vast number of drinkers who, even in that day of cheap liquor, could afford no such quantity in one purchase. This pre-Washingtonian law smells of the old mistrust of lower-class drinkers, for nothing in it kept the prosperous, who on the whole frequented taverns less, from buying all the wines and brandies they wanted. As resentment grew, a pamphleteer pointed out that thus to protect Society from the Demon was like protecting it from whoring by allowing "every one to be as licentious as he pleases, provided he will procure fifteen persons of ill fame at a time . . . in his own house." Some got round the law by buying fifteen gallons plus one gill, drinking the gill at once and selling back the fifteen gallons. One way or another this momentarily famous Fifteen-Gallon Law foundered on weak enforcement and was repealed—which should have warned other states of the basic weaknesses of prohibitory legislation, however disguised. It was thought that the emphasis on "moral suasion" among the Washingtonians and the Sons of Temperance in the early 1840's retarded the drive for "legal suasion." If so, the effect was temporary, for in 1846 the legislature of Maine, where both Washingtonians and Sons had been active, passed the first of the statewide Prohibitory Maine Laws that made the Pine Tree State as famous among Reformers as Paris is among dressmakers.

This [Prohibition] is Christ's work . . . a holy war, and every true soldier of the Cross will fight in it.

—NEAL DOW

It makes sense that Prohibition should have been New England's special contribution to the arsenal of anti-Demon weapons. The theocratic habit of confusing God's laws with man's and vice versa in the spirit of the Old Testament had always been strong there. But why should Maine have been the first of the states east of Greenwich, Connecticut, to inflict Prohibition on herself? The others all had lively movements to that purpose. The logical pioneers would have been Massachusetts or Connecticut, cradles of Yankee Temperance such as it was, instead of this Way-Down-East state consisting of a string of coastal ports and river-valley settlements backed by wilderness in which lumberjacks were encroaching on moose and porcupine. Neal Dow, the hot-Temperance Torquemada of Portland, thought his state stuck with the curse of drink because of this lagging backwoodsiness and because its lumber trade with the West Indies brought a cheap return flow of rum and molasses for local stills in Portland and Bangor. The solution may be simpler: Maine was at least as Puritan-minded as any other New England state and had been an outlying part of Massachusetts until 1820; and the "Father of the Maine Law" was a Massachusetts man, James Appleton of distillery-ridden Salem.

He seems to have been a standard, prim, energetic sort—a jeweler by trade—with heavy Syndromist-political leanings. His son's biography of him says that the notion of legal suppression of booze came to him as early as 1831, when he was attending a session of the Massachusetts legislature, "as a sudden revelation, as a discovery in morals, that the way to stop intemperance was to stop it. If the drinking of spirits was always wrong and dangerous . . . then it was not to be tolerated, nor dallied with by license laws, but put an end to." He worked hard for an abortive thirty-gallon law as opening wedge, then came out flat for categorical Prohibition not long before he moved to Portland and what proved to be greater opportunity for his ideas. Soon elected to the legislature, he headed a committee to study improvements of Maine's licensing laws in 1837, and filed a historic report plumping for statewide Prohibition as the only practical measure, saying:

"It is the inevitable tendency of shop and barroom to decoy men from themselves and from their self-control . . . experience under the license laws . . . has proved how hopeless it is that such places should exist and men not become intemperate. If the poison were not freely offered for sale under the sanction of the law . . . it could not . . . would not . . . be purchased . . . the law . . . has done much to fix on the mind of the public the impression that rum was necessary. . . . The objection will doubtless be made that . . . such a law could not be enforced . . . [but] prohibition would . . . render the traffic disreputable as well as unlawful . . ." and so on. In any case, though no law is ever completely enforced, any extent to which Prohibition were enforced would be clear gain for society.

Nine years of able agitation for this cutting of the Bacchanalian knot, aided by the patent absurdity of the existing license/no-license system, got Maine that first statewide Prohibition—with amendments greatly handicapping enforcement. Five years later the law was given teeth: ban on manufacture as well as sale and keeping-for-sale; jail for third offenders; right of search and seizure on complaint of three residents; confiscation of illegal supplies. . . . This tougher law of 1851 became the benchmark from which the history of Prohibition law dates, said a Dry historian of Temperance. "This thing is of God," cried Lyman Beecher in Boston's Old South Church. ". . . God's work every step of the way, perfect as we go along . . . the powers of hell are in dismay. That glorious Maine Law was a square and grand blow right between the horns of the Devil. . . . I seem to see him falling back—stubborn and terrible but falling back; and the consecrated host of God's elect press close upon him . . . until they shall push him over the battlements and send him back to Hell." Millennial Reformism never spoke more clearly.

Dr. John Jewett personally took part in the first exercise of the search-and-seizure clause, which occurred at Hallowell. A mob gathered but took it out in glaring and muttering. Gloatingly Jewett noted that though the guilty rumseller was soon out on bail, confiscation of his stock-in-trade and fixtures would make repeated offense unprofitable without that three-times-means-jail provision.

ஜூ

The steady fight that Maine has made . . . against decent rum, has been worthy of a better cause. Who hath woe? who hath sorrow and some more things of that sort? He that monkeyeth with Maine rum. . . . Those desiring the most prompt and vigorous style of jim-jams at cut rates will do well to examine Maine goods before going elsewhere.
—BILL NYE, "Down East Rum"

The Prohibition experiment soon came to hang on a hellishly energetic Portland businessman named Neal Dow who rallied early behind Appleton and then for forty years wore out everybody but himself keeping successive Maine Laws calked and at least afloat. In him one sees with growing distinctness the connection between Prohibition and paternalistic economics, in both politics and industrial relations.

Dow was Quaker born and reared but turned to Congregationalism on being "read out of meeting" for rejecting Friends' pacifism. John Calvin certainly suited his style better than George Fox even in his taste in clothes which, until he tried a pseudoclerical garb late in life, was anything but Quakerish: his fine blue coats, laced and embroidered vests and curling brown hair got him called "the jackdaw mayor of Portland" by a Wet legislator. Amateur boxer, keen oarsman, he made his way readily in the local volunteer fire companies and, early active in the pre-teetotal phase of Temperance, came close to drying them up city-wide. He not only ran the family tannery ably but found occasion to prosper in banking, railroads, Portland real estate and upstate timberlands. By 1829, aware of the economic as well as spiritual virtues of sobriety, he headed a widely successful movement among Portland employers to abandon the customary booze-breaks morning and afternoon at the boss's expense. In the early 1840's he worked behind the scenes to foster a Portland

Washingtonian society "spontaneously" organized among workmen with a sea captain as president and a joiner as vice-president. And when Appleton pressed hard for his "Act for the Suppression of Drinking Houses and Tippling Shops"— the loaded title of several versions of the Maine Law—Dow and his loyal wife (as adjutant among the ladies) were mainly responsible for the 40,000-odd signatures on the petitions that persuaded the legislature to knuckle under in 1846.

Today he would have been called "Mr. Maine Law." He put through its successive stricter versions; crisscrossed the nation outside the Deep South lecturing on its incomparable merits and exhorting other states to go and do likewise; and as chief Temperance man in Maine and off-and-on mayor of Portland moved heaven and earth to show the world that Prohibition could succeed in a sizable city. As national symbol of that pious hope in the war of the "ramrodders" against the "rummies" he acquired numerous tribute-trophies: Bangor's Temperance folks, for instance, gave him a silver pitcher engraved with about as much Temperance iconology per square inch as Homer put on Achilles' shield—police bilging casks of liquor, an empty jail, a ship under sail and "a cottage embowered in a grove of trees, with a fountain of playing waters in front." Two years later a great meeting in Trenton, New Jersey, came up with another pitcher stiff with bilged casks, spurting fountains and the Goddess of Liberty with the arms of Jersey and Maine quartered on her shield and the paradoxical motto, *Salus Populi Suprema Lex*. Maybe the most appreciated item was a gold medal presented at a dinner in New York City by General (and Congressman) Sam Houston, once the "Big Drunk" of the Indians of the Southwest but now a devoted and highly articulate teetotaler. During the proceedings Horace Mann, the first great American educationist, called Dow "the moral Columbus." The Rev. John Marsh, eminent Temperance zealot, went that one better with "the Napoleon of Temperance!" It was not inappropriate: Neal Dow was pint-size, one of his own greatest admirers and certainly left a sizable mark on his world.

In due time Portland was favored with a downtown window display of all this pious hardware presumably cele-

brating reform of the town's disreputable drinking habits.
The gesture was premature and remained so, for the zeal with
which Portland's rumsellers evaded the successively tough-
ened Maine Laws pretty much equaled that with which Dow
sought to suppress them. What he hoped would be a national
showcase for Prohibition was more like a comprehensive
dress rehearsal of the troubles that would beset the Volstead
Act seventy years later. His initial crackdown met with such
subtle resistance from the town's hotels that Portland's Prohibition was never more than an inconvenience. A Portland
man wanting a casual snort could pay a set fee for admission
to a room in the wall of which a wheel revolved and came up
with a glass of rum poured by unseen hands. Storekeepers
stopped selling drinks but charged three or five cents for a
soda cracker and threw in a drink free. A rumseller in Ded-
ham, Massachusetts, in the days of the Fifteen-Gallon Law,
had already begun to enrich the language by setting up a tent
at a militia "training-day" within which the public could have
a look at that rare animal, a striped pig, for six-and-a-quar-
ter cents. The pig was there right enough, painted in stripes,
and a free drink went with each admission. Elsewhere the
nominal attraction would be a blind pig, or a blind tiger in
the shape of a stuffed striped alley-cat with a blindfold. . . .
    The "bootlegger" began as a walking grogshop selling in-
dividual snorts up the alley from a bottle carried in the boot
top. Smuggled liquor flooded into Portland by the case, labeled CROCKERY or DRYGOODS or hidden in barrels of genuine
flour or sugar. Dow's police seized many such shipments but
more got through. There was trouble when zealous search
damaged lawful merchandise and the moment Dow busied
himself with some other duty, of course, the police proved
highly corruptible. Sale-by-the-drink spread into private
drinking clubs set up by fast young men and into the shanties
of Irish railroad labor whose vocabulary already included
"shebeen." Regularly Temperance forces demanded a
cleanup of the 300-odd drinking places that normally defied
the Maine Law in Portland; somebody—usually Dow—would
be elected on a Dry platform and crack down in good faith;
then vigilance would relax and within a year 300-odd drink-

ing places would be back in business down among the shanties, up the byways and in the best hotels.

Law itself abetted the evaders when federal courts held that, whatever state statutes said about sale of beverage alcohol within Maine, the Maine drinker could order liquor shipped to him from outside provided it came to him in "the original package"—a phrase thenceforth much bandied about in Temperance lore—which took care of the needs of the prosperous. Maine sprouted numerous "express companies" that did practically all their business in liquor shipments, soliciting orders more or less openly and maintaining "on-hand" stocks enabling them to deliver whiskey to the customer within an hour though it presumably came from outside the state. And the various Maine Laws themselves conspired against proper Temperance by allowing municipalities to set up agencies to sell liquor for medical and industrial uses. Numerous doctors, whether venal or humane, prescribed liberally for patients suffering from drought. Drink-minded communities sensibly entrusted their agencies to drink-minded officials who knew better than to ask questions about the exact industrial or medical purpose for which purchases were made. One heard of middle-sized towns that covered half the municipal budget with the profits of such agencies. In effect the state was licensing bootlegging in public hands provided it allowed no drinking on the premises—an approach that certain Southern states would try officially in the 1890's as the "dispensary system."

The "agency" device gave Dow and the Maine Law a disastrous setback in 1855. As mayor of Portland creating the town agency, Dow made the technical error of ordering its initial stock of out-of-state liquor in his own name. His Democratic foes made political capital of it. Hastily he corrected the situation. But the fat was in the fire as rumors burgeoned about how Neal Dow, a man known for quick grasp of a good thing, stood personally to profit from the liquor that the agency would sell. On the evening the affair came to a head several hundred members of the lower orders, mostly Irish and all staunch Dow and Temperance haters, were milling about and stoning the agency office on the ground floor of the municipal building. Dow called out a few score militia to help the scanty local police garrisoning the office. The militia disliked the assignment. Vacillating between orders to fire and even worse-advised countermandings and nervous delays, Dow made a botch of the emergency, which ended with half a dozen rioters wounded and one very dead—so far as I know the only male martyr to the Demon's cause in history. (The only female one to my knowledge was the married daughter of a Leavenworth, Kansas, speakeasy proprietor who was killed around the turn of the century by accidental explosion of a shotgun with which her father was seeking to resist a Temperance mob storming the place.) Dow was unlucky with firearms. At the age of fifty-seven he went gamely off to the Civil War and was soon a brigadier general. But because he and his commanding officer, Ben Butler, had no use for each other—and as between the two, give me Neal Dow—he saw no action until the siege of Port Hudson. Dow's first engagement there netted him a bungled attack, a bullet through the thigh and, thanks to his own carelessness, capture. He put in most of the rest of the war as highest-ranking officer in Richmond's Libby Prison, squabbling with other officer captives and the prison authorities.

Efforts to hold him criminally responsible for the rioter's death came to nothing. But the affair gave the Temperance cause a fine black eye in the national press. Within a year, as Frank L. Byrne's recent biography of Dow points out, the Dry governor of Maine was defeated for reelection; the legislature revised the law to allow innkeepers to sell by the drink, and a limited number of retailers to sell for home use; and the parade of states adopting Maine-type laws abruptly ended. Dow presently went to England to enjoy a hero's welcome from Britain's newish Prohibition movement, which based its propaganda on enthusiastic hearsay about the effectiveness of the Maine Law. Throughout the great towns of England and Scotland he spoke and spoke, insisting that Maine's experience showed that outlawing booze sales was utterly practical; that its only troubles came of the corruption of the lower orders and the moral numbness of their superiors; and that even where slackly enforced, it made drink so much less accessible and rumselling so disreputable that the moral and economic tone greatly improved. That was thenceforth the Prohibitionist's basic case. Indeed, it had been formulated by James Appleton even before his dream-child Prohibition law was ever voted on. In England and at home after his return Dow kept making it with special shrillness because he had so much emotional capital sunk in the cause that he could never even contemplate the possibility that he was wrong.

His approach to "legal suasion" anticipated several attitudes later important: Temperance legislation was bound to involve the movement in politics as the Rev. John Pierpont told the World Temperance Convention in New York City in 1853: "We ask at the hand of our civil legislatures a prohibitory law which we cannot get except at the hands of political action. It is therefore . . . absurd to renounce or reject all pretensions to mingling in politics. We mean to carry it to the polls. . . . We have up to this time been timid before politicians. We have said, 'We did not mean you.' We say now, 'We do mean you, and will put you down, if you do not give us what we ask.' " And Neal Dow sometimes spelled that out in terms that the anti-Saloon League would revive a generation later: the way to make politicians vote right, he said, was to threaten the candidates of the regular parties with crucial minorities of Dry voters. He also had an invidious if probably justified habit of attributing rumselling in defiance of law largely to the foreign-born in Maine's population, at that time principally Irish, mostly urbanized and typically voting Democratic. The 1850's saw the dislocating results of the first great waves of Irish and German immigration into the States. That decade was therefore the heyday of the Native American ("Know-Nothing") Party founded on mistrust of immigrant aliens and carrying a strong Temperance flavor, and Dow worked so closely with the Know-Nothings that he was strongly suspected of belonging to their secret Order of the Star-Spangled Banner. In Maine as elsewhere the Temperance forces in politics, anti-Democratic by force of circumstances, naturally became one of the strands woven in with

Know-Nothings, "Conscience" Whigs and Free-Soilers to make the soon-to-triumph Republican Party.

The new party turned its back on Temperance as soon as it could do without it. But, having nowhere else to go, Temperance retained a hankering after Republicanism for generations in spite of the striking success of the Anti-Saloon League in what it called "nonpartisanship," of which more later. And as big business and the Methodist-Baptist kind of churches bulked larger in the picture after the Civil War, Temperance's anti-alienism grew yearly stronger. Dow, the pious, Republican (ex-Whig, ex-Federalist) businessman driving out the Demon to satisfy Yankee moral values as well as to raise the efficiency of Portland's Irish (alien and Catholic) labor supply was a figure of many significances all in one bundle.

> King Alcohol is quaking,
> His throne is crumbling fast,
> And all his petty princes
> With terror stand aghast!
> "Down East" they have been routed,
> "Up West" we'll rout them too;
> From Maine to California,
> We'll scout the red-nosed crew;
> With the "Maine Law" banner o'er us,
> Our hosts are ever true. . . .
> —*The Maine Law Banner*, ANON.

Our federal system has the incidental advantage of enabling individual states to make experiments from which the rest may profit. Trial of a compulsory-seatbelt law in State A shows State B what it may accomplish under more or less like conditions. But Temperance was too much in a hurry, too excited to give Maine time to show realistic results, in a mood altogether too go-thou-and-do-likewise. Early reports had the new broom sweeping clean, and long before the bootleggers and shyster lawyers could get their feet back under them,

Prohibition crusaders outside Maine were assuming that success was assured. Within a scant three years all New England plus New York, New Jersey, Delaware and several states beyond the mountains had imitated Maine by either legislation or referendum, and in Pennsylvania and Illinois, referenda had come within a squeak of success. Some such laws went further than the original: Vermont's, for instance, compelled arrested drunks to tell where they got the liquor. Nor was it only Temperance men who thought Prohibition likely to work: When Massachusetts' Maine Law went into effect many a groggery in Lowell hung black crape on the door with a sign SPIRITS DEPARTED.

The exultant righteous dreamed of the whole nation's going dry by piecemeal. But human perversity, common sense and legal technicalities soon enabled the Demon to catch his sour breath. New York's Maine-type law of 1854, for instance, was vetoed by Governor Horatio P. Seymour (later Democratic presidential nominee in 1868) because he thought some of its enforcement clauses unconstitutional. Seymour was a teetotaler, and Dr. Delavan, still Mr. Temperance upstate, scrupulously assured his followers that, however wrongheaded, the governor's stand was sincere. But the Empire State had long been a cradle of Temperance, and Seymour was made to look bad by the capers of the liquor interests who, stupid as usual, fired a 365-gun salute to celebrate his veto. He lost the next election to a Know-Nothing-minded Temperance stalwart. A fresh Maine-type bill persuasively entitled "An Act for the Prevention of Intemperance, Pauperism and Crime" was passed, signed and put into effect. The Demon had the last word, however: The state appellate courts vindicated Seymour by throwing it out.

Maine stubbornly reenacted Prohibition in 1858; Vermont and Massachusetts stood firm. Elsewhere it was the New York story as legislatures had second thoughts, sometimes sensible and sometimes corrupt, and courts killed or crippled the drastic Maine Law pattern. In the 1850's, Wisconsin led off a flurry of "personal damage laws" entitling wives or other dependents of drunkards to collect compensation from the guilty rumsellers, which, it was smartly pointed out, spared the taxpayer the support of such dependents. The victims' timidity and the courts' failure to make the verdicts really hurt usually made the notion a dead letter, however. Local or county laws against selling for drinking on the premises might be quietly ignored; or the rumseller might put up his blue ruin in two-ounce bottles, sold over the bar for the price of a drink, to be taken outside the door, emptied down the hatch and returned for another round. By the time of the Civil War, one way or another the first great accumulation of statewide Prohibitions had eroded to a discouraged bump, and auxiliary laws to slow the Demon down had lost potency. Temperance was gloomily retreating to the county and township level, where sledding was harder than ever partly because the war and its attendant strains distracted the public from virtue, partly because new methods of evasion were making a fool of the law even where downright blind pigs were kept under.

> Some enterprising people,
>   In our cities and towns,
> Have gone to organizing clubs
>   Of men that's fallen down . . .
> The temperance reform club,
>   Forever may it stand,
> And everyone that loves strong drink
>   Pray, join it heart and hand.
>   —JULIA A. MOORE
>   ("The Sweet Singer of Michigan")

Maine's inability to make Prohibition prohibit anywhere but out in the bushes was so marked that Portland and Bangor, her chief cities, produced the nation's most conspicuous individual pledge-signing movements of the 1870's—Francis Murphy's Blue Ribbon movement and Dr. Henry A. Reynolds' Red Ribbon counterpart. Both men were salvaged drunkards exploiting their dissolute pasts as had Hawkins and Gough. Indeed both were in effect reviving Washingtonianism stiffened with the nondenominational, Protestant prayer-meeting type of religion that would later be the principal stay of the "rescue mission" Temperance work on Skid Row.

Born in Ireland (Wexford) and reared as a Catholic, Murphy had anomalous preparation for close identification with Protestants. How the transition came about appears in no record I can find. He married young, moved from Ireland to Montreal to York State to Portland, and fairly early was heavy drinker enough to trouble his young wife, though he sometimes managed stretches of abstinence. When he had a chance to go into hotel-keeping in Portland, Mrs. Murphy objected because the house bar would be a standing temptation. But for ten years he held out against the Demon and became a sleek, fat-mustached minor success who looked rather like Grover Cleveland.

Toward the end of the 1860's, however, the Demon managed to trip him and he went downhill fast, losing the hotel, going bankrupt, opening a low dive, killing a customer accidentally in a drunken fall, acquitted but soddenly down and out anyway. In his subsequent career as Temperance lecturer none of this lost in the telling in his luxuriant, brogue-tinged oratory. It was genuine misery for all that, a Temperance tract acted out in hangover-haunted shame. To secure him a good drying-out, friends arranged to have him sentenced to the Portland city jail. At the time, an amateur Temperance missionary had free access to the captive audience therein, and one of his Sunday prayer meetings for drunkards got through to Murphy. Suddenly assured of God's help in resisting drink, the poor devil regained self-respect and showed a great talent for Temperance preaching. His new-found eloquence converted every one of his fellow prisoners. Released in the spring of 1873, he made a great pledge-brandishing speech at the city hall, chose a bit of blue ribbon in the lapel as his converts' badge, and spent the rest of his life verbosely, earnestly and not unprosperously trying to impose the teetotal pledge on all the drunks in the country. Forty thousand pledged in Pittsburgh; 50,000 in Philadelphia under sponsorship of John Wanamaker, the righteous merchant-prince. His methods—mass meetings, Sunday breakfasts for bums, elaborate personal testimonies, heavy use of evangelical hymns concerned little with Temperance but much with salvation, home and mother—soon resembled those of the renowned soul-saving team of Moody & Sankey.

Reynolds' story was much the same though his background differed. He had been a Harvard M.D. doing well enough in Bangor but presently taking to drink. After two years of the Civil War as surgeon of the First Maine Heavy Artillery, he returned in better moral shape and became city physician. Gradually, however, the old trouble came back and he became an abject periodic drunk, sober for long intervals broken by sprees lasting for weeks. What straightened him out was Bangor's version of the Women's Crusade which apparently had the ladies praying not with rumsellers but with their outstanding victims. One day they invaded Reynolds' office and swept him off to a prayer meeting where he signed a religion-tinged pledge—and managed to keep it. Like Murphy he took at once to the platform—a handsome, black-bearded fellow with a slashing forensic manner and the prestige of a genuine M.D. behind his irresponsibly extravagant abuse of all forms of alcoholic beverages.

"Dare To Do Right" was the motto of his string of "Reform Clubs" of redeemed drunkards modeled on a similar movement beginning a few years earlier in Gardiner, Maine. The badge was a red ribbon knotted into the lapel and never to be untied. Reynolds was particularly successful in the Lake states. In Jackson, Michigan, a rumseller saw the red ribbon on a stranger-customer obviously breaking the pledge and refused to serve him. For that matter, in Elmira, New York, a barkeep once told a young man ordering one slug too many to go to the Murphy meeting down the street and sign the pledge. Murphy and Reynolds, very friendly rivals, were both notorious for neglecting to slander saloonkeepers as a group. Their worst heresy, however, their really perverse agreement, was in steadfastly repudiating "legal suasion," whether local option or Prohibition. It was no use trying to tell them about the Maine Law's triumphs and virtues as so glibly described by Neal Dow and the new-founded Prohibition Party. They were both Down Easters, had done a disastrous lot of drinking in that very State of Maine, and they knew.

As a physician Reynolds must have been especially aware of both the abuse of Maine's liquor-dispensing "agencies" and the role of chartered bootlegger played by that ubiquitous institution, the drugstore. Though Dr. Rush had come out strongly against "tinctures" (of alcohol) in his medical lectures, and in spite of Temperance's insistence that prescription booze often set patients on the road to ruin, most doctors still recommended wine or spirits as tonics. State Prohibition laws or local-option ordinances usually allowed sale of liquor for medicinal purposes, therefore. That loophole turned many drugstores into groggeries patronized by persons happily aware that the owner sold by the drink without stuffy insistence on prescription. The thing got into the professional humorist's stock-in-trade: Bill Nye, in his time second only to Mark Twain as popular jester, replied to a fictitious young pharmacist inquiring whether Kansas offered openings in the drug business: "If you mean by the drug business the sale of sure-enough drugs, medicines, paints, oils, glass, putty, toilet articles and prescriptions carefully compounded, I would *not* go to Kansas . . . if you would like to . . . sell the tincture of damnation. . . . It is a temperance state, and no saloons are allowed there. All is quiet and orderly, and the drug business is a great success. You can run a dummy drugstore there with two dozen dreary old glass bottles . . . and a tall red barrel in the backroom . . . and in a few years sell enough of this justly celebrated preparation for household, scientific and experimental purposes only to fill your flabby pockets with wealth."

Or a physician scenting a lucrative sideline would bypass the pharmacist, setting up his own drugstore to dispense *Sp. Frumenti* by drink or bottle on his own say-so. Ladies buying mustard plasters and Castile soap at the counter could not see into the partitioned-off backroom. But everybody knew that the sporty young lawyers who sauntered in and disappeared back there were not asking what to do for hangnails. In such communities "Doc" replaced "Deacon" as the standard title

of John Barleycorn's right-hand man, and "℞" had succeeded
the sign of the Sickle and Sheaf. In 1866 the Massachusetts
State Constabulary reported that in Boston there were 107
drugstores (not the accredited state agencies) selling liquor
freely, with Sundays their best days.

. . . and all those deacons who never drank anything
stronger than Hostetter's Bitters.
—GEORGE ADE, *The Old-Time Saloon*

The shades of national Prohibition were falling fast when,
in 1918, Don Marquis devoted his daily *The Sun Dial* to "A
Kansas Tragedy," a freehand ballad of how a devoted lover
dashed across Kansas in a Model-T Ford to a place called
Nicodemus to pay off the mortgage on his sweetheart's home.
The ingredients of this low-keyed masterpiece were: Kansas
was a famously Dry state; wartime shortage had moved her
governor to freeze sales of gasoline to individuals; and the
hero had the inspiration to fuel his flivver with various
highly alcoholic patent medicines freely available in Kansas
drugstores: Stutter's Stomach Bitters, then Stewroona, Doctor
Bunkus's Discovery for Kidneys, Lily Gingham's Discovery,
Siwash Indian Soorah—a Remedy for Liver Trouble went
into the gas tank to keep the motor roaring all the way to
Nicodemus. But

> Alas! Alas! Alas!
> Elvira did not clasp me in her sturdy Kansas arms,
> She sniffed the air and said:
> "I never will be wedded
> To a man who reeks with liquor!
> Give me Uncle Jethro's money!
> And don't you leave that drunken flivver
> On the streets of Nicodemus . . ."

Your grandfather would have recognized the originals of
all those fictitious nostrums. For generations the Demon had

been disguising himself as patent medicine sold across drugstore counters without prescription, yet containing alcohol—plenty of it. "Bitters," of course, was Phase One. Anise, clove, snakeroot, were some of the presumably health-giving aromatics used by housewives in homemade cordials taken before breakfast and sometimes passed round at women's gatherings. By the 1840's, ready-prepared commercial bitters had a growing market. Hostetter's Stomach Bitters (44% alcohol) was advertised everywhere as "harmless as water from the mountain spring," based on "vegetable curatives" instead of "mineral irritants" (a cut at the contemporary doctor's dependence on calomel), good for dyspepsia, ague, dysentery, colic, nervous prostration. Its many rivals, though usually a worse money's worth in jolt per dollar, also did well: There were Faith Whitcomb's Nerve Bitters (20.3%); Burdock Blood Bitters (25.2%); Drake's Plantation Bitters (33.2%); Flint's Quaker Bitters (23%); Luther's Temperance Bitters (16.6%); Hooflander's German Bitters (25%), "entirely vegetable and free from alcoholic stimulant". . . . The names mostly hinted vaguely at herbs, Indian lore or old-wives' "blood-purifiers." Many bars sold Hostetter's candidly by the drink. The others, ranging in strength from that of light sherry to that of today's British gin, often made it well worth while to enter the drugstore business in a local-option town.

Since these tipples commanded whiskey prices or better, and until 1905 the Bureau of Internal Revenue exempted the makers from the federal taxes paid by the drinking-liquor industry, the profits were gloriously high, like many of the customers. "Josh Billings" (Henry Wheeler Shaw), the most acid cracker-barrel humorist of the day, took a fall out of the Vegetable Bitters Man who, steeping rhubarb root, catnip and tanbark in cheap whiskey, "goes headlong into the liver-renovating business . . . offering to make the blind talk and the deaf see . . . for a dollar and twenty cents the bottle." The racket soon expanded beyond mere "bitters" into generalized "tonics" and specialized nostrums for women's and children's ills: Carter's Physical Extract (22%); Hooker's Wigwam Tonic (20.7%); Howe's Arabian Tonic (13.2%), "not a rum drink." Golden Liquid Beef Tonic (26.5%) was impudently "recommended for the treatment of alcoholic habit." "Sarsaparilla," which now means an old-timey carbonated soft drink, was originally sterner stuff flavored with exotic herbs, the alleged restorative powers of which may have owed much to its 26% alcohol. Paine's Celery Tonic, almost equally good for that run-down feeling, had 21%.

The best-known nostrum for female complaints was, of course, Lydia Pinkham's Vegetable Compound. Its inventor, Mrs. Lydia Estes Pinkham of Lynn, Massachusetts, derived from her Quaker mother intense interest in Temperance,

Abolition, women's rights and other Syndromisms including the herb-minded "eclectic" school of quack medicine. As wife and mother she developed an eclectic remedy for the aching back and other miseries associated with the recurring exigencies of female systems, soaking true unicorn root, black

cohosh, life root plant, fenugreek seed and so forth in alcohol "solely as a solvent and preservative." In 1902, government analysis found that apparently 21% alcohol was needed for such dissolving and preserving. For some twenty years Mrs. Pinkham just made and gave away her remedy where it would do her suffering sisters the most good. But when the panic of 1873 wiped out the family's substantial real estate holdings her sons had the happy idea of making and selling it wholesale as "The Greatest Medical Discovery Since the Dawn of History." First hawking it themselves store to store, then going into intensive nationwide advertising backed up by a direct-mail health-advice service for ailing women—Mrs. Pinkham's letters in reply were always signed "Yours for Health"—they worked up a substantial fortune and made their mother's name and picture as well known as Abraham Lincoln's.

"It revives the drooping spirits," said their leaflets, "gives elasticity and firmness to the step, restores the natural luster to the eye, and plants on the pale cheek . . . the fresh roses of life's spring." No doubt it did—maybe barring that firmness of step—for physiologically it had two-thirds of the kick of a Manhattan cocktail. Equally eminent among general tonics for both sexes and all ages was Dr. S. B. Hartman's rather stronger Pe-Ru-Na, advertised as strictly a cure for catarrh— only by the time the label got done defining catarrh, it was responsible for anything that might ail you: pneumonia, tuberculosis, appendicitis, Bright's disease, heart trouble, all were catarrh in its amazingly protean forms.

No doubt many women used Lydia's Compound in good faith for genuine female troubles as well as those suggested in the fine old song:

> Mrs. X had bosom trouble,
>   She was flat across the bow;
> Then she took three bottles of Compound,
>   Now they milk her like a cow!
> Oh we sing, we sing, we sing
>   Of Lydia Pinkham, Pinkham, Pinkham
> And her love for the human race!

And no doubt the alcohol in Pe-Ru-Na helped many consumptives through the terminal stage of the disease in a muz-
zily reconciled frame of mind. Acquaintances of William
Lloyd Garrison, as ardent a Temperance man and as confirmed a hypochondriac as he was an Abolitionist, smiled
when he recommended Dr. Church's Anti-Scrofulous Panacea because one felt it "permeating the whole system in the
most delightful manner." Samuel Hopkins Adams, who exposed these patent medicines in *Collier's* Magazine sixty years
ago, heard of a lady leader of the WCTU who wept reproach-
fully when her brother came home with liquor on his breath
but needed a large daily intake of Kilmer's Swamp Root for
herself. It outraged her when told she was obviously tipsy.
James Harvey Young, modern authority on all this, is willing
to believe that many such naïve persons, often of Temperance leanings, did not know the score. Certainly the manufacturers did all they could to preserve such innocence with
palaver about "purely vegetable ingredients"— ironically
true, of course, as far as it went. Such deceptions were easier
in those days before federal food-and-drug laws required
label-identification of ingredients, alcohol included.

The trade had another wide market, of course, in denizens
of Dry territory who used such products to pull the wool over
the eyes of the law and their fellow citizens if not themselves.
For his $1.10 the buyer of Pe-Ru-Na got a half-pint of
straight alcohol cut with a pint of water flavored and colored,
equal to eight two-ounce highballs made with 100-proof
whiskey. While Uncle Sam's revenuers refrained from taxing
the stuff because it was medicine, his Indian Service forbade
sale of it on reservations because it was so easy to get drunk
on. A Midwestern friend of mine recalls his doctor-father's
sardonic tale of finding a huge heap of empty Pe-Ru-Na
bottles in the barn of old John So-and-so, eminent local
Temperance leader, just dead of what had to be diagnosed as
acute alcoholism. Adams found the "Pe-Ru-Na jag" widely
known in West Virginia, and a New York City doctor told
him that many of his women patients had gone alcoholic by
way of Paine's Celery Tonic as well as Mrs. Pinkham's Compound.

Certainly Adams had good reason to believe the physician-expert on patent medicines who said that in the early 1900's when so much of the nation was already Dry—long after the deacon's keeping up his strength with Hostetter's Bitters had become a national joke—Americans drank more bulk of alcohol in such "medicines" than in tax-paid hard liquor. Whether Mrs. Pinkham was aware to what human failing she owed so much of her benevolent prosperity is now known only to the Recording Angel. Druggists still stock her Compound. But these days the alcoholic content is down to 13.5%. The label still mentions black cohosh and life root plant, but the true unicorn root and fenugreek seed are omitted; and the whole is stylishly hopped up with Vitamin B_1. I strongly suspect that it tasted better in the old days; indeed, a veteran schoolteacher who used to club with her normal-school roommate in convivial evenings with a bottle of Compound tried my modern bottle, bought in 1963, and made a face, saying it didn't used to be anything like so nasty. Other guests to whom I've given it after dinner as an exotic liqueur haven't set foot in the house since.

8

M.D.'S AND D.D.'S

. . . a middlin' doctor is a pore thing, and a middlin' law-yer is a pore thing; but keep me from a middlin' man of God.

—OWEN WISTER, *The Virginian*

SWICHEL: The fact is, every time I look at old Slade, I'm afraid of spontaneous combustion.

—*Ten Nights in a Bar-Room,* V, 1

PHYSICIANS whose venality helped to undermine no-license laws made up for some of the damage done by other physicians who gave Temperance pseudoscientific support. Sir Ashley Cooper's tales about beer were no taller than those of other mid-century doctors—often British—as zeal sharpened fancy and lulled feeble intellectual consciences. Thus Sir William Gull of Guy's Hospital, London, had seen corpses so rich in gas from beer drinking that it could be lighted as it escaped from skin punctures. Other eminent doctors told of spirits drinkers' breath containing enough alcohol to catch fire. Dr. Rush—pioneering here too— had already topped that with a drunkard who belched near a candle flame and was "suddenly destroyed." A certain Dr. Kirk found the fluid in the brain cavities of a Scottish workman killed by a drunken fall alcoholic enough to burn. In another such case in London the brain fluids smelled (and *tasted*) so of gin that the doctor tried a lighted match and sure enough. . . .

Temperance laymen on both sides of the water eagerly passed these yarns along. Nowadays they would be self-defeating, among doctors at least. It is too well known that at body temperature, let alone room temperature, an aqueous solution of alcohol much under 40 percent by volume will not ignite; and that no drinker can work up any such concentration in blood, breath or brain fluids because a mere fiftieth of that, say 0.7 percent to 0.8 percent, would long since have stopped his drinking by killing him. In that day, however, medicine knew precious little about the bloodstream and, as we have already suspected, most of what doctors said about the Demon a century ago, favorable or unfavorable, was invalid. Otherwise they would hardly have countenanced the frightful legend of Spontaneous Combustion:

Dickens did much to fix it in the popular mind. His widely read *Bleak House* (1853) tells of a gin-soaked junk dealer found charred down to a blackened torso, with "a smouldering suffocating vapour in the room, and a dark greasy coating on the walls and ceiling," implying that a living organism could grow so impregnated with alcohol that it would take fire from within like damp hay in a barn and smolder itself away in a kind of hideous destructive distillation. When certain readers of the novel in serial form questioned this, Dickens gave the book a Preface citing thirty-odd such cases—all more than a century old, from an age even more credulous and with even lower scientific standards. They impressed him, however, and millions of readers through him. He is not as much to be blamed as the French physician named Lair who had collected these cases from musty European archives; and Dr. Thomas Trotter, retired British army surgeon, who had borrowed and translated Lair's compilation for his *Essay . . . on Drunkenness* of 1810.

It makes grisly reading. No dog would touch bread smeared with the sinister soot pervading the room after Spontaneous Combustion disintegrated an Italian noblewoman accustomed to daily baths in brandy. A very old Frenchwoman who had drunk only spirits for years began spontaneously to combust in her chair; they threw quantities of water over her but the flameless fire within persisted till the flesh burned from her bones though the chair was hardly scorched. . . . The victims listed were all women but by the time the legend was naturalized in North America the other sex was also afflicted. A Dr. Schofield of Upper Canada (now Ontario) described a heavy drinker found standing like a human candlestick in "a widely extended, silver-colored flame" unquestionably from Spontaneous Combustion, for there had been no fire in the smithy where he was thus smitten while drunk.

Dr. Nott, who helped disseminate these whoppers, suggested that habitual drunkenness, being "a violation of the laws of life," was visited in the providence of God by such "signal tokens of His displeasure." Soon enough these lurid materials were inextricably woven into the folklore of drinking along with DTs and Jersey lightning. In our own time George Bernard Shaw, informed that a hard-drinking actor of his acquaintance had perished in a roominghouse fire, said: "Must have been spontaneous combustion."

I must abjure the Balm of Life, I must. . . .
—*The Rubaiyat of Omar Khayyam of Naishapur*

Many responsible physicians, such as Dr. Holmes, failed to join the witch-hunt after Rum. But to the admiration of the righteous and respectable many others rode the hobby of alcohol-slandering intemperately hard. They coined learned terms like "mania *a potu*" (Greek-plus-Latin for "frenzy from drinking") and "dipsomania" (Greek for "thirst-frenzy") to mask their actual vagueness about the abnormalities so labeled. Though they lacked both the germ-theory of disease and modern statistical tools to make a case with, they nevertheless assured the public that practically all persons dying in the epidemics of cholera that terrified the nation in the 1830's and 1840's had been habitual drinkers, whereas teetotalers went scatheless. Washington, D.C., took that so seriously that she closed local groggeries for three months during an epidemic. Some of these omniscient doctors ascribed the inebriate's craving to alcoholic irritation of the stomach lining, which demanded frequent restimulation like an itch demanding scratching. Finding alcohol detectible in the drinker's urine as well as breath, they rashly assumed that all of it was eventually excreted. Therefore none of it was metabolized in the body; therefore Dr. Rush was right, it had no food value—a position that none took more firmly than Dr. Nathan S. Davis, dean of the Northwestern University Medical School and a founder of the American Medical Association. Therefore, in view of its known toxicity, alcohol was to be regarded as strictly a poison like snake venom, any intrusion of which in the bloodstream was by definition harmful. Its observable effects, such as flushed skin, faster pulse, were taken as symptoms of the body's emergency effort to get rid of the stuff before it was too late.

Already in the 1860's there were sound laboratory reasons to doubt all that. Within thirty years the Committee of Fifty's unimpeachable medical experts pointed out that if alcohol deserves the name "poison," it "must be a very slow [one], since many have used it up to old age with apparently no prejudicial effects. . . ."; that the caffeine in tea is also a poison; that, grossly overused, common salt becomes one; and unequivocally asserted the food value of alcohol as source of energy for the system. (That set Mr. Dooley warning Mr. Hennessy that "ye'll read in the' pa-aper that 'Anton Boozinski, while crazed with ham an' eggs, thried to kill his wife an' childher . . . they'll be places where a man can be took whin he gets th' monkeys from immodhrate eatin'. . . .") But Temperance went right on calling alcohol an unqualified, categorical poison clear up to the Volstead Act.

Temperance's pet doctors set forth none of these dicta as tentative but spoke as if they were as well established as the circulation of the blood or the nine months of human gestation. They knew no other way to talk—a trait persisting in some of their successors, especially psychiatrists. So naturally their extravagances lost nothing when retold by the food faddists, phrenologists, Dry preachers, reformed drunkards and others making careers of abusing the Demon. Even when Galen Lancet, M.D., sought properly to qualify his statements, Areopagus Homily, D.D., dropped all caution when pounding the pulpit in the good cause. Blithely he gave the congregation his solemn word that babies suckling mothers who drink can become infantile alcoholics, and that French babies are known to refuse to nurse from any woman who was sober . . . that the untoward effect of alcohol on the circulation causes ulcerated lungs, ossified heart, cancer, hemorrhoids . . . that the milk of cows fed on spent mash from distilleries causes the high infant mortality of large cities . . . that habitual use of alcohol so lowers "the principle of vitality" that the shock of merely drinking a glass of cold water can kill (shades of W. C. Fields!); that a teetotaling sailor on an arctic expedition escaped scurvy, whereas all his shipmates who took their grog ration came down with it, and his name solemnly recorded, was Adam Ayles. . . .

Inevitably Temperance doctors revived another of Dr. Rush's indestructible hints: ". . . drunkenness resembles certain hereditary . . . diseases," and warned that drinking parents risk passing alcoholism on to their offspring as if it were red hair or a Roman nose. The nineteenth century, lacking Mendel's keys to these matters, was hopelessly confused about them, so there was no danger of scientific challenge. *Post-hoc* reasoning, drawing wishful conclusions from the observed frequency with which drunken ne'er-do-wells have drunken, ne'er-do-well fathers, had a field day. It was particularly impressive when Dr. B. W. Richardson, august British leader of Temperance medicine, stated with elaborate caution that, in his observation, the degenerative effects of parental drinking on offspring might die out after the *third* generation provided child and grandchild were kept teetotal. To heritable degeneracy brought on by drink he traced not only alcoholism but much epilepsy, tuberculosis, idiocy, insanity and criminality. Nor could moderation in drinking reduce these genetic hazards. In 1884, Dr. A. B. Palmer, professor of the practice of medicine at the University of Michigan, endorsed a "phsyiology" text prepared by the WCTU which told schoolchildren:

> . . . sometimes one is sick or suffers very much because of wrong things that his parents or grand-parents did. . . . Over in the poor-house is a man who does not know as much as most children four years old . . . because he is the child of drinking parents whose poisoned life blood tainted his own. Many men and women are insane because they inherit disordered bodies and minds, caused by the drinking habits of their parents; and *the descendants of "moderate drinkers"*

differ in this way as well as those of the drunkard [italics mine . . . . This is called the law of heredity . . . one of God's laws, and just like earthly laws, helps right living and punishes those who disobey.

From inebriate forebears, said this outrageous work, the English and Americans derive such a craving for alcohol that brandy sauce or wine jelly may trigger it and doom the taster to a drunkard's grave. (It also has a clear working sketch of a simple still and advises running hard cider through twice for applejack of proper strength. Can it have been aimed at another public outside the schoolroom?) Eventually a Dry pamphleteer summing up allegedly accepted medical findings stated that the offspring of parents both of whom drink are invariably either insane, tuberculous or alcoholic; citing cases of small children with an hereditary yen for alcohol so strong that the mere sight of a bottle shaped like a whiskey flask brought them whining for a nip.

The one thing to be said for all this is that it did incline people to think of drunkards as suffering from a disease to be handled as such—which prepared the way for modern approaches to the problem. Offering an early gleam of sense, Dr. Holmes, though leaving room for rare hereditary factors, thought most drunkards victims of their own emotional and intellectual emptiness. At Massachusetts' legislative hearings on the liquor problem in 1867, several other eminent doctors from the Harvard Medical School cast chilling doubts on the exuberance of Temperance's scare-propaganda. Dr. Davis, for all his championing a Maine-type law for Illinois, saw the typical drunkard as a maimed or unstable personality and said that nineteen in twenty alleged hereditary cases he had seen had obviously acquired the habit from home influences, not heredity at all. But such discretion had small chance against a theory so simple and yet so flashy. Temperance spellbinders snatched at wild anecdotes about despairing victims of inherited craving for drink and fancied them up with pseudoscientific jigsaw work. One reformed drunkard-lecturer insisted that his brother and he had both gone alcoholic because their pioneer parents had "exhausted their nervous force by excessive hard work" before begetting them. An eminent phrenologist taught that alcoholic stimulation of "the animal propensities" was what made offspring of drinkers so deficient in morals and brains, "quarrelsome and vicious and the pests of society." Nor did this heredity theory fail to keep acquiring endorsement from great names, such as Dr. Willard Parker, first American to perform an appendectomy, and Charles Warren Eliot, president of Harvard.

Not until well past 1900 did Temperance literature begin unobtrusively to admit that later—and sounder—research had shown the alcohol habit not to be heritable. Most Temperance crusaders probably never heard of these shy retractions. Captain Richmond Pearson Hobson, USN (ret.)—of whose Temperance career more later—went right on shouting his extravagant version of the heredity theory. Robert W. Chambers made it the plot basis of his popular novel of Bar Harbor–style high life of 1906, *The Fighting Chance*. Thanks to disingenuous publicity and noisy doctors, in fact, most of the Demon's enemies continued to believe and preach well into Prohibition that alcoholism was about as heritable as spyhilis.

That was the case against drink for those planning progeny. The celibate and the middle-aged were told that alcohol was not only poison in all contexts and concentrations, however dilute, but peculiarly vicious among poisons because of its "unnatural" origin. It is not found in living nature, Temperance said, only in dead vegetable matter undergoing fermentation—a form of decay which is a function of death— and it takes man's perverse invention of the still to extract it. No wonder it was fatal to body and soul, for it sprang from death and corruption. Instead of being "water of life" it is "water of death . . . the juice of decay," wrote Gough's biographer. A preacher named Woodend asked: "Shall we turn away with loathing and disgust from the . . . vulture gorging itself with carrion all quivering with putrescence and then drink [wine] sparkling . . . by reason of a like work of decomposition going on within?"

Even at the time that was poor science. Then as now, overripe wild fruits ferment and naturally create alcohol without man's help; and butterflies, ants and wasps get tipsy on it without needing man to show them how. (An expert from the Bartlett Tree Research Laboratories tells me yellow-jackets fall over drunk and take hours to sleep it off. The notion of a yellow-jacket with a hangover is appalling; those I've met were savage enough sober.) Nobody brought that up, however. Challenge waited until Pasteur showed that fermentation actually teems with life and naturalness as yeast cells flourish on the natural carbohydrates of grape juice, apple juice and malt with alcohol as one by-product. Then the Committee of Fifty's doctors pointed out that alcohol is both naturally and normally present "in the healthy [human] organism," being somehow spontaneously manufactured in the enteric tract.

So Temperance dropped "unnatural" and took to scatology. Dr. Winfield S. Hall, professor of physiology at Northwestern University, pronounced alcohol "the excretion of a fungus." That was the stuff to give the troops. As Hobson exultantly noted, it "removed all glamour from the cup and produced a reaction of loathing," as well it might among semantic innocents. Apply the same rhetorical trick to the ripening of cheese and you will never eat Welsh rarebit again, let alone Roquefort. The sighs of the poet's lady-love can be described as loaded with "excrement"—the carbon dioxide that her respiratory system exhausts through her lungs. The appetizing odor of baking bread comes of alcohol, that same excrement from yeast, and yeasts are no more and no less fungi than the mushrooms on a beefsteak. But the connotations of "fungus" are dank and nasty, and for most of us "excrement" applies to dung and urine only. So Temperance developed this joyfully: "When the grape is broken in the wine-press," said a Dry sermon of 1913, "[yeasts] . . . gorge themselves and leave their liquid excrement. That is what alcohol is. Now sing of your ruby wine!"

But the old reliable body of medical old wives' tales was already collapsing on Temperance's hands, and by our time those hair-raising lists of allegedly alcohol-caused diseases have shrunk to three or four: DTs, yes, due to brain damage from excessive drinking, sometimes recurring without it when the subject meets a high fever or a general anesthetic. Cirrhosis of the liver, yes, again from prolonged abuse; but teetotalers can get it too. Chronic gastritis, yes; "drunkard's nose." . . . That's about it, though the malnutrition and poor physical condition that go with too much drinking naturally weaken the subject and may open the door for many other ills. It remains true that, since mother and un-born child share the same bloodstream, child gets as drunk as mother and must share her hangover, which is most unfair but at least there is some reason to believe that child's misery may be less severe. Once born, however, the breast-fed baby runs no risk of going alcoholic from mother's milk, no matter how hard she drinks. Worst blow of all for Temperance, neither geneticist nor statistician can yet find evidence that the most destructive drinking can distort heredity. It is hazily possible that alcoholism may sometimes be one symptom of a general emotional or metabolic inadequacy with a genetic twist to it. But suppose such a factor demonstrated—there is no present indication that it will be—even so, parental drink-ing could not increase nor parental teetotaling reduce its genetic effect. There are many good reasons for not drinking too much, and for not drinking at all if you don't like or can't handle it. But the old-fangled "hereditary taint" of the WCTU textbooks is not one of them.

What key will unlock the door to hell? Whis-*key*.
—*National Temperance Almanac,* 1878

Doctors are of several kinds. The issue whether alcohol is "natural" tempted M.D.'s to encroach on the sphere of D.D.'s, and Ph.D.'s too, for it raised knotty problems: Are things to the making of which human agency is indispens-able—Rum or the *Iliad* or the internal-combustion motor—therefore "unnatural"? They may be no more artificial than the mathematically precise honeycomb of bees or the cleverly engineered nests of orioles, yet birds, bees and all their works

are thought of as highly "natural." Then, even supposing alcoholic drink "unnatural," is the term as much of a reproach
as the minds of that time and ours tend to feel? Further, since
fermentation and the resulting alcohol obviously occur naturally, that is, without man's agency, "unnaturalness" can begin only where the still takes over—which leaves winebibbing, cider swilling and beer guzzling, with their attendant
drunkenness, dismayingly in the clear. But Temperance
D.D.'s are very eager to call alcohol a human perversion of
God's natural world, not at all His doing or His responsibility, because that would disqualify it as one of those "good
creatures of God" that the Apostle Paul recommended as innocent.* Otherwise the parson had to wriggle on the di-
lemma so well stated about the time *Ten Nights in a Bar-
room* was first staged:

> "Why, be this Juice the growth of God, who dare
> Blaspheme the twisted Tendril as a Snare?
> A Blessing, we should use it, should we not?
> And if a Curse—why, then, Who set it there?"

Today it sounds strange that a few words awkwardly translated from a Near Eastern preacher named Paul 1,800 years
dead should so critically modify human behavior. Consider,
however, that Temperance had taken shape before "The
Higher Criticism" and Darwin had flawed literal acceptance
of the Bible. A few agnostics altogether denied its authority;
divines disputed the meaning of obscure passages; ordinary
persons disobeyed one or another of its clearest injunctions
off and on. But its essential prestige was pretty much unflawed. The devout might still use it for divination, opening
at random and taking whatever text the eye first lighted on as
Heaven's answer to a vexing problem. Certainly in any question of morals in the English-speaking world, particularly its
North American division, what the Bible said or seemed to
say about an issue mattered greatly to laymen as well as cler-
ics.

* "For every creature of God is good, and nothing to be refused, if it be
received with thanksgiving." (I Timothy, 14:4)

Birth control was hampered early—still is in the Catholic context—by reference to the vengeance that God took on Onan because though it was his familial duty in terms of his day to beget children of his late brother's widow, he spilled his seed upon the ground to avoid doing so. It embarrassed antislavery men that chattel slavery was clearly accepted in both the Old and the New Testaments; and the zeal with which Abolitionist parsons sought to explain this away—and failed—was equal only to that with which Southern parsons rubbed it in. Paul's remarks to Timothy about "suffer not a woman to teach" was a principal reason for barring women from speaking in good-cause meetings. And it was highly awkward for teetotal Temperance that a little further along Paul also advised his young friend: "Drink no longer water but use a little wine for thy stomach's sake, and thine often infirmities." True, that might be represented as mere medical advice; even Maine Laws left room for medical use of alcoholic drinks. But no such loophole marred Moses' earlier and equally inspired advice to the Israelites to spend their money on "whatsoever thy soul lusteth after," with "strong drink" as one suggestion. Worse, Christ's first miracle consisted of turning water into wine at a marriage feast when— the chronic dread of hostesses—the supply ran low. Worst of all, the Last Supper, prototype of a sacrament of the Church, made wine as well as bread the vehicle of the basic Christian mystery.

None of that was cripplingly embarrassing while Temperance denounced only drunkenness generally and spirits specifically. From Adam's ale to Timothy's wine the Bible knew not distilling. Plenty of passages, notably in the Old Testament, scolded drunkards—early Temperance's prime targets— or told of the disgraceful consequences of drunkenness: Noah, drunk from the wine of the first vineyard, exposed himself so indecently that only cursing one of his sons to the end of time could adequately vent his chagrin. Lot's daughters plied their father with wine to get him to sleep with them. But when Temperance went teetotal, tabooing both drinks with any detectible alcoholic content and anybody daring to try moderate drinking, zealous parsons were hard put: "The Son of Man came eating and drinking," said the New Testament to distinguish Him from John the Baptist, His ascetic harbinger. "Go that way," says the Old Testament, "eat thy bread with joy, drink thy wine with a merry heart." Where did such passages leave the new doctrine, favorite of the all-or-nothing mind, that any ingestion of alcohol was a poisonous sin and alcohol itself a sinful poison?

Well, the Bible did sponsor teetotalism for special groups like Moses' Nazarites, who were ascetics forbidden to shave or touch wine or grape juice, raisins or fresh grapes. (Actually more like a general vine-taboo of obscure origin than a specific gesture against alcohol?) John the Baptist, a most holy man, was a Nazarite. The three children in the fiery furnace were Rechabites, the teetotaling nomads whom we have already met in that secret Temperance order of the 1840's. Yet the practice of such eccentric minorities might not justify what Temperance hoped to impose on all wishing to be thought Christians. In desperation Temperance's D.D.'s denied that the wine used by the righteous in the Bible was alcoholic, professing to deduce from internal evidence that it was unfermented grape juice. Only the unrighteous had let grape-squeezings ferment with such shameful consequences as overtook Noah and Lot to warn posterity. Or maybe the unrighteous spiked their unfermented juice with unspecified nonalcoholic narcotics to make the "strong drink" of which many Old Testament texts took so dim a view.*

To back up these hypotheses it was represented that the original Hebrew and Greek texts of the Bible had several different terms for grape drinks, all usually lumped as "wine" in the King James Version that *was* the Bible for most Tem-

---

* Samuel I, 1:14–15 leaves no doubt that, whatever the shortcomings of translation, the Old Testament Jews had both an intoxicating wine and some other "strong drink": "And Eli said unto her, How long wilt thou be drunken? put away thy wine from thee. And Hannah answered . . . I have drunk neither wine nor strong drink . . ." Dr. William Dock of Downstate Medical Center, Brooklyn, N.Y., believes that "strong drink" was a fermentation of honey or palm juice which would come out more intoxicating than wine from Holy Land grapes.

perance laymen, variations reflecting differences in toxic content and state of preservation of the drinks meant. This left room for hoping that the "wine" of Cana, the Last Supper and St. Paul's prescription was innocently unfermented. Scholars invaded the kitchens of their houses to conduct experiments to persuade themselves that the ancient Jews could have known how to keep jars of grape juice from fermenting in the climate of Palestine. Their purpose was not only to prove it possible but also to create a theologically acceptable substitute for alcoholic wine at Communion in seasons when fresh grapes were unavailable. Eventually such efforts founded the American grape-juice industry as a minor economic result of Temperance.

Fresh grape juice as a staple of Solomon's diet was too implausible for scholars less eager in the Temperance cause. They denounced the notion in the pulpit and in print. Champions of grape juice reacted violently, and for a couple of generations after the 1830's reverend gentlemen beat one another over the head with sermons and pamphlets using exotic words like *yayin* and *oinos* in very bad temper. Lay churchmen got into it; some, like Dr. Delavan, because they were incapable of staying out of a Temperance fight, others because of intraparochial disputes whether to buy port for Communion or ask the ladies to put up a year's supply of sterilized grape juice. Temperance writers ground out fictions about sextons or promising young ministers dragged down to drunkenness by the standing temptation of the sacramental wine in the vestry. An unedifying squabble widely and deservedly deplored. Even Gough, stern Methodist though he had become, thought it unbecoming to run to the Bible for pettifogging justification of every detail of what his soul told him was right—or wrong. Yet its rumblings persisted down to the triumph of national Prohibition, and Don Marquis' Old Soak had the last word on it with his own kind of internal evidence: His wife tried to tell him that "the liquor drinked in the Bible wasn't nothing but unfermented grape juice . . . like hell it was . . . how about that there book that says vanity, vanity, all is vanity? Well, I ask you, did you ever get that way in the morning after you had spend the night before drinking the unfermented juice of the grape?"

ATTENTIVE: But that which is worse than all, [drunkenness] also prepares men for everlasting burnings.

WISEMAN: Yea, and it so stupefies and besotts the soul, that a man that is far gone in Drunkenness, is hardly ever recovered to God. Tell me, when did you see an old drunkard converted?

—JOHN BUNYAN, *The Life and Death of Mr. Badman*

As biologists ruling on the unnaturalness of alcohol or as scholars twisting obscure Hebrew nouns into meaning what they should, these Temperance parsons were unimpressive. So far their churches would have done better to learn from the Hardshell Baptists of New Salem, Illinois, who simultaneously expelled one member for drunkenness and another for advocating teetotalism; or, like Islam a thousand years earlier (or the Mormons of a later day) to impose abstinence by dictatorial order with no ifs, ands or buts. Actually they hardly needed to appeal to pedantry and what passed for science. Their real strength lay in Christian ethics first and then in mystical considerations common to many religions—matters much better suited to the pulpit.

The ethical point we have already seen used against moderate drinkers. It too relied on St. Paul, first: "Let . . . no man put a stumbling block, or an occasion to fall, in his brother's way. . . . It is good neither to eat flesh, nor to drink wine, nor any thing whereby thy brother stumbleth or is offended, or is made weak." Second, Paul elsewhere listed drunkards along with fornicators, homosexuals, idolaters, thieves, extortioners, as by definition excluded from the Kingdom of God. These considerations might well obligate those of true Christian sensibility to give up their own drinking and do their best to see alcoholic liquors outlawed lest they be the occasion, even in small degree, of countenancing or promoting what would send weaker souls to hell. Given the premises, the reasoning is good and such Christianity is sound; only so subtle a sense of Christian duties is even rarer now than when John Wesley, quoting Paul, applied it in support of Temperance two hundred years ago.

That drunkenness damns was so plain to the Rev. Dr. Armstrong, cofounder of that first Temperance society, that for him alcohol was worse than unnatural—it was the Devil's own special invention for destroying the Church of God. He proved it from the Scriptures.* Less sensationally John Woolman deplored Rum in the harvest field lest it spoil "that calmness and serenity which we should endeavor to live in . . . [and] disqualify [us] from successfully following Him who is meek and low of heart." The Rev. Dr. Justin Edwards shouted it: Carnal gratification, in his view, is at best a notorious hazard to the soul and distraction from the glory of God, and man's cultivated appetite for alcohol presumptuously adds another fleshly indulgence to those with which God has already seen fit to saddle His universe, which amounts to rebellion against God and is damning in itself.

The Rev. J. H. Danforth, crying in the bibulous wilderness of Washington, D.C., in 1830, got nearer the gist of it by calling drinking "a habit which estranges the soul from the means of grace." Annual reports of the American Temperance Society in the 1830's argued the point well: Drink keeps sinners from "God's illuminating and purifying power. It tends directly and strongly to make men feel, as Jesus Christ hates—rich spiritually, increased in goods and in need of nothing. . . . As the salvation of the soul is the greatest of all blessings, that which tends most to hinder this is among the greatest of evils. . . . A quantity [of alcohol] that does not deprive a man of reason . . . may nevertheless prevent the effect of divine truth, and keep him in a state of hardness of

---

* "When the enemy shall come in like a flood, the Spirit of the Lord shall lift up a standard against him." (Isaiah, lix, 19) "And the serpent shall cast out of his mouth water as a flood after the woman, that he might cause her to be carried away of the flood. And the earth helped the woman, and the earth opened her mouth, and swallowed up the flood which the dragon cast out of her mouth." (Revelation, xii, 15–16)

heart and blindness of mind . . . in direct opposition to the Holy Ghost."

Those theological values were more familiar to our great-grandfathers than to us. Their essence translates rather well into the terms of universal mysticism: When such theologians spoke of "grace" they referred, beneath the jargons of their particular sects, to the state of communion and identification with the Infinite Something (God, in their view) that mystics are skilled in achieving. In Buddhist or Quaker, Jew or Chippewa, the emotional symptoms sound so much the same that the underlying reality, whatever it may be, is also likely to be the same. The "Holy Ghost" of Christian theology puts a quasi-metaphorical name on the sense of possession by an outside power that is nevertheless a function of oneself—or vice versa—which, according to those who have experienced it, ushers in these ineffable states of mind. Here "salvation" means the privilege of arriving at such a state intermittently and arduously in this world; permanently, the subject hopes, in the next. For the generalized mystic the Christian symbolic legend of redemption only masks and dramatizes a reality that the Christian shares with fellow adepts of many cults. Yet for the adept Christian, the legend remains valid even though cognate to parallel elements in others.

Aldous Huxley, lay guide in these matters, considers that the yearning for such "grace" comes of a "deep-seated urge to self-transcendence . . . as men and women [try] to escape from the tormenting consciousness of being merely themselves." Whether or not that yearning sways us all to some extent, as Huxley, William James and others seem to assume, it certainly exists in enough individuals to make it an important fact of human experience.

Now recall the Indians seeking self-transcendence from alcohol here, peyote there, prayer and fasting elsewhere, preferring one such means to another because it is traditional among them but readily turning to alien approaches, such as exhaust fumes, under changed circumstances. Western minds tend to be less catholic. In their view all self-transcendence is not necessarily a proper "state of grace." Huxley, in his Epilogue to *The Devils of Loudun,* classes alcohol along with opium, coca, elementary (impersonal) sexuality and the mob-emotions as "Grace-substitutes"—the capitalization maybe emphasizing his feeling that, though taking the subject out of himself right enough, they do so with a coarser, deleterious content, "invariably downward into the less than human, the lower than personal." In that light the likely results are doubly disastrous according to mystic and theologian too: The subject not only degenerates from normal sinfulness (or self-containment), to the extent that he calls on a Grace-substitute to help him soar into self-transcendence, it walls him away from the more-than-human, higher-than-personal kind of self-transcendence that is conversion-*cum*-salvation. That is what Temperance parsons were getting at when warning that the Demon Rum hardened the heart against the Holy Ghost and led the soul to damnation. Alcohol inoculates against a state of grace.

There somewhere lies the sound reason for abstaining from and even denouncing drink. Other reasons are either inapplicable to most temperaments; or pharisaical; or hypersolicitous; or spurious. The D.D.'s theology far outdid the M.D.'s physiology.

9

"HE DRINKS!"

'Mid pleasures and palaces though we may roam,
Be it ever so humble, there's no place like home.
But there is the father lies drunk on the floor,
The table is empty, the wolf's at the door,
And mother sobs loud in her broken-back'd chair,
Her garments in tatters, her soul in despair. . . .
—NOBLE ADKISSON, *Ruined by Drink,* II, 2

THE Civil War banked but did not extinguish the fires of Temperance. In 1862 the cause won a minor but long-sought victory as the U.S. Navy abolished spirits-rations for enlisted men, restricting the Demon to the officers' euphemistically named "wine mess." It was also handy for Temperance, if not for him, that the first Union casualty in line of duty was the conspicuous Col. Elmer E. Ellsworth, protégé of Abraham Lincoln, organizer of "Zouave" light infantry and priggish teetotaler. Shot dead in Alexandria, Virginia, by a civilian from whose roof he had torn down a Confederate flag, Ellsworth was an overnight hero. The American Temperance Union made haste to circulate an "Ellsworth pledge" among the troops binding them to abstain from drink for the duration, which was enterprising; and proof that Ellsworth really existed still remains in a memorial tablet on the base of the flagpole in New York City's bar-dominated Sheridan Square.

Several important commanders, McClellan, Banks and Butler included, took more or less severe measures to keep sutlers from selling, and personnel from drinking, any but ration liquor. Banks gave extra leave to Sons of Temperance who chose to throw the ration away. Other generals got ungenerously maligned as examples of the evils of drink: Temperance propagandists not only gossiped about Grant's thirst for whiskey but encouraged rumors that what happened to McDowell at Bull Run and to Hooker at Chancellorsville came of too much Dutch courage in the general. Actually McDowell was a teetotaler; Hooker, though fond of his drink, probably owed his fatal confusion at a critical juncture not to

the Demon but to shock resulting from a solid shot striking
the veranda post on which he was leaning his head.

With further disregard of military morale the American
Temperance Union kept after the high brass with a tract,
Our Generals and Subordinate Officers, saying that if anybody needed such "aristocratic luxuries" as drink, it was the
rank-and-file: "It is not for you, generals, . . . to drink. . . .
Give wine to the bleeding soldier in the ambulance." The
enlisted man's interests were served by other tracts: *The Soldier's Crown; The Sick Soldier; The Temperance Soldier.*
. . . But it stands to reason and is pretty clear in the record
that, in spite of such reading matter reinforced by uncer-
tainty of supply, the boys in blue got in plenty of drinking,
more than those in gray—for logistic if not moral reasons
booze was often sadly scarce for Johnny Reb. There was
probably more drinking in Northern cities too as job oppor-
tunities increased along with pay scales, and wartime emotions and activities set zealous Temperance types doing other
things.

A lasting mark was left on the good cause when Uncle Sam
inaugurated federal taxation of liquor to help pay for the
war, as had previously been done in the War of 1812. That
tax was repealed in 1817 but its successor of 1862 is essentially still in force a hundred years later. Temperance did not
mind its creating the classic picture of the revenuer beating
the laurel for the moonshiner; its raising the price of whiskey
might even be taken as a blow against the Demon. But it also
made Uncle Sam to some extent a partner in the profits of
the distilling and brewing industries and so would discourage
him from helping to exterminate them. Within a few months
of the passage of the Internal Revenue Act of 1862, fore-
sighted brewers, so dominated by Germans that the inaugu-
ratory proceedings were conducted in German, had formed
the still existing United States Brewers Association to look
after the new situation—the Demon's first formal gesture of
defense.

The Act also required all liquor dealers, wholesale or re-
tail, to take out a federal tax-license. That greatly confused
things in nominally Dry states like Massachusetts where the

owners of blind pigs in trouble with the police tried to maintain that they could too sell booze in defiance of state law since here was a federal license permitting it. Supreme Court decisions in 1864 and 1865 cured them of that delusion, after which the Demon's foes found that part, at least, of the new law very handy. Few rumsellers, licit or illicit, wanted to get in trouble with Uncle Sam so they usually took out federal licenses, and in Revenue Districts where the Commissioner felt obliging, a local chief of police wanting to know just where the blind pigs were and who owned them had only to run his eye down the list of license receipts. Some states were so unsporting as to make possession of such a license *prima-facie* evidence of violation of state Dry laws.

On the whole, however, Temperance stalwarts were right to see the years since John Brown had raided Harpers Ferry as low-water for their cause. As yet they were unaware of the great service the war was doing them as preparation for future glories: It was showing American women—the very ones likeliest to value Temperance—their previously neglected talents as militant organizers.

In many respects—use of armored men-of-war; World War I–style entrenching; aerial reconnaissance; entertainment troupes in camp; privileges for newspaper correspondents—the Civil War was modern, and one of its most modern touches was its voluntary civilian auxiliaries organized largely on women's initiative. Before the flustered War Department had taken up the problem, Dorothea Dix, great lady of asylum reform, was in Washington asking leave to recruit women nurses—the homeliest available—for military hospitals. Clara Barton not only collected medical supplies for battlefield use but personally made sure they were expended to the best advantage. The North's ablest propaganda spellbinder was Anna E. Dickinson, a brash little Pennsylvania girl, who came early to fame by calling McClellan a traitor after the battle of Ball's Bluff, then became a sort of fishwife Joan of Arc trouping the country with eagle-screaming orations useful to the Republicans as well as to the war effort. Women's Righters organized a Women's National Loyal League avowedly to teach women the causes and aims of the war but also with the purpose of bedeviling Mr. Lincoln into admitting it was a war on slavery, hence into freeing the slaves.

Wider and most significant was the "soldiers' relief" movement. Husbands, sons and brothers left woman-run homes for man-run camps. Mothers, sisters and wives assumed—rightly— that they would need a great deal that Uncle Sam would neglect to furnish; that up to then, indeed, soldiers had seldom had. All over the country, most notably in New England, women got together sewing-bee–charity-bazaar fashion to make and ship to camp the supplementary things that those impractical generals would never think of: better-than-rations food; extra socks and woolies; spare remedies for toothache and sore feet; personal help for men traveling on furlough and, as problems arose, for the families whom they had left behind or were trying to reach. Dr. Emily Blackwell, pioneer woman physician, correlated these sporadic improvisations into a Women's Central Relief Committee in New York City. Hastily recognizing a sound idea, Uncle Sam gave it official standing as the U.S. Sanitary Commission, precursor of the Red Cross. Its nominal male heads, particularly F. L. Olmsted, creator of New York City's Central Park and sound observer of slavery, were able men. But as aforesaid the bulk of the necessary time, energy and town-by-town organizing was women's work. West of Pittsburgh, in fact, those things were almost altogether handled by women who, an amazed New York businessman wrote, "evinced talents which, in other spheres and in the other sex, would have made them merchant-princes or great administrators of public affairs."

For instance, Mrs. Mary A. Livermore, head of the Northwest Sanitary Commission with headquarters in Chicago, correlated 4,000-odd local branches in operations following the Union armies all the way down the Southern rivers. Mrs. Annie Wittenmyer of Keokuk, Iowa, who ignored Confederate fire at the siege of Vicksburg, organized diet-kitchens for the wounded so well that Grant made her and them an official arm of his western command. Mrs. Eliza Daniel Stewart of Springfield, Ohio—alias "Mother Stewart"—was as well known in Union army hospitals as Florence Nightingale at

Scutari. Behind such chieftainesses were formidable thousands of local organizers like Mrs. Mary Ann Reese of Steubenville, Ohio, who found time to write inspirational war poetry while managing a Soldiers' Relief—and ten years later was jailed in Pittsburgh for praying on the sidewalk outside a saloon. After the war all the ladies here mentioned, plus many more thus acquiring stimulating experience, took part, heads down and heels flying, in the great Women's Crusade that turned into the National Woman's Christian Temperance Union.

Where had these able women been up to then? Frustrated in outer darkness, working up a snarling hatred for the Demon that boded him no good if anything, such as a civil war, should release their potential.

> No matter what anyone says, no matter what anyone thinks,
>   If you want to be happy the rest of your life,
>   Don't marry a man if he drinks!
>   —*Temperance Song*

Back when Temperance was young and full of gristle a tavern in Montgomery County, New York, burned down. General Ashbel Riley heard a woman in the crowd say: "Glory to God! I prayed for that!" He told audiences that that fervent blasphemy was what set him against the Demon. Though a professional Dry, Riley likely enough did hear something of the sort. Many women have had reason to feel strongly about gin mills. At about the same time (1833), in nearby Delaware County, a woman was arrested for setting fire to the barn of a man who went on selling drink to her inebriate son. It should be said, however, that such punitive arson was rare. Prayer was woman's first and favorite weapon against the Demon, its weight often increased by combining it with log-rolling and obstruction of traffic.

Whatever the choice of weapon here or there, it remains true that had women failed to take a large hand in Temperance, we would probably never have embarked on national Prohibition. It depended heavily on the impulse to stop backing, filling, fact-finding, hemming and hawing and *do something* regardless that often overcomes women with strong feelings about problems, private or public. Call it the Carry Nation complex. But the hatchet-happy terror of Kansas was only last and most conspicuous of a long series of women anticipating her taste for violence and lacking only her psychotic talent for getting jailed.

Canny Prohibitionists eventually came to understand that women were indispensable—and in any case had to be given their heads because their hearts were untamably stirred. That was realized only after years of sporadic antics, however, had made it ever clearer that members of the more headstrong sex were right in casting themselves as Temperance's shock troops; that, given rein, they would overwhelm King Alcohol's intrenchments as impulsively as the boys in blue had carried Missionary Ridge.

The chief obstacle was cultural, of course. The early nineteenth century, when Temperance was shaping up, defined "woman's sphere" too narrowly to allow her much organized activity outside the curtained parlors that sheltered the ladies' auxiliaries of missionary or Bible societies. The examples of such exceptional women as Elizabeth Fry in prison reform were bearing fruit, true, but very spottily. The founder of that Allentown Sober Society was a woman, but nothing came of her enterprise. It still caused great dissension among antislavery men in Boston in the 1830's when the achingly respectable Grimké sisters, highborn daughters of South Carolina, spoke before Abolitionist women's meetings that came to include a few equally respectable men. The Congressional Temperance Society of 1834 resolved that "the influence of woman . . . [is] essential to the triumph of every good and great cause" and would make the triumph of Temperance "certain and complete." But "influence" was the limiting keyword. "Woman" in the abstract singular, two-dimensional as a paper doll, was expected to remain up there in the stands as smiling inspiration while her knight battled the Demon in the sweaty lists.

She had had gallant warning from the Rev. Dr. Eliphalet Nott, president of Union College, wealthy inventor of the coal-burning stoves that turned American sitting rooms into sweatboxes, whose *Temperance Lectures* were an acknowledged handbook. He would not if he could, he said, persuade women to become "public, clamorous advocates of . . . temperance." Theirs rather to set "open, willing, visible example, enforced by that soft, persuasive, colloquial eloquence which, in some hallowed retirement and chosen moments, exerts such controlling influence over a husband's, a son's, a brother's heart . . . you [women] have a heaven-appointed armour, as well as a heaven-appointed theatre of action. The look of tenderness, the eye of compassion, the lip of entreaty are yours." That is, Woman, cajoling the male world into laying off the stuff, was to be a sort of B-girl in reverse. Further, since she ruled fashion, she could "remove at once and forever, temptation from the drawing-room and the dining-table . . . loathsome, brutal drunkenness will be compelled to exist, if it exist at all, only among those vulgar and ragged wretches who, shunning the society of woman, herd together in the bar-room, the oyster cellar and the groggery."

> I saw a little girl,
>   With half uncovered form,
> And wondered why she wandered thus
>   Amid the winter storm.
> They said her mother drank of that
>   Which took her sense away,
> And so she let her children go
>   Hungry and cold all day.
>   —Mrs. Lydia Huntley Sigourney

A basic assumption of Temperance propaganda was that essentially Woman was above Man's coarse taste for alcohol. The facts were less flattering:

Dr. Nott may not have realized that Woman could set that "open, willing example" only by going on the wagon herself—which implies that she had previously been drinking more or less. Such hints are rare but all the more significant for the variety of contexts in which they occur. Lady alcoholics turned up in the literature from the beginning. Dr. Rush cited two, seemingly of respectable social position. The Rev. Mr. Marsh wrote of another who blamed her trouble on having had wine at table as a child. President Franklin Pierce's mother was alcoholic and it darkened his own struggle with the Demon to suspect that he had inherited the tendency. Backwoods women used spirits along with their men: "The girls' eyes shone with fun and whiskey," wrote H. H. Hadley recalling a frolic in pioneer Ohio. At the other end of the social scale, ladies in Tidewater Virginia took wine at dinner and punch at parties. The human organism being what it is, disastrous addiction probably resulted in a certain proportion of these instances.

Temperance was hardly moving before the Rev. Dr. Heman Humphrey protested that "to get intoxicated now and then is too often passed over, as a kind of venial fault, which by no means disqualifies persons of *either sex* [italics mine] from genteel and virtuous society." In the 1820's the old crone who ran the "dame school" that little Mary Rice (Livermore) attended in Boston sent her out every morning at eleven to fetch her dram of rum. Albany County, New York, reported that three out of four women admitted to the almshouse in 1833 "were intemperate . . . half grossly so." That needs thinking over: Alcoholics of either sex are likely to slide downhill: Sally Snoozle, a fictional wench scolded by the Rev. Thomas P. Hunt because she would not join his Cold Water Army, "was fond of riding out with young men, who would stop at taverns, and treat her with wine and hot punch." Eventually she married Dick Guzzle, had drunken fights with him, "went from sin to sin [and] is now in the work-house." On the other hand, then as now economic misery—no part of Sally's downfall—can drive women of certain temperaments as well as men to drink.

Clearly, in any case, American women of 1830, say, had no categorical immunity to the Demon's blandishments and those of fair to high social position were still flirting with him and sometimes got badly burned. The Rev. Mr. Abner Clopton, founder of Temperance in Virginia, abjured drink because he heard that "a female of respectable connections" whom he knew and thought well of had been carried home dead drunk. Harriet Martineau, whose writings about the States caused a commotion at this period, was much abused for writing that she knew personally of "seven or eight cases . . . of intemperance . . . among women of station . . . in the higher classes of society . . . in one of the most enlightened parts of the country"—which everybody took to mean Boston, and correctly. Denials would have sounded better if L. M. Sargent, a contemporary Bostonian of irreproachable prestige, had not already printed that many a lady at evening parties drank to the point where "she solicits or permits familiarities . . . which she would not permit, still less solicit, were it not for the champagne."

Here is a new notion of one's Beacon Hill ancestresses if any. In less exalted but still decent circles the Pennsylvania Society for the Suppression of Ardent Spirits expressed alarm over the amount of hard liquor drunk at quilting-parties around Pittsburgh—which certainly sheds new light on why Nellie had to be seen home from Aunt Dinah's. A generation later the New York *Tribune* complained that, in spite of well-known new institutions for lady alcoholics and the growing evil of dosing female ailments with nostrums of high alcoholic content, American men's "sense of chivalry toward the weaker sex and faith in their purity" still blinded them to heavy drinking among smart women. In corroboration a responsible Temperance writer was then estimating that nearly two thousand among the applicants for a new inebriate asylum opened in Binghamton, New York, were "rich men's daughters."

For forty years, however, Temperance tracts had sounded, to cite Sargent again, "as though . . . the crime of drunkenness [were] impracticable by females." Temperance leaders of both sexes had shared whatever conspiracy of silence was needed and looked the other way, assuming that alcoholic excesses were confined either to the coarser sex or to the coarsest, usually vicious women. The temptation to pharisaism would have been irresistible even had mentors like Dr. Nott failed to recommend it. Susan B. Anthony, soon to be the most brilliant leader of the Women's Rights movement, told the Daughters of Temperance at Canajoharie, New York: ". . . were [women] en masse to discontinue the use of wine and brandy at both their public and their private parties, not one . . . who has any claim to the title of gentleman, would so insult them as to come into their presence after having quaffed of that foul destroyer of all true delicacy and refinement. Ladies! There is no neutral position for us to assume." In well-to-do circles here and there, primmer hostesses began to omit punch and wine at large parties.

The larger the town, the more worldly its tone, the less such squeamishness took hold, of course. Before 1919 there never was a time when many smart parties in great cities were even nominally dry. But the infection spread rapidly up and down from the important middle stratum of sermon-heeding women. By 1878 a Temperance writer could say: "Society sees that it must at least in theory frown on the alliance of the drinking habit with . . . polite life, and many fashionable assemblies occur without the host thinking it necessary to furnish wine. . . . The New Year's festival is rapidly emerging from the blight and disgrace, which a few years ago made the anniversary sad and ominous . . . now the rivalry is not who shall make the most alluring display of wines, but who shall furnish the strongest coffee and purest lemonade." That was in the middle of the presidential administration of General Rutherford B. Hayes, an abstemious man of Temperance but not Prohibitionist principles, whose wife came gracelessly to fame as "Lemonade Lucy" because she barred alcohol from all White House social functions, saying: "I have young sons who have never tasted liquor. They shall not receive from my hand, or with the sanction that its use in the family would give, the first taste of what might prove their ruin. What I wish for my own sons I must do for the sons of other mothers."

There was uproar. Ill-natured rumor had it that her motive was stinginess, not Temperance. "At the White House," said an unidentified wit, "water flows like champagne." But Lucy Webb Hayes, the fine flower of Chillicothe, Ohio, had got away with such a ban when Hayes was governor of Ohio and saw no reason to alter her stand. Hayes seems mildly to have approved of it. So did the WCTU—so strongly that they had her portrait painted and presented to the White House as permanent monument to her consistent courage. But there is probably something in the notion that it threw cold water on Hayes' political career. He was not renominated, and decades later Mr. Dooley (Finley Peter Dunne), the Irish barkeep-satirist, called him "Th' most onpopular prisidint we iver had . . . because whin people wint up to th' White House they got nawthin' to drink but sparklin' wather, a bivridge, Hinnissy, that is nayether cheerin' nor innebratin', but gives ye th' most inconvaniant part iv a debauch, that is th' hiccups. Fr'm 8 o'clock, whin they set down to dinner, to 8:30, whin th' last southren congressman ran shriekin' down th' street, this gr-reat but tactless man pumped his guests full iv imprisoned gas. An' whin his term expired he wint back where he come fr'm an' I niver heerd iv him again. . . . He went down, as ye might say, to a wathry grave."

The natural consequence of such highminded gestures was a genuine if not universally honored taboo with special feminine aspects. It had begun merely as a shyness of taking and then of serving anything alcoholic. But among respectable women of limited background it soon expanded into a feeling that potable alcohol was on their account The Unclean Thing—exactly what Elizabeth Cady Stanton, queen of Women's Rights, labeled it in 1852. To taste, see, smell or touch it polluted female virtue as contact with pork pollutes a follower of the Mosaic law. In this extreme but very widely held view a woman who as much as entered a room harboring the stuff was, so to speak, insulting herself. In due season the ladies proceeded to take even higher ground. They came to feel and proclaim to men that what wasn't sauce for the goose shouldn't be sauce for the gander.

> . . . speed the day . . . when no young man . . . who pollutes his lips with the drunkard's cup shall presume to seek the favors of our precious daughters.
>   —Susan B. Anthony

It was a mass demonstration of The Fox That Lost His Tail. The logic was: Decent women refrain from drink. Therefore drinking must be somehow essentially indecent. Therefore it must also be indecent for men.

Actually, of course, it was a matter of rising emotional temperatures, illogical in even those broken-backed terms. Cultural jealousy was likely one of the emotions cropping up: Crypto-feminists came to resent this minor (and self-imposed) but strict double standard. This is no subtle deduction from reading between the lines and hoping one knows how women work, but a thing often spelled out in each generation between the Missouri Compromise and the Volstead Act. Says the young wife to her Southern-planter husband in an early Temperance tract: ". . . while so many other husbands were not satisfied with their wives . . . constantly running to taverns for company and pleasure, you appeared to look for pleasure nowhere but in me and your little family. But . . . you never seem to be happy with us now. . . . You order your horse and go away, leaving me here . . . to solitude and distraction. . . . I see gamblers and sharpers . . . pressing you to drink . . . winning your money. . . . I see the creditors coming to tear every thing from us . . . turning my poor boy and myself out of house and home, to starve and beg." Almost a century later Jack London explained it to his wife in frank anthropological terms: "I reminded [her] of the canoe-houses from which she had been barred in the South Pacific . . . sacred precincts taboo to women under pain of death. As a youth, by way of the saloon, I had escaped from the narrowness of women's influence into the wide free world of men."

Women kept warning one another of this unflattering eagerness with which men let them fastidiously withdraw from the tavern. Here is the Eternal Feminine waiting up for the Eternal Masculine in a Temperance giftbook "Annual" of 1851:

> Why don't he come?—the morning light,
>   In amber rays, breaks from the east;
> He said he would come back last night,
>   Nor tarry at the midnight feast.
> Ah that the revel and the song
>   Should lure him from my smiles away,
> The vigil why did he prolong
>   In Politicians' idle fray. . . .

Another lady writer of that day besought sisters to plot to keep their brothers home evenings with fun and games: "I know no more agreeable and interesting spectacle, than that of brothers and sisters playing and singing together those elevated compositions in music and poetry which gratify the taste and purify the heart, while their fond parents sit delighted by. . . . Sisters should . . . walk, ride, visit with their brothers. I have been told by some [brothers] . . . they have put aside the wine-cup . . . because they would not profane with their fumes the holy kiss, with which they were accustomed to bid their sisters goodnight. . . ."

In T. S. Arthur's *The Bar-Rooms of Brantly* the son of a moderate-drinker father grows to the age of twenty-five unsullied by the Demon. But then he spends a week in New York City on business, meets and likes drink, and on his return "his mother saw the first change in him which gave her the alarm. . . . From this time . . . her eyes were on him in his going out and his coming in . . . fighting with her fears at every step, the sad and sorrowful conclusion forced itself upon her mind that . . . every day he seemed to be going a little away from her. The lovelight was fading in his beautiful eyes, and the tenderness out of his voice. . . ." At about the time that was published the newly created National Woman's

Christian Temperance Union was choosing its membership badge—a bow of white ribbon. It should have been a silver cord. Encountering a "barroom nude" on one of her early smashing forays, Carry Nation "told [the barkeep] he was insulting his own mother by having her form stripped naked and hung up in a place where it was not even decent for a

woman to be in when she had her clothes on. . . . It is very significant that the pictures of naked women are in saloons. [Woman is] stripped of everything by them . . . her husband . . . her sons, her home, her food and her virtue."

The possibility of "if you can't lick 'em, jine 'em" never occurred to most Temperance women. Their grandmothers might not have seen anything wrong with having flip with the old man in a tavern; but it shocked granddaughter to see

a German family, mother, daughter and all, relaxing in a
beer garden; or a respectable French matron, probably as
severely garbed as any president of a Ladies' Aid in Vandalia,
Illinois, taking a vermouth on a café terrace. Granddaughter's
reaction was louder screams for the total banishment of the
Demon, citing the glaring damage that alcoholism among
breadwinning men wrought on marriages and families; the
close association between drinking and whoring; and the
pulpit's vague but daunting warnings about the eroding
effect of alcohol on the soul.

Few such she-zealots can have read or heard of *Lysistrata*. It
was their own sense of tactics that led them to a less explicit
version of sex boycott long before it was proclaimed in song
that "Lips that touch Liquor must never touch mine." In
1829 the lady members of an Ohio Temperance society resolved to discountenance all "addresses . . . with a view to
matrimony" from men known to drink spirits at all. One of
Gough's best bits was the one about the sweet young lady
standing up to be married, detecting alcohol on the groom's
breath and, when the parson asked "Wilt thou . . . ?" saying
No. The parson expostulated but she told the groom: "You
have deceived me. . . . You said you would not drink . . .
and the prospects for me, if I become your wife, are so dreadful, that my own safety and future happiness demand that I
shall say No." Taboo! Taboo! She would have fared better, or
anyway spared herself embarrassment, had she patterned herself on the heroine of "The Maiden's Refusal," a lissome
number from *The Temperance Musician;* a chord, please,
Professor:

> Go, Henry, go! the scene is o'er;
>   And we must now forever part;
> Those twining cords are now unloosed
>   That bound thee closely to my heart;
> For I will ne'er consent to be
>   The wife of one whose reckless soul
> Is led by passion's ghostly form
>   To drink from out the poison bowl. . . .
>
> I spurn the wine-cup and its friends,
>   And feel determined not to link

My destiny with one whose deeds
　　Would place me soon on ruin's brink.
Yes, go! and I'll be free again;
　　For I had rather spend my life
In loneliness upon the earth
　　Than be a loathsome drunkard's wife.

Her ideal would have been the preacher passenger on the canal boat who, they told Miss Martineau, was so strict Temperance that he had refused to drink water from Brandywine Creek.

Behold that wretched female form,
　　An outcast from her home,
Bleached in affliction's blighting storm,
　　And doomed in want to roam;
Behold her!—ask that prattler near
　　Why mother is so poor;
He'll whisper in thy startl'd ear,
" 'Twas father's 'One Glass More!' "
　　　　　　　—ROBERT STEVENSON COFFIN,
　　　　　　　"The Boston Bard"

"He *drinks* . . ." —iambic monosyllables uttered with deep relish of the seriousness of the charge and the scandal of it. The culprit was not necessarily charged with overfrequent drinking, nor yet with damaging his economic potential by ill-timed sprees. The charge could be no more than being known to take and enjoy a glass of beer. That was enough because it broke the taboo. In some men the consequences of that sort of rearing could be scarring: When some of his young comrades threatened to force a shot of whiskey down the throat of Clement Vallandigham, fanatic Copperhead-to-be, he vowed that if they succeeded he would kill himself. In view of the traits he showed in later life no doubt he would have done it—the analogy being a girl with virtue violated.

The doctrine of shun-the-drinker could not avoid the punitive: "Let a mark of infamy be set upon the [drunk-

ards's] forehead," advised Dr. Humphrey, "which nothing
but tears and repentance can ever efface. If he is hungry, feed
him;—but shun him as you would a pestilence . . . and thus
teach all others what to expect, if they become intemperate."
Strange talk from a minister of the gospel that tells of the
Good Samaritan. No wonder that Washingtonian spokesmen
for the despised alcoholics resented it. But it appealed
strongly to the holier-than-thouness to which women are as
prone as others. It underlay the singing Hutchinson Family's
reaction when a slaveholding Cuban accidentally spilled wine
on sister Abby in the steamer going to Europe: ". . . his pro-
fuse and distressing apologies coming from such besotted lips,
were much worse than the wine stains on the silk shirt." The
Rev. H. D. Kitchel, eminent creator of Temperance propaganda, soon demanded that "Intemperance, *with all that
produces and sustains it*," be made a crime; and called for a
society in which "the use of [intoxicating drinks] by any
man . . . is looked upon as . . . trifling with his own well-
being *and that of all around him*. For a man to put himself
into a state of intoxication, *or make any voluntary approach
toward that state,* is a . . . mad and criminal act." [Italics
mine] How dare husband or fiancé criminally imperil wife
or lady-love by taking a glass of sherry? Since Society could
never be sure in advance that a first drink would not lead to a
bottle-throwing, wife-beating, alcoholic delinquent, Society—
in the shape of purer, clear-sighted, more spiritual Woman—
determined to take no chances.

As foil for this righteous Woman, Temperance propagandists created a stock character: The thoughtless, beautiful,
virtuous but giddy temptress who refuses No for an answer
when asking the young fellow to take wine with her: " 'This
is not exactly *wine*,' " she tells the callow New Year's caller.
" 'It is pure juice of the grape . . . not like drinking anything intoxicating, you know! . . .' Miss Marvin turned her
bewitching eyes upon him. 'Surely you will not refuse to
drink with *me*—many happy returns of this day!' Leander
tried to gain his attention but poor Clayton had eyes only for
the beautiful syren who was luring him so steadily to his
ruin. Another glance at the charmer, then seizing the goblet,

he drank his first glass of wine!" His ensuing alcoholism led
him to murder a friend; and as the law escorted him to Sing
Sing by rail, "a gaily dressed *lady* rudely jostled him, saying
to a companion in sneering tones: 'How very democratic . . .
when a lady must be brought in contact with a "jail bird." '
Miss Magnolia Marvin . . . failed to recognize in the man-
acled criminal the acquaintance of better days. Clayton, how-

ever, knew her at a glance and whispered through clenched
teeth . . . 'Viper indeed!' " Or as in T. S. Arthur's "The
Circean Cup," the girl's father mistrusts a teetotal suitor, advises daughter to give him a little brandy now and then . . .
and it all winds up with young husband's selling his wretched
family's stove to a bartender for a drink in the middle of the
winter. Anything that isn't red-hot or nailed down. . . .

Thus to cast Woman as even occasionally culpable tended
to keep her self-righteousness from flowing too free. The
Temperance writer usually stuck to The Drunkard's Wife,

however, making her not more sinned against than sinning but not sinning at all, a shattered but stainless victim of
the Demon's skill at exploiting Man's coarseness and heed-
lessness. Hence my favorite scene in the stage version of *Ten
Nights:*

MORGAN: Thank you, dear one! O God, what a wretched
slave have I become! Fanny, I could not blame you were you
to leave me to die alone!

MRS. MORGAN: Leave you—no! Though you have banished
relatives and friends from your door, though you have drawn
the contempt of the world upon your wretched head, though
you are a mark for the good to grieve at, and the vain to
scoff at, still, still, I will never desert you. The name of husband is not lost though it be coupled with that of—

MORGAN: Drunkard! Yes, end the sentence—'tis too true.

MRS. MORGAN: Oh, think how I have suffered, to see you day
by day sink from your once exalted station, until you have
reached the wretched footing of the outcast, your temper
broken by that infatuation which my heart sickens to think
of, and my lips refuse to name. [Knock heard off L.] Try and
compose your feelings, Joe. Come in! . . .

Or consider the treatment of The Drunkard's Wife in an
anonymous Temperance monologue, "The Drunkard's
Daughter":

Go to my mother's side,
    And her crushed spirit cheer;
Thine own deep anguish hide,
    Wipe from her cheek the tear.
Mark her dimmed eye, her furrowed brow,
The gray that streaks her dark hair now;
Her toil-worn frame, her trembling limb,
And trace the ruin back to him
Whose plighted faith, in early youth,
Promised eternal love and truth;
But who, forsworn, hath yielded up
That promise to the deadly cup,
And led her down from love and light,

> From all that made her pathway bright,
> And chained her there 'mid want and strife,
> That lowly thing, a drunkard's wife!
>   . . . my very soul
> With strong disgust is stirred
> Whene'er I see, or hear, or tell
> Of the dark beverage of hell!

That states Mrs. Stanton's taboo so mawkishly that one almost forgets that there really were—and still are—many handsome and hopeful women whose lives alcoholic spouses ruin; and that, other things being equal, the lot of the alcoholic's wife was far worse when divorce was more difficult and more frowned upon than it is now. It made sense for Women's Righters to give higher priority to agitation for divorce on grounds of habitual drunkenness. Woman's mistake lay not in seeing alcohol as a major problem in intersex relations, which it can be, but in dramatizing herself in relation to it as either Victim of the Drinking Sex or Pure Lady-Savior of same.

Her early and, as we shall see, thwarted efforts to turn "public, clamorous advocate" of Temperance (against Dr. Nott's wish) were usually in terms of her duty to save from the Demon the menfolks or "the lower orders," maybe indirectly her suffering sisters of a nameless class . . . but whatever the reference, it was always *de haut en bas*. An early meeting of the Daughters of Temperance at Rochester, New York, must have waved their handkerchiefs with particular zest when a visiting Son of Temperance offered, presumably in water, a toast to

> The Daughters!
> Our characters they elevate,
> Our manners they refine.
> Without them we degenerate
> To the level of the swine!

Forty years later, William Jennings Bryan explained why, though as yet no Prohibitionist, he had omitted wine from a Bar Association dinner at Lincoln, Nebraska: "It was a question of having the banquet without wine or without women. Many of the guests . . . could do without wine, but none . . . could do without the refining influence of women, so wine was abandoned and women triumphed." Dr. Janet Giele, a sociologist pondering these matters from the vantage point of 1960, has Woman thinking of Man as "given to moral weakness . . . [having] inadequate moral resources . . . incapable of controlling the strength of his desire," owing any moral changes for the better to Woman as "the real dynamic for change—the initialer, the guide, the satisfied teacher when he [has] learned."

That woman's hand that puts away the cup
Is fair as Joan's with the sword lifted up!
—GEORGE W. CABLE in praise
of Mrs. Rutherford B. Hayes

Dr. Nott's rule of fair-lady-above-the-battle long hampered the forces fated to create that ruthless horde of Valkyrie, the WCTU. As we know, the Washingtonians' ladies' auxiliaries were, though benign, not militant. The Temperance press took little note of the early Temperance speeches of hyper-articulate women like Mrs. Stanton and queer, soon psychotic Abby Kelly Foster. In the 1840's certain Pennsylvania women, maybe under Quaker influences, publicly advocated local-option legislation and formed associations inviting speakers on their own. But the Independent Order of Good Samaritans and Daughters of Samaria, which admitted women to full membership, stayed insignificant. When the question of admitting women split the Sons of Temperance, the keep-them-out segment was the large, victorious one; the Templars of Honor and Temperance, formed by secession of the losing minority, duly going coeducational, cut much less ice.

The problem recurred in the 1850's when strong-minded ladies of the Stanton stripe in upper York State—again!—

formed sporadic lodges of "Daughters of Temperance" and sought formal affiliation with the Sons. At first the Sons countenanced joint meetings, and their gilt-and-scarlet yearbook carried a salute to

> Daughters of Temperance! noble as thou [sic] art,
> Thy influence cheers the desponding heart;
> Thy words of hope and love cheer Temp'rance on,
> And bid the dreaded "tyrant-fiend" begone.
> Woman—God's best gift—thy influence pure
> Our army's certain triumph will ensure! . . .

They even allowed the Daughters to send observer-delegates to their New York State convention at Albany in 1852. But cordiality dwindled when one of these lady delegates sought actively to join in offering resolutions and so forth instead of modestly listening and no more. Snubbed, the Daughters withdrew, held a rump meeting with some men allies that created a separate Women's State Temperance organization, and defiantly held their first convention a few months later.

One of its principal acts was to appoint two lady delegates to the upcoming New York State convention of all Temperance organizations. Great tumult ensued when that same Daughter-delegate again sought full man-style rights, as she had at Albany, and was again rejected. Next year, again representing the stubborn Daughters, she again battled for a rightful place on the platform of a meeting planning a World's Temperance Convention to go with the World's Fair at New York City in 1853. The consequent row lasted two days. Police had to be called in to clear the hall of unauthorized voters against a resolution that "the common uses of society . . . exclude women from the platform." Among those shouting for the women was Wendell Phillips, radical Abolitionist, doubtless mindful of how in a parallel unedifying struggle a few years earlier the antislavery ladies had secured at least a partial victory. The Sons of Temperance, however, still permeated by the Washingtonians' conservatism, were less subject to Syndromist influence and the weaker sex were routed. When the

World's Temperance meeting opened that fall they tried
again, and after another uproar were again denied standing.

Thereupon Mrs. Stanton's father, Daniel Cady, a rugged
upstate Syndromist, set up a heterosexual Temperance order
called the Knights of Jericho, which gave lady members the
curious title of "Sister Knights" and seated them, winningly
bareheaded, in a special section near the desk of the Worthy
Chief Knight. It had some success, particularly in the South,
but petered out in the 1870's. Generally, Mrs. Stanton wrote
in reminiscence, the Sons' lack of gallantry caused "Most of
the liberal men and women [to withdraw] from all temperance organizations, leaving the movement in the hands of
time-serving priests and politicians."

This may not be the most objective testimony but it remains true that until the 1870's women were little more than
sleeping partners (if the phrase is allowed) in the diminish-
ing Temperance effort. No doubt they went on exerting soft,
persuasive, colloquial eloquence in hallowed retirement at
chosen moments, as Dr. Nott suggested. To judge from Temperance literature they certainly got great mileage out of the
lip of entreaty. But only locally off and on did they act on
their own. The Sons had much to answer for in thus driving
doughty volunteers into the wilderness. Had women's eagerness against the Demon been better utilized in the 1850's, the
movement might have been better consolidated before the
Civil War, hence would not have lost so much momentum
during the war years.

Note again that the heads of that New York State Women's
Temperance organization were Mrs. Stanton, high priestess
of Women's Rights; the lady delegate so churlishly denied
standing three times was Susan B. Anthony, coadjutor high
priestess; the lady delegate ejected from the World's Temperance Convention was the Rev. Antoinette L. Brown, pioneer lady preacher and Women's Righter; at her third defeat
Miss Anthony's fellow ejectee was Mrs. Amelia Bloomer of
bifurcated fame, owner-editor of *The Lily,* a paper bent as
much on Women's Rights as on Temperance; and that the
Demon was a favorite lecture subject of plump little Lucy

Stone, first to insist on retaining her maiden name after marriage.

Until the rebuffs described above, Miss Anthony had been unsure whether to focus her career-to-be on Temperance. But soon it was clear to her and Mrs. Stanton that Woman should concentrate on acquiring the vote and man-style legal rights, after which her righteous strength at the polls would annihilate the Demon along with other social menaces. So that formidable pair opted to major in Women's Rights, so to speak. Thenceforward sometimes on the surface, sometimes far below publicly acknowledged strategy and tactics, the fight against the Oppressor Man and that against his disreputable crony, the Demon Rum, had much in common. That built-in association strongly affected the future of Temperance by helping to shape the policies of the WCTU and the Prohibition Party.

It was a fine example of Syndromism, logical to the brain and satisfying to the emotions. It reflected how thoroughly Woman had identified the Demon with all that she was out to eradicate by the ballot: corrupt politics, fornication, prostitution, gambling—the whole bag of snares awaiting mother's blue-eyed, curly-pated boy, the evil communications that turned sons into coarsened men right under their mothers' sorrowing eyes. It was the Demon who kept men out late in that goatish, tobacco-reeking, sawdust-sprinkled, gas-bedizened world of their own that tempted them away from the chaste Currier & Ives amenities of Home, from the cherishing of devoted wife or mother and the pure delights of the prattle of one's own offspring. In the hyperpragmatic thinking of too many strong-minded women the right to divorce a drunken husband and the right to prohibit the Demon were opposite faces of the same holy purpose. "The movement that finally resulted in Prohibition," wrote Brand Whitlock, thinking it over in 1930 in the light of what he had observed as boy and newspaperman in Ohio, "was a maneuver in the Great General Strike of the Women, which is almost as significant an event of our time as [World War I] itself."

10

SAUCE FOR
THE GANDER

. . . the next war in this country will be between women
and whiskey, and though there will not be much blood shed
. . . rum will flow freely in the gutter.

—New York *Tribune* (1869)

TEMPERANCE slacked off as the 1860's approached but women's emotions did not. The rising generation of wives and mothers had been reared in a climate of extravagant denunciation of the Demon in hymnbooks, prayer meetings and the local weekly press, always equating alcohol with sin, pauperism and wife-beating to widen the gulf between decent women and anything convivial. In many places statewide Prohibition or some form of local option had bitterly disappointed women who, though unable to vote, had fervently thanked God when the men finally summoned the law to support righteousness. Law was often still nominally there. But usually, as we have seen, the Demon continued to do fair business at the old stand or round the corner or just over the town line. The resulting exasperation sometimes stirred women into action of a sort that caused gin mill keepers to wish it really were true that no lady could conceivably set foot in the place.

The Women's Righters, Miss Anthony, Mrs. Brown, *et al.*, were still trying to crack the sex prejudice of Temperance men in 1853 when Mrs. Margaret Freeland of Syracuse, New York, who seems to have had no theories but a talent for action, used a club to smash in the bar door of a local rumseller and break up his bottles and glassware. Duly arrested, she explained that her husband was so devoted a customer of the place that his brutalities had several times required police interference; that she had often begged the rumseller not to sell him the stuff that was ruining him; and that the last refusal had moved her to take matters into her own hands. Local Temperance men procured her counsel. Threats of prosecution for illegal selling led the rumseller to withdraw charges. What became of him or the unhappy Freelands I do not know nor is it important. The important thing was the lady's being first to show how women could *do something* in good physical earnest.

She had been alone though obviously more than a match for the startled rumseller. The next step—collective action—had a humorous touch next year: Mrs. Amanda M. Way, a brisk Methodist turned Quaker because Quakers let women preach, resented the way the saloons of Winchester, Indiana, played up their rival free lunches. Mustering other right-minded local women, she rounded up hungry tots whose fathers drank too much and sicked them on one bar after another, saying go to it, children, that sign in the window says FREE LUNCH! Action was more violent in Michigan where state courts had recently found the new state Prohibition law unconstitutional, which shifted the burden back to local option—which worked no better there than elsewhere. Otsego, Michigan, had the usual story of lackadaisical enforcement tolerating numerous joints; and the usual alcoholic husbands and their frantic wives begging barkeeps not to serve them and meeting the usual bored rebuffs. The evening of December 12 an Otsego husband came home drunk once too often. His wife enlisted a similarly plagued neighbor woman and sent word to local prominent citizens that she was on her way downtown loaded for bear and they had better back her up. Ax in hand, urged on by a knot of respectable men, she crashed into a saloon, stove in its kegs of liquor and used the barkeep's own poker to break the bottles back of the bar. That not only made her feel better, no doubt, but inspired "all the respectable women in town"—a terrifying notion!—to march next day in a body on every local groggery to force the owner of each to pledge in writing to close up for six months.

Their mass-foray from bar to bar began at 8 A.M. on a winter morning when courage among those who stay up late is likely to be low. Most owners were dauntedly willing to sign. It was good judgment. The first rumseller who locked up and refused to heed the ladies' shouted threats had his door smashed in with axes and the place carried with a rush. He knuckled under. Another attempt to resist collapsed when a local hardware merchant presented a shiny new hatchet apiece to each lady in the shawled and bonneted mob. Brandishing these, they gave that stubborn rumseller five minutes to sign—or else see them go to work on his stock and fixtures. They actually used the hatchets a few days later when, hearing that the joints were faithlessly reopening, the mob gathered again and made a clean sweep of every keg and bottle in every identifiable bar.

No arrests ensued. There had been none in Livingston, Michigan, that spring when a small rising raided a grocer who had tempted a local alcoholic trying to stay on the wagon; his wife, and who's to blame her, led the storming party. The local press approved: "The officers of the law ought to be made ashamed of themselves . . . leaving to respectable females the rough work of seizing and destroying contraband liquor . . . as the spirit of the law was adhered to, the women will be sustained. Certainly no *men* would allow them to bear any legal expense that may arise." Such a raid in Clinton, Illinois, the next year did lead to legal proceedings. An eminent Illinois lawyer, Abraham Lincoln, volunteered to defend the ladies and got them off with a mild reprimand that put none of the spilled whiskey back in the broken bottles. In 1856 the women of Rockport, Massachusetts, marched on local illicit bars under a white banner bearing the device of a black hatchet, did a job still lively in local memory, and found themselves in court for, among other charges, breaking and entering. But appellate courts ruled that places where liquor was sold illegally were common nuisances that private citizens could abate by force.

In any case the women involved were seldom likely to be severely handled even when law was invoked, for they were wives, sisters or mothers of eminent citizens—banker, ministers, staider lawyers, maybe the owners of feedmill, sawmill or dry-goods store. Sometimes, as in Otsego, men of local standing informally backed up their womenfolks. Indeed, supposing any such husbands or brothers mistrusted the ladies' high-handed methods, they were unlikely to say so lest they be accused of defending the Unclean Thing and maybe even lusting after its attendant train of vices. Besides, Temperance was already a most respectable cause, so the support of most of these local oligarchs was wholehearted if a little sheepish because the women were so dashingly doing what the presumed leaders of the community had neglected.

Another such smashing affair at East Weymouth, Massachusetts, is the only other instance in New England known to me. Generally this episode in Woman's feud with the Demon was a Midwestern affair and petered out with the 1850's. Since every county seat west of Pittsburgh probably had Otsego's kind of problem, since Otsego may have got the motion from Livingston, Clinton from Otsego and so on, a fine regional carnival of aggressive self-righteousness might have come of such infectious examples. This was before the boys went Tramp, Tramp, Tramping, however, and the ladies had not yet discovered their own strength. Nor—to introduce the single person who did most to crystallize matters—had the right women yet been stirred up by the indispensable man, a red-bearded, ruddy, large and incredibly energetic fellow, Dr. Dio (short for Dioclesian) Lewis.

꩜

Dr. Dio Lewis, so hale and hearty, so profoundly confident in the omnipotence of his methods and the uselessness of all others.

—T. W. HIGGINSON

He combined intelligence, ignorance and a sort of innocent quackery well suited for spreading his Syndromist ideas. That "Dr." stood inspection little better than many of his notions. It was only honorary, and homeopathic to boot. Lack of funds cut short his first year at Harvard Medical School; for further training he had only several years' apprenticeship with homeopaths in upper York State. Such study was still a legitimate way to become a physician then, however, and the dilute doses of mild, usually herbal drugs preferred by homeopathic medicine often did less damage than the heroic bleedings and purges of the more august "allopathic" school of Dr. Rush and his successors.

Temperamentally Dio Lewis was more the allopathic type. He knew not moderation in treatment or in Temperance. For his wife's tuberculosis he invented a therapy calling for long walks in thick-soled boots and flannel skirts so heavy that she used men's suspenders to hold them up; and much firewood sawing because "the harder you saw the deeper you must breathe." (Deep breathing is now thought to be bad for tubercular lungs.) Loyally she refrained from making her husband look bad by dying. That doubtless strengthened his belief that any notion of his was several times sounder than anybody else's, so it deserved universal application. He could be good-natured about it but firm, as intellectual and moral duty demanded, and once in four or five times a pet idea of his proved durably valuable. For instance, he did a great deal to persuade those in charge of girls' schools to install regular, rhythmic exercise. On the other hand he was spiritual father of the WCTU. It is a nice question whether the first did more good than the second did harm.

Upper New York State, of course, was where he came from. His size, vigor and impressive voice may have come from his Grandfather Barbour, a strapping, booming Welsh carpenter who settled near Clarksville in Cayuga County—a deacon of the church as well as the best-known local distiller of peach and apple brandy, which was, as we saw, nothing out of the way c. 1810. Daughter Delecta married one Lewis who soon proved to be alcoholic. Like many another sorrowing wife in Temperance stories—for they could be true enough in essence —she had to support her four children by sewing, odd-jobbing and selling produce under the handicap of a husband who was less than no use. Nobody could blame her for the pronounced anti-alcohol sentiments that led her to foment her own holy war on the Demon. In Clarksville as elsewhere, groggeries were both a social nuisance and a hindrance to godliness. Under a banner showing a child drinking from a bucket, presumably of water, this distiller's daughter and alcoholic's wife organized the local women to raid barrooms in forays of massed prayer that, as son Dio liked to tell it, shamed the rumsellers into closing the neighborhood up tight as a drum, dry as a desert. But no smashing—it appears that Delecta Barbour Lewis was the kind of woman needing no weapons but her own withering glance.

All her children did well. All were understandably hot-Temperance. The second son, Loran, who became a judge, began his forensic career as a precocious Washingtonian lecturer. Dio, the redheaded eldest, quit school at the age of twelve to earn for the household as a polisher in a tool-handle plant, but within three years had taught himself enough—those country schools required little—to turn schoolmaster. Already nonconformist and eagerly picking ideas out of the air through which the winds of change were blowing, he puzzled his pupils' parents by renouncing corporal punishment and using songs and games as learning means. He also found time for speechifying on Temperance at local gatherings. Soon he ventured westward to Lower Sandusky (now Fremont), Ohio, and set up an academy so successful that the pleased patrons put up a new building for it called "The Dioclesian Institute." (Rutherford B. Hayes was a pupil.) But Midwestern chills and fever pulled him down. He came back east and began to study medicine under the physician of the famous State Penitentiary at Auburn, New York; then had his abortive year at Harvard; then his apprenticeship in what passed for medicine in homeopathic circles.

Seeking a milder climate for his ailing wife, he shifted to Fredericksburg, Virginia, in the early 1850's. There he joined the Sons of Temperance, though deploring their failure to denounce tobacco and their narrow-minded refusal to admit women, and there in the town hall he launched himself in the growing lecture business. His subject was "The Influence of Christian Women in the Temperance Cause"; he seems to have described his mother's anti-groggery war in Clarksville and gone on into eloquent generalities about the ladies as potential battlers against all aspects of the Demon.

He was a striking platform figure, large and genial, robustly charming, "at home with himself and all the world," said a contemporary newspaper that also called his lecturing "intimate parlor conversation between the speaker and his audience." His position on moderate drinking was: ". . . men . . . who drink now and then in a respectable and gentlemanly manner without exposing themselves to reproach . . . are the recruiting officers in the devil's army." After a successful lecture in Richmond he widened his repertory, adding medical lectures defending homeopathy and hygiene of the cracked-wheat-and-flannel school already well launched by "Dr." Sylvester Graham. Soon he had quit medicine for a lecturing career, working through Kentucky, York State and so on. Hygiene was the weekday pitch, women-and-Temperance on Sundays when, with luck, some or all local churches would cancel evening service in his favor. By now he called that number an "Address upon the Power of Women's Prayer in Grog Shops" and sometimes urged his lady hearers to imitate his mother, march into the barrooms and pray till shame closed them down. Several times in Illinois and Michigan in 1858 the ladies did thus descend on the groggeries two by two, singing hymns and praying like all possessed, often with temporary success. In Battle Creek, Michigan, such an array marched past Lewis' hotel bearing as token of victory a large SALOON sign. But though the motor thus coughed now and again, it was not quite ready to start.

Toward 1860 Lewis was distracted by a new hygienic hobby, organized rhythmic exercise specially for females. Stern German émigrés had already infected the States with heavily disciplined calisthenics but only among men. Lewis visited Europe and came back with light wooden dumbbells, wands and so on to modify the cult for the weaker sex. He personally invented beanbags for throwing back and forth in rhythm and—borrowing from the Women's Righters' dress reform—created the gym bloomers that disfigured two future generations of young American womanhood. Such exercise-minded celebrities as Dr. Holmes, T. W. Higginson, James T. Fields, editor of the *Atlantic Monthly,* and President Felton of Harvard endorsed his Normal Institute for Physical Education in Boston. Nathaniel Hawthorne's daughter Una was one of the high-minded girls attracted to the cult of beanbags, no corsets and the good life at the diet-and-exercise school that he set up at Lexington, Massachusetts, along with a "health institute" for ailing adults. And his lecture on "Our Girls" became the most popular item in his repertory.

He kept his Temperance zeal, however. He lost money for years trying to make a good Temperance hotel pay in Boston. In "Our Girls" he often interpolated the story of his mother, the tone severe: "Women rule in the social sphere and are responsible for its vices. . . . There is no spectacle so bewildering and so sad, as this queen of the social sphere living in the midst of drunken howls, the sickening fumes of tobacco, and in a hot-bed of licentiousness, and hiding the magic wand with which she might dispel every social iniquity, and then standing before a mirror, paint her cheeks . . . adjust her curls. . . . God will hold her responsible for all this silly, shameless abandonment and betrayal of her high and sacred trust." His syntax got away from him a little, and "hot-bed of licentiousness" may not have been just the way to describe the level of social occasion he had in mind. But finally, after his twenty years of dogged effort to incite women to righteous riot after his mother's example, that peroration worked. The ensuing prairie fire started in upper New York State—where else? The women of America were at last taking the field, horse, foot and artillery, against the Demon.

> We're coming, Father Lewis,
> Three hundred thousand strong!
> We're burnishing our weapons
> Of Faith and Prayer and Song;
> We do not stop for scorning;
> We do not stop for taunts;
> But follow, night and morning,
> The rum fiend to his haunts. . . .
> —P. H. Myers

Like most earthquakes this one had premonitory tremors. In 1866 the Sons of Temperance had given in and admitted women; within a year or so they outnumbered men mem-

bers. In 1871 the newly formed Massachusetts Total Abstinence Society installed nine women as members of its board
of thirty-eight, including eminent feminists like Lucy Stone
and Mrs. Mary Livermore. In Greenville, Ohio, in 1868 a
well-thought-of youth was killed by a stray bullet fired by one
of a drunken crowd, and a mob of seventy women cleaned
out every saloon in town. Next year the women of Perryville,
Ohio, remonstrated with a rumseller planning to open up in
their previously unpolluted village and when he paid no
heed, rushed the premises and broke up his stock-in-trade.

Dio Lewis never countenanced bottle-busting, however.
Delecta had done without such rowdy methods. Her followers had merely crowded in and prayed—for the drunkard's
soul, for his miserable wife and babes, for the rumseller that
his hard heart might be softened ere he corrupted himself
past redemption, oh hear us, Lord! Evening after evening in
the early 1870's Delecta's eldest was telling audiences, often
in interdenominational meetings, about his mother and the
plucky ladies of Battle Creek, never mentioning that in a
matter of weeks the bars closed there had reopened as lively
as ever.

Why the spark delayed so long is unaccountable: Maybe it
needed the sense of insecurity even among the godly and well
established caused by the sweeping economic panic of that
year; maybe it was just that the church he spoke in was more
overheated than usual that evening, inducing febrile emotions. Anyway, on a mid-December Sunday in 1873, Lewis
was holding forth in Fredonia, New York—in a district since
famous for grape (and wine) growing—on women and Temperance and his mother's rousing example, and when he finished:

"There was not a loosely strung nerve in that audience of
nearly a thousand people," reported the Fredonian *Censor*.
More than a hundred rose when Lewis asked "if the women
were inclined to organize," and what was also ominous, their
husbands and brothers also rose to pledge "moral support
and money, if necessary." Next morning the ladies, anything
but cooled off overnight, mustered some three hundred at an
organizing meeting at the Baptist Church. Shortly before

noon "over one hundred wives of our most respected citizens, venerable and revered matrons as well as young ladies" led by a judge's wife and a minister's wife sallied from the church basement while their menfolks remained to pray and take up a collection. They flooded into the saloon of the Taylor House, nearly filling it. Forewarned, all three partner-owners were there. The ladies read an appeal summoning them to drop the most profitable part of their business because the Lord wished it; sang a hymn, repeated the Lord's Prayer. . . . When Taylor, the principal partner, said he approved of Temperance and did not drink himself but "felt obliged to keep liquor in his hotel . . . the ladies said they did not come for argument but urged him by the promises of God . . ." and so on, his partners striving to brace up Taylor, who finally said that he would close up if the druggist down the street would stop selling on the pretext of medical need. The ladies assailed the druggist and had his surrender by nightfall. They planned nightly prayer meetings and Sunday Temperance conferences "till the work should be accomplished." The local paper shrewdly predicted that "this movement . . . if not abated, will end the liquor traffic in our midst," adding that it would be "a great educator for women. By the time that band has tramped a week . . . not many women will say: 'I have all the rights I want. Don't ask me to vote.' "

While that stately flood of she-Christians was inundating the Taylor House, Lewis was leaving the other hotel for Jamestown, the county seat. After his lecture there, his landlord asked "in great trepidation . . . what I had seen in the management of his house which required prayers, that I had set a thousand women on him." Soon enough, after vain effort to persuade the ladies that at least beer was harmless, he too was promising to close his bar. Diligently spreading the word, Lewis soon had fifty women on the prowl in Jamestown. A week later he had so thoroughly roused Hillsboro, a county seat in southwestern Ohio, that this "Women's Crusade" is usually, though erroneously, said to have originated there. Its leader, Mrs. Eliza Jane (Trimble) Thompson, was the locally prominent daughter of a Temperance-minded former governor of the state. Her own account of how she got involved beautifully conveys the flavor of these goings-on:

She had been prevented from attending Lewis' incendiary lecture but when the ladies there present blazed up like their sisters in Fredonia and chose a steering committee for the morrow's loin-girding, Mrs. Thompson's name was high on the list. Her teen-age son, who had been there, came home eagerly telling her: ". . . they've got you in business! You're on a committee . . . the Presbyterian Church at nine o'clock, and then the ladies want you to go with them to the saloons." Understandably this startled Thompson, who was trying to have a peaceful Sunday evening lying down. He raised on one elbow and said: "What tomfoolery is that?" Son made off; wife said that it might be the Lord's will, not tomfoolery; husband and wife discussed it, not without heat, and Mrs. Thompson managed to promise not to do anything foolish.

After breakfast next morning son brought the matter up again and his sister came to sit on a little stool by mother and urged her to go. Thompson, disturbedly walking the floor, laid a hand on the family Bible and said: "Children, you know where your mother goes to settle all vexed questions. Let's leave her alone." Mrs. Thompson was on her knees in her room praying for guidance when daughter, playing Babe-and-Suckling to the hilt, knocked and showed mother, with streaming tears, that her own little Bible, opened at random, had come up with the 146th Psalm: "The Lord . . . relieveth the fatherless and the widow; but the way of the wicked he turneth upside down."

Unable to resist so clear a summons, Mrs. Thompson donned hat and cloak and repaired to the Presbyterian Church to be chosen president of the projected organization to turn the way of the wicked upside down. The men present helped to draw up formal appeals to Hillsboro's saloonkeepers, hotel owners and druggists, rather like declarations of war. Then the Methodist minister's wife struck up the old hymn, an Abolitionist favorite, "Give to the winds thy fears!" Mrs. Thompson formed her command into columns of twos, shortest first, tallest last like European schoolgirls out for an airing, and said, "Let us proceed to our sacred mission, trusting alone in the God of Jacob." Methodists, Baptists, Quakers, Presbyterians, were the backbone of the ensuing Crusade. Episcopalians and Lutherans seldom, Catholics very seldom, took part.

The ladies blooded themselves on the druggists for, unless they were dried up, rumsellers would have too good an excuse for recalcitrance. Scanning the seventy faces crowded in, the druggists saw the wives of their best customers, not unlikely also of their lawyers, bankers and landlords. Three soon gave in; the fourth, who held out, had reason to regret it. Next day the Crusaders tackled saloons. The owner of the fanciest one, an Englishman locally considered urbane and witty, admitted them, got behind the bar and said he'd like to have a talk with this Dr. Dio Lewis. Mrs. Thompson answered loftily that Dr. Lewis had nothing to do with it, this was the Lord's scheme: "We have come not to threaten," she said, "not even to upbraid; but in the name of our Heavenly Friend and Saviour and in His spirit to forgive and to commend you to His pardon if you will abandon a business that is so damaging to our hearts and homes. . . . Let us pray!" And there on his knees, doubtless betrayed by vestigial memories of a pious rearing at home in England, was clever Robert Ward, rumseller no more.

Others persisted in hardheartedness. Denied access, the ladies knelt on the sidewalk in supplicating clumps, which forced intending drinkers to run the gantlet of their disapproving stares to reach the swinging doors. Once inside, they probably needed several snorts to get over feeling like sheep-killing dogs. It was the last week in the year, and kneeling in snow, slush or cold mud for prayerful hours was no joke even for ladies wearing several flannel petticoats; but they kept it up as doggedly as Grant had beleaguered Vicksburg. A correspondent of a Baptist paper grew lyrical over the spectacle of Mrs. Trimble kneeling in a cutting north wind on the steps outside a Hillsboro gin mill: "The plaintive, tender tones of that pleading wife and mother were carried to every heart. . . . Passers-by uncovered their heads, for the place whereon they trod was holy ground . . . not a man who saw them kneeling there but felt that if he were entering heaven's gate and if one of these women were to approach, he would stand aside and let her enter first."

The ladies meant business: When a rumseller locked his door against them, Mrs. Judge Foraker, second in command, borrowed a doormat, put it on the top step and knelt and prayed vociferously through the keyhole till the ruffian gave in. (It is sad to record that U.S. Senator Joseph B. Foraker, her eminent politician-son, acted as principal representative of the distilling industry in its fight against the Food & Drug agitation in the early 1900's.) To bring that hold-out druggist to terms, the ladies got their menfolks to build them what they called a "tabernacle"—a roofed, three-sided shelter on skids with a small stove. Planted on the sidewalk at the drugstore door, it warmed and shielded them from winter much like the "facing camp" of their pioneer ancestors, enabling them to pray, sing and exhort in comparative comfort. The druggist sued for $10,000 for trespass. He got a directed verdict for five dollars and costs and an injunction against what amounted to mass-picketing, a word new then among labor. But Hillsboro's best people financed an appeal and by the time the case reached the state's highest court, the druggist was bankrupt and the referee chose to drop the suit.

Lewis had long since taken the Crusade, as it came to be called, to nearby Washington Court House where the ladies went at it hammer and tongs and closed the town down in a week; then on into other Ohio county seats. "Mother" Stewart, whom we last saw supervising nurses in Union Army hospitals, was active in spreading the idea up and down the state. Partly by such individual missionarying, partly through hearsay imitation, the grisly spectacle of pious womanhood on the warpath visited some hundreds of municipalities as the Crusade lapped over eastward into Pennsylvania and westward through Indiana. Granted, it took pluck for a godly woman to walk into a barroom where, in her view, no decent female would let herself be seen; where, if rumsellers were the brutes that Temperance teaching depicted, she risked insult and maybe physical assault. In these small towns, however, as in those undergoing smashing raids in the 1850's, the ladies could and did rely with utter lack of scruple on the psychology of unhand-me-sir!, of none-but-a-coward-touches-a-woman-save-in-the-way-of-kindness. The local rumseller was aware that he dasn't even shove a lady, let alone kick her away from the bar door, and the ladies exploited this taboo with the aplomb of professional blackmailers. They always had known in their bones that they were the superior sex, the spiritual sex, with privileges vouchsafed direct from heaven, as the Trimble girl's Bible showed. Those doubting had only to come along and see how big, brutal barkeeps quailed before pure womanhood while their menfolks merely stood on the other side of the street admiring them for doing what men could never have done themselves without provoking violence—even had they had the gumption and imagination to try.

"Who is left to [suppress saloons] but God and the Women?" crowed the *Crusade Temperance Almanac* (1875), its cover showing a smartly gowned and coiffed lady spiking a bottle-shaped great gun marked RUM. "It becomes men to be either helpful or dumb," which was indeed putting the cruder sex in its place. When the Crusade closed all saloons in Chesterton, Indiana, thirsty residents ordered beer delivered to their homes from nearby Valparaiso. The ladies learned of this sneaky defiance and set a watch for the beer wagon, the first spying it to run and ring the church bell as signal to muster and work the driver over. The record does not tell what they did or said to him on his next appearance but the day after, when a man in Valparaiso offered him a load of strictly nonalcoholic merchandise for Chesterton, he said shuddering: "I wouldn't go back to Chesterton for a thousand dollars."

Sporadic resistance appeared especially among rumsellers of German background, of whom the Old Northwest had many. Sometimes it was the owner's thick-accented wife who screamed abuse at the interloping ladies. One defiantly fetched her small boy and fed him beer in full sight of the appalled "praying band." The sinfulness and barbarism of these foreigners were duly emphasized in the many self-admiring accounts of these matters that the Crusaders wrote. With utter lack of chivalry German barkeeps opened doors and windows and put out the fire in the stove to freeze the invaders out; or plugged up the stovepipe to smoke them out; or threw pepper on the stove to make them sneeze and weep; or flooded the floor with dirty water; or threw it on them—But between shower baths and sneezes the ladies kept on praying and singing and returned next day and the next for more of the same, while their presence kept away the customers of what was, after all, meant to be a paying business. Even brass bands to drown them out proved futile in several instances.

Nor could appeal to law be counted on. It looked promising in Bucyrus, Ohio, where the ladies were convicted for disorderly conduct in "unlawfully and wilfully hallooing, vociferating and singing" in the street. But the state Supreme Court, considering that to be no polite description of a lady singing hymns and praying, ordered a new trial and prosecution was dropped. At Morrow, Ohio, a rumseller seeking an injunction against the Crusaders was denied on the grounds that, since he had been openly violating local liquor ordinances and allowing gambling, his premises were a public nuisance that citizens were entitled to abate by force if no breach of the peace occurred. That was always and everywhere the saloon's weak spot: The owner had seldom resisted the temptation to increase his takings by ignoring local regulations forbidding selling after midnight; or sale to minors; or sale by the drink; or gambling; or unobstructed view of interior from street. And that put him at the mercy of Temperance's lawyers any time he got into court, unless he could bribe or use influence at expense greatly reducing the profits of his transgressions.

Big cities gave the ladies much occasion to say unhand-me-sir! In Cleveland a "praying band" kneeling outside a saloon was mobbed and some of its members got kicked. After the mayor forbade use of sidewalks for demonstrations the Crusade dwindled into a campaign to indict rumsellers for flagrant breaches of local law. Pittsburgh turned fire hoses on the ladies, threw in their faces the tobacco-soggy sawdust from barroom floors and arrested some who persisted in defying the outrageous principle laid down by an Indiana judge

that "Mob law enforced by women is no better than mob law
enforced by men." Cincinnati, full of distilleries, breweries,
Germans and disregard of chivalry, resorted to longstanding
ordinances against obstructing sidewalks and arrested forty-
three Crusaders, who walked demurely to the station house
two by two. For their trial "We all put on our best things,"
wrote their leader, the Mrs. Leavitt whom we have already
met as blue-eyed Little Willie's mother, "and, though I say it,
were forty-three of the prettiest-looking women you ever
saw"; she was equally exultant about their social status: "Six
were ministers' wives, three wives of rich bankers . . . the
rest of wealthy citizens." Maybe on that account they were
released with a mere scolding from the bench. But thenceforth they had the discretion to stop mass demonstrations and
confine themselves to visiting saloons by twos and threes.

Mrs. Leavitt's delight in the prestige of her troop was part
of the smug arrogance that went with the Crusade. Occasionally it tempered zeal with mercy, helping a closed-up rumseller to go into a decent business and seeing it was well patronized; or attending the sale of his stock and fixtures to bid
them so high that, in effect, the ladies' husbands financed
whatever new venture he turned to. Glassware and lamps
thus acquired became heirloom souvenirs of the days when
Grandma was a heroine. The gavel that Frances Willard used
in presiding over WCTU meetings was said to be a bung
starter from a Hillsboro saloon. But beneath their skim of
meekness and charity the Crusaders were wonderfully harsh.
They never deigned to reason with their victim but joyfully
bludgeoned him with hymns of self-righteous tenor and
prayers and tears and patronizing assurances that God knew
best and what-He-wanted-and-was-going-to-get-or-know-the-
reason-why was a complete, voluntary shutdown of this
smelly soul-trap. They never grasped what Judge Alphonso
Taft of Cincinnati (founder of a distinguished family) meant
in saying: "It is an objectionable feature of the present crusade that it intrudes religious observances on those who do
not ask for them. Prayer with or for those who desire it is
commendable; but when forced upon the unwilling it is a
mockery of God. . . ."

The judge might have seen further mockery of God in the ladies' superstitious use of the Bible as a device for divination and in their ghoulish pleasure in what they took to be His manifest judgments on those who failed to knuckle under to the Crusaders: Thus the husband of that woman who gave her child beer to scandalize the ladies committed suicide a few months later. So did one of the holdout rumsellers of Bucyrus; another was thrown from a wagon and killed. Within a year most of the coarse ruffians who held a mock prayer meeting in front of the Crusaders in a saloon in Piqua, Ohio, had died "violent and awful deaths." In Williamsport, Pennsylvania, "The man who was the most insulting to us has shot himself. Two others have found a home in the insane asylum . . . [another] now goes about a cripple . . . [whereas] those who aided us in the work have generally prospered." The ladies warned a hotelkeeper that unless he closed his bar, God might "bring him to the truth of His judgments" by "taking" his handsome little son. He was stubborn and in a month the boy died. . . . In a different context and two centuries earlier a thing like that might have got the ladies burned as witches.

As Crusading spread—eventually into both New England and California—it tended to lose classic form. Some local variations were clever, such as the notion of stationing a lady or two at the door of a given saloon, peaceably but ostentatiously noting for some undisclosed but no doubt unpleasant use the name of each man entering. As the impulse vented itself in mass meetings seeking Sunday closing of saloons here, in anti-Demon, pro-local option petitions there, less and less remained of the old presumption that organized Women seeking to do good should do so strictly out of sight in the church basement.

The issue of permanence of results was troublesome in the Ohio valley where the fever had risen highest and the most towns had been assailed. A character in Arthur's *Woman to the Rescue*, his novel about the Crusade, asked: ". . . what is to hinder a return to the old order of things?"; and the answer was lame: "Nothing [if] the town goes back into her old indifference. But [our women] know that 'the price of liberty is eternal vigilance,' and do not mean to sleep." Actually, as the ladies ruefully saw and sometimes admitted, most of the closed bars had reopened by fall, 1874. Highly important residual effects remained, however. For among the supplementary projects of the Crusaders' "praying bands" here and there was organization of local and state leagues federating and making them permanent. In August, 1874, a great gathering of the Sunday school-minded at Chautauqua, New York, only a few miles from fateful Fredonia, naturally included many women who had been high in—and high on—the Crusade. There they decided to federate all local and state outfits into a national organization. For that purpose they called a convention to meet in Cleveland in November barely eleven months after the first raids. That assembly did a solid job worthy of its able, experienced delegates—many of whom had won their spurs in the Sanitary Commission—and when the time came, choice of name was easy because several state organizations had already severally adopted a good one, calling themselves Woman's Christian Temperance Unions.

WCTU—initials as ominous for the United States as K.K.K. In a few years the ungodly had good reason irreverently to interpret them as standing for: "We see to you."

11

LAW, ORDER
AND THE MARTYRS

We wash our hands of the liquid foe,
  The offspring of perdition,
And to the ballot yearly go
  To vote for Prohibition;
For no man has a moral right
  To deal out to another
A licensed curse to swell his purse
  Regardless of his brother.
—*National Temperance Almanac* (1878)

Three hundred fifty persons signed the pledge during the recent Temperance meetings in Frenchtown. Stick to it, boys, even if sometimes you feel like kicking the dog or upsetting the dinner table . . . how you will laugh at the others in the bye and bye when the whole country goes dry!
—Hunterdon County (N.J.)
Democrat, September 11, 1888

AS HOLY mob rule intimidating small-town authorities the Women's Crusade was essentially illegal. Before and after its rise and fall, Temperance-minded members of the more orderly sex—ministers, pious employers, praying politicians—often resorted to legal weapons against Rum. Some were new, some had already been tried and discredited here and there but that made no difference. Temperance was always so sanguine and earnest that not only would it try anything once, it would try it again and again no matter how signally it failed in this state or that county. Its history was full of pledge-plugging, badge-waving crusades that burned out in a few years, leaving the affected towns pretty much as sodden as before; and of futile pendulum-swings as local or state no-license laws were shattered by application, repealed in disillusion, revived in revised form after some years of wide-open guzzling, then repealed again. . . .

Temperance men craving help from the law but squeamish about downright Prohibition often clutched at the Colonists'—and Dr. Rush's—hope to blunt the Demon's claws by issuing fewer licenses to sell drink. It was assumed that, other things being equal, the more bars in business, the worse their influence because, with so many competing for the local nickels and dimes, each had to cut corners to keep up the necessary volume of business. That meant urging customers to drink more and oftener; lowering price-per-drink, hence worse liquor; ignoring laws against serving known drunks or those already intoxicated; harboring whores as added attractions; evading rules against sales on Sunday and to minors. . . .

Cutting down number of licenses reduced competition, however, and made rumselling more profitable—which led straight to bribery and corruption of the officials granting or renewing that limited number of licenses. To cure that in the period after the Civil War, "high license" was invented. The idea was to make license fees so stiff that only a few bars doing a rushing trade among respectable drinkers could stay in business. Ten such large places each paying $1,000 a year would not only combine fewer licenses with higher ethics but also bring county or township far more revenue than a hundred frowsy little gin mills paying only ten dollars each. Free of the demands of competition, each rumseller could afford to stock good liquor in a decent atmosphere at reasonable markup while observing all local regulations. The relatively small numbers of bars would reduce the inordinate temptation to youth and the weak-willed that lay in seeing a saloon on every corner. It was even contended that such high-toned rumsellers would cooperate with the authorities in smelling out blind pigs.

Those possibilities attracted milder Temperance men as well as legislators. Indeed, the father of high-license was John B. Finch of Nebraska, later to be a Prohibition Party nominee for President. In practice high-license did, as per promise, confine legal drink-selling to responsible, not unrespectable hands, often in the bars of decent hotels. But, as Nebraska learned after Finch and friends induced her to try it in 1881, it was otherwise a disastrous compromise with the Demon. One of its former advocates called it "a whiskey Devil in Temperance garb." For it was about as fertile as Prohibition itself in encouraging blind tigers, speakeasies, "dark-lantern hotels," or whatever local slang called places selling illegally. Omaha was found to have ninety-one residents paying federal liquor-seller's license fees without state licenses to match. That obviously meant ninety-one blind pigs in town. Doubtless the silk-hat atmosphere and high prices-per-drink of the legal bars put off the flannel-shirted hod carrier, the farmer in town to sell a load of hogs, and the low-paid drygoods clerk. Nor did legal license holders show any eagerness to ferret out and squeal on illicit rivals. So the lower orders—the very group whose drinking high-license was supposed to discourage—could make it well worth while for lewd persons to sell by the drink behind more or less tightly closed shutters at popular prices. When a raid occurred or something slipped —maybe as an occasional sop to public opinion—local dislike of Dry-tending laws usually kept judges slack, witnesses reluctant or perjured, and juries blind to evidence. It might come to be informally understood that a given joint would be raided say three times a year and the owner fined $100 each time—a sort of unofficial, tourist-class high-license. In Maine this was known as "the Bangor system" after the city in which it came to flower as a way to ease the rigors of statewide Prohibition.

Once again difficulties in enforcement had crippled a promising method of civilizing the Demon. He was, in fact, as hard to civilize as Huckleberry Finn—or Huck's Pap. Militant Temperance scorned high-license anyway because in effect it put the municipality into partnership with rumsellers. The truth of the charge became clear in 1867 when Massachusetts almost passed a proposed law allowing townships to nullify the state's Maine-type law by local referendum as a way to save Temperance's face and yet give large towns high-license revenues. Presently Iowa, almost as hot-Temperance as Maine or Kansas, did pass such a "mulct law," leaving statewide Prohibition unrepealed but allowing local referenda to nullify it on condition of no Sunday sales and huge license fees to the state. The large, sinful river towns hastily voted to be "mulcted."

Such legislative hypocrisy outraged Temperance the worse because in places like Burlington high-license failed—as usual —to keep out blind tigers; and because in any case it implied that bar-type drinking could be tolerable under decent conditions. In a sermon on "High-License, the Monopoly of Abominations," the Rev. T. DeWitt Talmage of Brooklyn, New York, a conspicuous Presbyterian spellbinder of the 1870's, shouted that the better high-license worked, the worse it would be for the world. Its success would make "rum-selling and rum-drinking highly respectable. . . . It is not the rookeries of alcohol that do the worst work. . . . Where did that bloating, ulcerous, wheezing wretch that staggers out of a rum-hole get his habits started? At a glittering restaurant or the bar-room of a first-class hotel . . . the disposition is to stop . . . small establishments, which are only the rash on the skin of the body politic, and then to gather all the poison and the pus and the matteration [*sic*] into a few great carbuncles which mean death. I say, give us the rash rather than the carbuncles!" When a Massachusetts legislative committee asked a parson from Woonsocket, Rhode Island: "Do you wish to be understood as saying that you prefer that liquor should be sold by disreputable persons in groggeries . . . ?" he answered: "Yes, sir!" The orthodox Temperance position had been that of the Hoosier judge who tucked into a decision in a liquor case the *obiter dictum* that (echoing John Hawkins) "The decent, respectable saloon is as impossible as a virgin prostitute."

Temperance-minded laws, like other well-meant social measures, often troubled the righteous by having unexpectedly deplorable side effects. The classic case was New York State's Raines Law of 1895, which, on condition of especially high license fees, allowed hotels of at least ten bedrooms to serve Sunday drinks to guests ordering meals. John Raines, its author, was a respectable lawyer-politician unable to foresee that, since Sunday business was crucial to urban rumsellers, many of them would build on ten bedrooms minimum-size—the law specified at least 8' x 8'—to qualify their saloons as hotels; and that to recoup that expense and the higher license fee they would naturally put those criblike rooms to obvious use seven nights a week. In no time Brooklyn's number of "hotels" jumped from thirteen to over 2,000, and worthy Senator Raines proved to have done more than any other man before or since to foster prostitution in New York City. Among curious minor results was the famous "Raines

Law sandwich"—never eaten, seldom edible, just two dried and curling slices of bread and a sliver of moldy cheese, it was always set at the Sunday drinker's elbow as the "meal" he had implicitly ordered, the waiter making it clear that while cash had to be paid for drinks, food came on credit, take the rest of your life to pay.

Or consider the sheriff of Norfolk County, Massachusetts, who seized the stock-in-trade of a speakeasy and, as the law required, sold it at auction for the benefit of the state. The owner's lawyer studied the statute, noted that it made any sale of liquor categorically illegal, and had the sheriff arrested for selling. He was duly convicted and sentenced to the county jail of which he himself was official keeper. When Somerville, Massachusetts, bordering on the august sister suburb of Cambridge, went no-license in the 1880's, a local rumseller named Dewire built a handsome new saloon to take care of his old customers just across the Cambridge line on Kirkland Street—a neighborhood rife with Harvard faculty and elderly gentlewomen of private means and prim standards. When Dewire applied for the proper restaurant and bar licenses, Kirkland Street objected strongly. The Cambridge city government in the person of one J. J. Kelley, who probably shared the chronic lack of mutual esteem between the Cambridge Irish and Harvard, replied that the city budget needed $35,000 from saloon licenses and though the number necessary to make up that sum was obviously "in excess of legitimate need," he was going to grant them, Dewire's included. Here was license law proliferating not blind pigs this time but legal saloons as sources of revenue.

Dewire prospered though the coarse nature of his clientele greatly distressed Professor Francis James Child and neighbors. Then Cambridge too went no-license by a narrow margin. Dewire kept his place open regardless, and his uncouth patrons continued to troop across the town line. (Being the world's ranking expert on the balladry of the Scottish-English border, Professor Child should have looked more kindly on lawless goings-on across boundaries.) It took the best people on Kirkland Street a year to amass evidence to get Dewire raided and sent to the House of Correction. Nightly in all weathers the gentlemen residents had huddled in shrubbery across the street peering through binoculars to catch occasional flashes of goings-on in the heavily shaded interior of Dewire's premises. The eventual raid found the bar equipped with electric bells with which sentries alerted the boss to intruders, and a large picture that swung on hinges to mask the secret entrance to the main liquor supply. Doubtless there still are those who think that it was the Volstead Act that created the speakeasy.

Thenceforth Cambridge voted no-license every time the issue came up. Local Temperance men said that such consistent action slackened the hold of booze on local politics, lightened the work of the police and, by driving bars underground at least, rid the town of so many "traps for the unwary, temptations to the weak, allurements to young men." Had not Boston been both nearby and wet, it might have been a different story. As it was, youngsters from Harvard and any other thirsty Cantabrigians had only to board a horsecar to do their drinking legally on the other side of the Charles. Three of every four arrests for drunkenness made by the Cambridge police occurred on those cars or on the bridges. The apparent lesson was that the best way to get reasonable enforcement of no-license was to have a large wet city next door. That soon came to be known as the "safety-valve theory" of Temperance legislation. It worked so well that Professor Hugo Münsterberg, Harvard's eminent German psychologist, kept saying that though he was no Prohibitionist, he hoped that Cambridge would go on serenely voting no-license forever.

○○

I do not believe that a man who sells ardent spirits . . . will faithfully carry out any license laws that may be enacted. . . . I may be wanting in faith in humanity, but I have very little faith in that portion of humanity that is engaged in the liquor traffic.
—THE REV. WILLARD SPAULDING (1867)

Those damp spies in the shrubbery represented a second reason why no-license worked better in Cambridge than

elsewhere. There vigilante spirit was carried on by respectable local volunteers organized as a Law and Order League
who did much to make no-license stick by gathering and pre-
senting in court watertight evidence against Cambridge rumsellers trying to stay in business. Law and Order Leagues had
originated in Chicago where a civic leader, Andrew Paxton,
conspicuously banded the righteous together to raise funds,
hire detectives and work up cases against saloons selling to
minors. For a while Paxton had a national movement going,
with annual conventions and flare-ups of temporary accom-
plishment from Philadelphia to Bangor to Sioux City. But
only in stubbornly consistent places like Cambridge did the
impetus last. Elsewhere it was eventually smothered, a Temperance authority said, by "the unbroken successes of the
saloon element at the polls" in getting license somehow
restored.

The notion of Temperance vigilantes actually went back to
the first Maine Law, which inspired a "Brotherhood of
Temperance Watchmen" to look for blind pigs, liquor-
smuggling and so forth and swear out complaints when local
authorities preferred to look the other way. Though such
Brothers were well within their legal rights, their activities
were bound to rouse bad feeling. "What is simply the duty of
a civil officer," a contemporary Temperance man said sadly,
"is often regarded as officiousness when done by a private
citizen." These self-appointed snoopers knowingly risked
having their horses painted in bizarre colors and, in rough
neighborhoods, their fruit trees killed by girdling, even their
barns burned. A Temperance leader in Standish, Maine, was
snatched out of bed one cold night and soused several times
in his own horse trough—to give him plenty of cold water,
said the masked men doing it. Portland toughs threw dead
cats and rum bottles into Neal Dow's carriage as it waited for
him, and once ruined Mrs. Dow's best carpet by throwing a
bottle of asafetida through his parlor window. In spite of
such capers men of rugged mind like the Rev. T. W. Higginson—the soldier-parson who became successively a ring-
leader in John Brown's conspiracy and a principal midwife
for Emily Dickinson's poetry—felt that good citizens had no

choice but to step in and snoop and give evidence when officialdom failed to suppress blind pigs.

Paid snoopers were added to amateurs by Thomas L. Carson, a determined York Stater who founded "Carson Leagues" of zealots hiring both detectives to gather evidence and lawyers to make cases against illicit Rum. Tacking his own name on the organization like a quack doctor's picture on a patent medicine, Carson personally edited its newspaper; worked hard in the campaign for New York's abortive Prohibition law; and best stated his principles in an atrocious pun: "The best temperance tracts I know are rumsellers' tracks to jail." What made him patron saint of Temperance militants, however, was his Brutus-like righteousness in having his own brother prosecuted for irregular sales of liquor at his hotel. Up to the Civil War, Carson Leagues cropped up here and there in New England too, usually led by parsons. One of them once assured a sniffy outsider that his League took every precaution to hire only detectives who were sincere teetotalers in private life.

Paxton's hobby of organizing Law and Order Leagues got him badly roughed up in several cities. He could hardly have been surprised. As Prohibition sentiment grew in the uneasy 1880's and private citizens like him egged the law on, violence began to erupt, shots to ring out and funerals to ensue, particularly in the newer states across the Mississippi and in the South. The largest group of such Dry victims consisted of ministers giving the Demon and his allies the rough side of their tongues in a fashion irksome to local corrupt politicians. Several others were editors of Temperance papers that trod too heavily on the toes of local political power. One way or another Temperance came to its great victory in 1919 sanctified by the blood of a good dozen civilian martyrs, which (if you except John Brown's men as aggressors) was many more than Abolitionism or any other Syndromist good cause could show.

Maybe the outstanding preacher-martyr was the Rev. George C. Haddock, Methodist, who took over a pulpit in Sioux City, Iowa, in 1885, full of zeal as a new convert to the Prohibition Party's ideas. The town's 100-odd saloons openly defied statewide Prohibition, and he went right to work on them. Teamed with a local pious lawyer, he circulated petitions urging local authorities to crack down; lectured up and down the neighborhood wherever he could find a platform; and wrote and distributed an outspoken pamphlet, "A City in Rebellion." He was asking for the trouble that Sioux City's liquor interests had long promised anybody daring to cross them. Returning late one evening from a country lecture, Haddock left his hired rig at the livery stable and set out for home on foot, alone. A crowd gathered round to hoot and hustle him. There was a scuffle, a shot—and the Rev. Mr. Haddock very dead. The affair made a stink elsewhere in the state but Sioux City was well under control. A local brewer was tried for the murder but got a hung jury under circumstances smelling high of corruption. At the second trial the jury acquitted him and then sat for a gloating group photograph with him as hero in the center.

It was much the same story for Roderick Dhu Gambrill, boy editor of the Jackson (Miss.) *Sword & Shield,* a Temperance paper. His Virginian parents, enthusiastic Drys as well as (to judge from their son's name) admirers of Sir Walter Scott, had moved to Mississippi in 1884, bought the paper and put the youngster in charge, though he was only nineteen. In the old tradition of editor-printer he set the type as well as writing the copy that called loudly for action against the many local speakeasies. They burned his printshop down. Within weeks he was back in operation, brash as ever. In 1886 Jackson had a local-option referendum. The pro-saloon faction was led by a state senator named Hamilton who set up a propaganda sheet in opposition to Gambrill's and lost prestige when no-license won. When Hamilton ran again for the state senate in 1887, Gambrill's paper called him "leader of the worst element in society" and partaker in recent state money scandals.

One night Hamilton, accompanied by the city marshal and a local barkeep, caught up with Gambrill on his way home from the shop. Just what happened was never clear: Several shots brought people running to find Gambrill, who seems to have been armed, dying on the ground with his face beaten in, presumably by the barkeep who was still holding a pistol all over blood. Hamilton had stopped two bullets and his coat sleeve was smoldering, presumably from Gambrill's point-blank fire. The righteous element of the community talked of lynching Hamilton & Co., which sounds queer only till one reflects that after all, this was Mississippi. Gambrill's father pled successfully for legal, fair trial. The result was neither fair nor legal: Hamilton alone was actually tried. A change of venue took the case to a county where the deputy in charge of jury lists was a henchman of his. Acquitted, he came home to a noisy triumph in Jackson. The sense of public relations among the Demon's friends degenerated as need for canniness increased. The U.S. Brewers' Association had already had the effrontery to felicitate the industry on that miscarriage of justice in Sioux City. Now this affair even more clearly identified the Demon with murder—just what Temperance had long been trying to accomplish.

Neither Haddock nor Gambrill had the luck of the Rev. R. E. McClure of the Pennsylvania Anti-Saloon League, who was shot at in 1913 by miscreants unknown but doubtless anti-Temperance. At the time, he had a Bible under his arm. The bullet penetrated no farther than the page carrying Moses' teetotal rules for the Nazarites.

❧

"But can ye iver enforce prohybition?" asked Mr. Hennessy. "Well," said Mr. Dooley, "Father Kelly says th' best they've done so far is to make dhrink wrong to take, hard to get, an' tur'ble bad whin ye get it."
　　—F. P. DUNNE, "Mr. Dooley on the Temperance Wave."

After the Civil War, Massachusetts was still saddled with a Maine-type Prohibition law. Temperance, reviving, soon pushed through a likely innovation—a special state constabulary to crack down on townships and counties failing duly to persecute the Demon. (This was essentially the nation's first state police.) The new broom went stiffly to work on Boston and other cities in a fashion irksome to rumsellers. The right course was to keep cool and let the new outfit wear down to the same slackness and corruption that already distinguished Boston's municipal force. But the respectable wing of the liquor interest, led by the lessor of the Parker House, which had the finest bar in town, formed an alliance with those who thought Prohibition was working out poorly, and tried to put across the aforementioned forerunner of Iowa's "mulct law." Eminent counsel headed by John A. Andrew, able war governor of the state, made the case for it. The consequent hearings before a joint legislative committee failed to make it look logical to keep a law on the books while allowing municipalities to nullify it. But they also presented a momentous analysis of the handicaps inevitable for Prohibition. Inevitable, that is, so long as doctors prescribed alcoholic drinks; express companies could ship them interstate; sinful men liked the effects of booze and were prone to accept bribes; yeast persisted in creating alcohol; and the application of moderate heat so conveniently released it from solution in water.

Most striking was the testimony about the utter breakdown of enforcement in the slums. Catholic parish priests; Protestant (usually clerical) social workers, including the nationally famous Father Taylor of the Seamen's Chapel; both the chief of the Boston police and the patrolman assigned to try to rehabilitate drunkards—all spoke of ten-room tenements where every room was a separate blind pig, of slum households' ordering and presumably selling six to eight kegs of beer a week and of the North End coppersmiths' rushing trade in small-scale distilling equipment. Or the local Irishman, unable to afford that, needed only a teakettle and a discarded gas pipe to turn molasses into rum that was signally powerful and, once you were used to it, potable. The police chief's list of 1,515 known places in Boston where one could buy liquor was unusually small, he said, because of the new state constabulary's zeal. At that, it was one for each 130-odd inhabitants of all ages, and he was confident that hundreds more stray shebeens and blind pigs were as yet unknown to his men. As to Cambridge, even Dr. Francis Bowen, professor of Natural Religion and Moral Philosophy at Harvard, knew (he did not say how) that it was as easy to buy booze there as bread. In Charlestown alone, said the local police judge, some 200 federal liquor-sale licenses had been taken out *after* the U.S. Supreme Court had made it clear that they gave no protection against state or local laws.

Evidence about other towns backed up the committee's majority conclusion: little liquor was sold in small places but "in all the large cities and towns it can be had without difficulty . . . sales are open . . . whenever by peculiarly vigorous efforts the open places are closed, secret places are established. . . . The fact that the business is contraband and liable to interruptions, and its gains hazardous, tends to drive the honest men from it and to leave it in the control of dishonest men." But meager sale in villages did not mean drinking there had dried up. Through mail-order for delivery by express, prosperous tipplers kept well supplied with wines and liquors from both Boston and out-of-state firms. Prosperous city men used the same means of supply; whereas the lower orders, usually lacking the cash to finance mail-orders, had to go without in villages—which they resented—or in the wicked larger places patronize the moonshine-bootlegger-blind pig complex. "I want to have the law carried out!" the chaplain of Charlestown State Prison told the committee, ". . . and not only on Patrick Murphy and Bridget Maloney but on the people who live in fine houses and drink their champagne!"

The hearings saw some humor: An ex-governor recalled three legislators, his fellow boarders at the elegant Tremont House, who had voted for the statewide Prohibition law in 1852 and then celebrated its passage with hot whiskey punch, assuring him that the measure was a mere concession to public tumult and could never conceivably be enforced. Haverhill's state agent for the sale of liquor for medicinal and industrial use testified that he sold $33,000 worth a year, meaning, at the prices of the time, well over 10,000 gallons. "Are your people peculiarly sick?" examining counsel asked solicitously. "No, sir, they are as healthy, I presume, as other places. . . ." "Any peculiar epidemic last summer?" "No, sir." Nothing more needed saying about the absurdities of the state-agent system that Massachusetts had borrowed from Maine—all the purchaser had to do was say that he needed a pint for medicinal purposes. The chief state constable had a list of 107 Boston drugstores wide open every Sunday with liquor a principal item. Large town after large town was shown to be just like Salem, the ex-mayor of which told the committee that there Prohibition was "a melancholy mockery and a solemn farce" that failed to lessen the number selling while increasing the number buying. Just like New York City as I saw it in 1926.

That was how it went everywhere in the first wave of statewide Prohibition laws. In 1866 a Temperance zealot disgustedly described Michigan's as "everywhere openly violated . . . nearly a dead letter" with 500 wide-open bars in Detroit, 300 in Grand Rapids, and big city hotels handing all patrons wine and liquor lists. The year after those hearings Massachusetts repealed her Prohibition law and embarked on experiments with licensing systems. But the hard-core Temperance mind could never learn. In that very same year the Order of Good Templars set up a political action committee aimed at forming a national Prohibition Party. If it didn't work statewide, try it nationwide.

The constitution is the only safe abiding place for a reform so fundamental as prohibition . . . [it] is the people's law, beyond the reach of professional lobbies and peanut politics.
    —*The Pocket Encyclopaedia of Temperance* (1916)

Dr. Billy J. Clark, still an oracle of Temperance at his shrine in Saratoga County in the 1850's, was one of the first to advise imbedding Temperance in state constitutions. The suggestion had tactical merit: Mere statutes like the Maine Law were too easy for a backsliding legislature to repeal as initial zeal ebbed and flaws in enforcement grew flagrant. But had the original enthusiasm been exploited to create an anti-liquor amendment to the state constitution, the Demon's

sneaky allies would have had a harder time getting it re-
scinded. To amend an amendment out of existence is a cumbrous process—usually calling for a statewide referendum after elaborate legislative action—giving Temperance forces
ample warning to rally.

The old gentleman's good advice did not get proper observance, however, until the young Prohibition Party endorsed the principle in 1876 and the newish National Temperance Society and Publication House got its propaganda
machine behind it. In 1880, Kansas showed the way for several states (Maine included, of course) by securing a stiff
amendment. Special credit for it went to a Quaker woman
preacher, Drusilla Wilson, who logged over 3,000 miles by
horse and wagon crisscrossing the Sunflower State militantly
and eloquently to promote the good cause. In Maine, it was
soon noted, the effect of constitutional amendment was to
make the State wetter than ever as enforcement officers and
public alike assumed that—as the Drys had promised—everything was now settled and little further effort needed.
Maine's amendment stuck, however; the mightiest effort to
repeal failed by some 700 votes in a referendum in 1911.
Elsewhere the effect was not as durable as advertised: Where
the Wets spent enough money and took enough trouble, re-
submission acts often went through legislatures smoothly,
setting up second-thoughts referenda in which repeal won,
which started the pendulum swinging again. South Dakota,
for instance, repealed the anti-Demon clause in her original
constitution after seven years of disappointing experience
with enforcement, only to restore it in 1916. Rhode Island
repealed after three years—1886 to 1889—and never tried
again.

Meanwhile Representative Henry W. Blair of Vermont,
Dry-minded Republican politician-with-a-conscience whose
other special concerns were Chinese exclusion, Sunday observance and federal aid to education, had let his sense of
logic take an ominous leap into new ground. Late in December, 1876, the very season when legislators would be acutely
feeling the effects of too much Tom and Jerry, he introduced
an amendment to the *federal* constitution outlawing sale,

manufacture or importation of hard liquor nationwide, with the usual exceptions for medicinal and industrial use. It was not to take effect until 1900, the start of the hopeful new century, which sportingly gave distillers a whole generation in which to mend their ways and liquidate their businesses. "Longer than [the twenty-one years] our fathers gave to the merchant marine . . . to remove its capital from the slave-trade," said Blair, who was fair-minded about those in the liquor trade. "Men like ourselves," he boldly asserted, "sometimes better than those who assail them."

That was more like Dr. Clark's notion. Amending the federal constitution really is cumbrous: It calls for two-third majorities in both houses of Congress plus separate ratifications by three-fourths of the states. Blair's amendment also promised more than mere entrenchment of Prohibition behind constitutional barriers. Others seeking nationwide Prohibition before him had always stuck on one point: Before the Eighteenth Amendment, the Federal Government had no direct power over rumselling within the states, could bar it only from such special federal jurisdictions as the Territories, Indian reservations and so on. Therefore, no matter how flagrantly booze and drinkers oozed across the boundaries of Dry states, Temperance had never sought a federal statute to impose Dryness on sinful states. Blair's amendment would widen federal powers in this respect, unshackle Uncle Sam, clear the way for a national Prohibition statute (like the Volstead Act-to-be) "which can wield an ax big and sharp enough to cut off [the Demon's] hydra head." It never got out of committee that time around. Later, as Senator from Vermont, he introduced a stronger version also banning beer and wine and, as chairman of the pertinent committee in 1889, personally steered it to a vote and 33-to-13 defeat. Not the defeat but those thirteen votes so early in the game is the surprising thing about that.

Only after another twenty-four years did all major Temperance forces come round to Blair's way of thinking. Yet his was the position into which, once law was invoked at all, fanatic logic necessarily drove anybody insisting on thinking teetotaling Temperance through without regard to other

social data. Now in 1964, with so much melted ice gone over
the dam in so many post-Prohibition cocktails, it can seem
half-gratifying that Blair lived on to see the Eighteenth
Amendment and the Volstead Act. His intellectual manners
were so much better than those of many other zealots who
helped to bring about those twin legislative calamities.

> Prohibition is the key-note of the hour, and will be the full
> chorus of the future.
> —CLARA L. ROACH in
> *The White Ribbon Birthday Book* (1887)

The Prohibition Party that anticipated Blair in plumping
for nationwide action was born of an oversanguine sense of
history. Its founders were seeking to emulate the success story
of antislaveryism: In the 1840's certain antislavery leaders
had broken with those who still hoped to keep their good
cause out of politics and set up a national Liberty Party dedicated to freedom for the slave. In its own name it polled piti-
fully few votes but it had a momentous future. Within a few
years it was one of the groups fusing into the broader-gauged
Free Soil Party, which in turn, during the game of political
musical chairs in the 1850's, merged with many Know-Nothings, many former Whigs and odd Democrats queasy about
slavery into the Republican Party, which, true to the Liberty
Party strain in its ancestry, fought the war that freed the
slave. The Prohibition forces that were also part of the original Republican blend got snubbed as the slavery issue
reached white heat. But now slavery's hash was settled, it was
hoped that Prohibition's turn was come.

So in 1869, delegates from twenty states met in Chicago to
launch the National Prohibition Party. The theory was that
this new single-cause party would stay a force-in-being, attracting few votes, no doubt, but ready when opportunity
arose to blend into and infect with Dry-mindedness a major
political group that would outlaw rumsellers as the Liberty

Party's giant grandchild had outlawed slaveowners. Nor was there any question that the Republicans were what the Prohibitionists had their eye on. In pre-Civil War jockeyings the Democrats of the Northeastern states had got too well identified with Wet or anyway anti-Maine Law sentiment. After the war the Democrats retained an inconvenient odor of Copperheadism and opposition to good causes. There would come a day when Southern Democrats and some in the North too would lick the boots of professional Drys—but these were the storm troopers of the Anti-Saloon League, not the Syndromist zealots of the Prohibition Party.

Its founding leaders came from the Right Worthy Grand Lodge of Good Templars with strong support from other Temperance orders—mostly men unknown outside their hometowns. But tireless old Dr. Delavan was there, and his chronic ally, Gerrit Smith, eight years recovered from his psychotic panic and laying down, apropos of Dry legislation, the illiberal doctrine that "in all matters . . . of fundamental morality, the ruler is bound to consult, not the will of the people, but the will of God." In 1870, Prohibition Party tickets appeared in some states under various names. Delavan and Smith called their entry in New York the Anti-Dramshop Party. In Massachusetts, Wendell Phillips, now espousing labor and Women's Rights as well as Temperance, ran for governor under auspices of both a workingmen's party and the Prohibitionists, getting 22,000 votes of which some 8,000 were credited to the latter. In its first national election in 1872 the Party put up for the Presidency James Black* of Pennsylvania—small-time railroad lawyer, former Republican, Grand Worthy Chief of the Good Templars, foe of hard cider, a founder of the Methodists' seaside paradise, Ocean City, New Jersey. The platform called for national Prohibition plus a mixture of liberal-leaning and conservative planks: for instance, election of President and senators by direct popular vote; but also the creditor-favoring step of restoring the gold standard. In 1876 the planks canted sharply toward the pious: abolition of prostitution; nation-

* This book owes a very great deal to the old gentleman's magnificent collection of Temperanceana now in the New York Public Library.

wide Sunday observance; compulsory Bible reading in public schools. . . . In succeeding years the piety persisted but was more and more obscured by mildly radical notions such as Women's Rights, railroad regulation, referendum and recall, as if embryonic Populism had been strained through a fresh-water Sunday school.

The Republicans, triumphantly waving "the bloody shirt," took care that up through 1900 their every presidential nominee had a solid record as a Civil War field officer. Bent on making a noise like a real party, the Prohibitionists did likewise. The roster ran: General Green Clay Smith (1876) veteran of the Mexican War, Kentucky Republican rising to brigadier general's rank before resigning in 1864 to get elected to Congress and come within half a vote of being Lincoln's second Vice-President. That means, of course, that he would have been President after April 15, 1865. On his own in 1876 he attracted only some 9,000 votes nationwide. In 1880, the party's candidate, our old friend General Neal Dow, was widely known but failed to do much better. In 1884 General John P. St. John, Forty-niner, Women's Righter, Indian fighter, governor of Kansas when she pioneered state constitutional Prohibition, got some 150,000 votes for reasons to be gone into later. That was slightly bettered in 1888 by General Clinton B. Fisk, Missouri businessman who, to his everlasting glory, had founded Fisk University in Tennessee during Reconstruction times. In 1892 the pace was maintained by General John Bidwell, pre-Forty-nine Californian, former Republican congressman, friend of the pushed-around California Indians, fruit rancher who uprooted his vineyards when he saw California wines causing so much drunkenness. Mark that all those were considerable figures, men of experience and ability. All also had significantly Republican backgrounds. But all except Dow had been of the "Mugwump" school of Republican—disgusted with the crass money-changers who had so shamelessly taken over the party of Lincoln and the Battle Hymn of the Republic. That was why the cleaner if slightly absurd and probably futile climate of the Prohibition Party had eventually seemed preferable.

The Party's only clear victory came in 1914 when it actually elected a congressman—from a Los Angeles district, of course. Indirectly, however, it left its mark through a steady drumming of propaganda that gradually accustomed the public ear to the notion of federal Prohibition—and through a political freak that showed the yet-to-be-born American Anti-Saloon League the way to conquer. For in 1884, the Prohibition Party came balefully to the notice of serious politicians as a principal reason why James G. Blaine, the Republicans' "Plumed Knight," failed to make the White House.

The trouble was that the Republican platform committee had snubbed an earnest Dry effort, led by St. John and Frances Willard, head of the already formidable Woman's Christian Temperance Union, to get some kind of anti-Demon clause into the platform. Indignantly St. John bolted the Party, accepted the Prohibitionists' offer of nomination, and set out to show it didn't pay to be impolite to the Kansas style of righteousness. In a tireless speaking campaign—and he was a major spellbinder with the finest pair of handlebar mustaches west of St. Louis—he concentrated on New York State, home of the nation's largest block of electoral votes, where he could hurt Blaine worst. He reaped 25,000 New York votes, a sixth of his national total. Blaine was in Mugwump trouble anyway but had hoped to recoup by creating a sizable Irish Republican movement. That was spoiled at the last minute by the famous blunder of the eminent Republican parson who alienated the carefully cultivated Irish by calling the Democrats "the party of rum, Romanism and rebellion." But even so it was touch and go in New York State because the Republicans had got Cleveland, the Democratic nominee, into very hot water by exposing him as father of an illegitimate child. Blaine lost the state—and as it turned out the election, New York's votes being crucial—by little more than a thousand votes. And it stood to reason that a few thousands of St. John's 25,000 came from men at least nominally Republican who might well have voted for Blaine had not St. John's riproaring campaign suggested protest votes for the Prohibition ticket.

The implied lesson was not lost. In 1893 the fledgling Anti-

Saloon League made such crucial minority votes the keystone of the strategy that culminated in Prohibition in 1919. Their unofficial, never published, seldom spoken, good word for candidates for office in any contests worth their attention might well have been: "Remember what happened to Blaine in 1884!"

12

BELOVED OCTOPUS

"Sure, politics ain't bean bags. 'Tis a man's game, an' women, childher, and pro-hybitionists do well to keep out iv it."
—F. P. DUNNE, "Mr. Dooley on Ward Leaders"

"Husband and wife are one,"
  Says the perfect law divine.
"That one the man," says human law
  With its distinctions fine.
But in the W.C.T.U.,
  New realm of law and life,
Husband and wife are often one,
  But that one is the wife."
    —JULIA A. WILLARD in
    The White Ribbon Birthday Book

WHEN a couple of hundred women from seventeen states met in Cleveland late in 1874 to form the National Woman's Christian Temperance Union, most of their leaders were, as noted, veterans of the U.S. Sanitary Commission and the Women's Crusade. Fittingly their national president was the redoubtable Mrs. Annie Wittenmyer; their national treasurer Little Willie Leavitt's style-conscious mother; their intellectual preceptress Mrs. Mary A. Livermore, who was making a lucrative career of feminist-flavored inspirational lectures. But their most momentous choice was not appreciated at full significance: Their recording secretary, up from the same berth in the Illinois WCTU, was Frances Elizabeth Willard of Evanston, Illinois, whose affair with the WCTU would get her called "The Uncrowned Queen of American Womanhood." As a girl, redheaded, slightly made "Frank" Willard had noted that next to being a saint, she'd like most to be a politician. Joining the war on the Demon as an alarmingly capable spinster of thirty-five years, she ended with a saint's reputation and a politician's arts.

There was something Napoleonic about the deliberation of her self-crowning. She was born in—this is really getting monotonous—upper New York State (Churchville, near Rochester) of Yankee stock in 1839. Her father, hoping to turn Congregational minister, took his growing family to Oberlin, Ohio, where the new Oberlin College spread just the kind of holy-Syndromist light that he sought. His wife also took courses and the good life was shaping well when his lungs began to hemorrhage and the doctor ordered outdoor life as the only recourse. Resignedly the Willards pulled up stakes and drove west to the southern fringe of Wisconsin to develop the farm—in later life Frank lyrically referred to it as "Forest Home"—where she had most of her rearing. Succumbing to the local religious climate, Willard turned fanatic Methodist. As his elder daughter embarked on her phenomenal way in the world, being a Methodist came in very handy for her.

The family stayed Syndromist, of course: antislavery and addicted to Temperance (in which Mrs. Willard was enlisted in Churchville by General Riley), calisthenics, phrenology, hydropathy. They treated sore throats with cold-water compresses. When Frank stepped on a nail, they warded off lockjaw by pumping cold water on the foot; when elder brother Oliver broke a leg, its knitting was promoted by cold-water bandages. Standards were stern *chez* Willard: Frank and younger sister Mary loved to play the parlor melodeon. One day Father, doubtless proud to be able to afford it, brought home a piano. When the girls preferred the familiar melodeon, he forbade use of it, and when they backslid, had it taken away and sold. The worldly habits of Oliver, who smoked and drank too much as a Chicago newspaperman, eventually editor-owner of the Chicago *Post & Mail*, sore troubled his mother. When he died in middle age and Frank rushed home to comfort the old lady, she proved to need no such thing: "Praise heaven with me," she said, "I've grown gray with praying for my son, and now to think he's safe with God!"

The 1850's considered hair as red as Frank's a calamity for a girl. When they yelled "Carrots!" at her, she ran to Mother for reassurance that as she matured, it would ripen toward golden-brown. It further strengthened her Ugly Duckling feeling that sister Mary was plumper and, it was thought, prettier. Actually a photograph of Frank at the age of nineteen shows her quite pretty too—a delicate, round-chinned, level-eyed face with a Cupid's bow mouth flicked upward at the corners. As her career progressed, the mouth dropped and tightened and the eyes hid behind a perpetual frost of pincenez lenses. Maybe her skinniness encouraged her in her chosen role of tomboy: She wore her red hair cut short and couldn't be got into long skirts till she was sixteen; liked tagging after Oliver to help with trapping and carpentry; despised kitchen chores; heroine-worshiped Margaret Fuller, the prototype American bluestocking; dreamed of being a lady doctor; scribbled precociously . . . just like the clever, not candybox-pretty but creative girls in the stories that, following Miss Alcott's lead, American lady writers of that time wrote over and over again.

This clever girl did well at a girls' academy in Milwaukee and at the North Western Female College in Chicago, a new Methodist-endorsed affair. On finishing, she taught school here and there as much to get away from home as because she had to earn a living—in Chicago suburbs; in Kankakee, Illinois; Pittsburgh; Lima, Ohio—always furbishing up her originally sketchy learning, steadily rising to upper echelon posts in well-thought-of schools. Soon after the Civil War she grew intimate with a younger colleague, a former pupil, whose rich father sent daughter and friend to Europe for two splendid years, enabling her to publish some "travel letters" in lay and religious papers and greatly enhancing her reputation at home. Not long after this trip she was made president of Evanston College for Ladies, set up by local women as an attempt at a Midwestern Vassar. When it merged into Northwestern University, which was gingerly toying with co-education, she went along as Dean of its Women's College. But just when she was becoming Cook County's equivalent of Tennyson's Princess, that cultivated cultivator of the peculiar excellences of women, her educator's career stopped short. Northwestern acquired a new president, Charles Fowler, whom she had once promised to marry when he was a callow young parson and then thrown over. Maybe because he still resented it—or her—frictions between president and dean grew until she felt forced to resign.

That was vexing but little more. She started lecturing on topics flavored with rarefied Women's Rights and was successful enough to show that between that and occasional soulful journalism she could support self and Mother. Though self-supporting women were far rarer then than now outside the needle, washtub and blackboard trades, trust Frank Willard to manage with one narrow nervous hand tied behind her. Only she thirsted for some nationwide equivalent of the career of Anna Dickinson, the little she-firebrand of the platform whom she had seen dripping public acclaim in Pittsburgh during the Civil War. Frank had to have renown, adulation, to be the focus of important, pervasive influences. Her defeat in Evanston turned her into ambition incarnate seeking a vehicle for expressing itself.

There was Women's Rights: She had dabbled in it but mistrusted the prevalent shrill version of that cause. (Actually she reversed the Stanton-Anthony school of thought: They had turned to concentrating on Women's Rights as a means to Temperance among other things. She turned to concentrating on Temperance as a pretext for organizing for Women's Rights in a widely inclusive sense.) As a Midwestern Methodist educated in bone-dry Evanston, she had been soaked in Temperance all her life. At the age of sixteen she had pasted a Temperance pledge in the family Bible for all to sign. In Europe, true, she had learned to take table wines freely as custom of the country, but on returning to the alcoholophobia of Evanston, she did not miss them. She had had no part in Chicago's watered-down version of the Women's Crusade; her only experience with it had been an afternoon at a prayer-raid in Pittsburgh. But she was a good friend of Mrs. Livermore, who headed the (anti-Stanton) Association for the Advancement of Women and embodied the affinity between Temperance and ladylike feminism. Miss Willard's sudden interest in militant Temperance, suggests her recent biographer, Mary Earhart,* came not so much "from moral conviction as from her interest in the woman's side of the movement." Maybe she sensed that many women of the 1870's would take more readily to the concrete, man-decrying idea of Temperance than to the abstract, responsibility-demanding idea of Women's Rights. Yet one hand could wash the other, Temperance supplying emotional drive, Women's Rights the vote necessary to batter the Demon down.

Anyway, the WCTU that Miss Willard personally created saw Temperance as combined bridge and ladder to help Man across the great moral gulf fixed between the sexes: "Drink and tobacco," she wrote, "are the great separatists [sic] between men and women. Once they used these things together, but woman's evolution has carried her beyond them; man will climb to the same level . . . but meanwhile . . . the fact that he permits himself fleshly indulgence that he would deprecate in her, makes their planes different, giving her . . . an instinct of revulsion." She saw woman "above [Man] on the hard-won heights of purity that she may lead him upward into freedom from the drink dominion . . . and that he may learn . . . a chastity as steadfast as her own." Enter the Double Standard inside out and backfiring. She saw marriage as tolerable only if men were reared woman-style. Her "Pledge for Boys" might come from *The Little Colonel* books for girls:

> I pledge my brain God's thoughts to think,
> My lips no fire or foam to drink
> From alcoholic cup.
> Nor link with my pure breath tobacco's taint.
> For have I not a right to be
> As wholesome, pure and free as she
> Who through the years so glad and free
> Moves gently onward to meet me
> A knight of the new chivalry. . . .

* *Frances Willard: From Prayers to Politics* (1944). I owe this book much for data and interpretation. It must not be held responsible for the tone of my sketch of the subject.

Her basic feeling appears in her fondness for an alleged Arab proverb: " 'A pure man is a brother of girls.' The brotherly man will . . . respond to the sisterly woman . . . when [Woman] stands before [Man] royal, crowned with heart of love and brain of fire, then shall come the new day. God grant that [Woman] may be so loving and gentle in it all, that there shall be no vanity, no pride. Evermore the grandest natures are the humblest."

The Uncrowned Queen's court ladies often tried to match her rococo rhetoric, which her platform charm seems to have made highly persuasive, and readily fell in with the delusions of sexual grandeur underlying her—and Woman's—special interest in Temperance. None ever knew the exact nature of the revulsion that caused her to hand young Fowler the mitten. The only other man in whom she was known to take substantial personal interest was, years later, Terence V. Powderly, engaging, idealistic and Temperance-minded leader of the Knights of Labor—and he was ten years her junior. Otherwise it must be said—without making too much of it, for her time and place were most ignorantly innocent in such epicene matters—that she showed an outstanding talent for schoolgirl crushes and carried their emotional values into her later life as a daintily charming spinster.

There survive letters from her pupils to their young teacher, implying responses of similar tone from her, that would make even an unusually cautious psychiatrist look wise as a treeful of owls. Hothouse gush and hair-down gurgles marked the stiflingly close relationship between her and her secretary-assistant-biographer, Anna F. Gordon. Things were mighty warm with Lady Henry Somerset, daughter of an earl, who separated young from her patrician spouse and went in for Peace, suppression of "The Social Evil," and Temperance. Also notable among the Queen's adulatory intimates was Mrs. Hannah Whitall Smith—mother of Logan Pearsall Smith, the finicky essayist; mother-in-law of Bernard Berenson and Bertrand Russell; and herself a Philadelphia Quaker amateur mystic and devotee of causes. Her Introduction to one of Miss Willard's prolix autobiographies has Apocalyptic—and maybe also Revelatory—overtones, calling her "the embodiment of all that is lovely, and good, and womanly, and strong, and noble, and tender in human nature . . . my queen among women. . . . There is a creature in the sea called the Octopus . . . with immense arms covered with suckers . . . that stretch themselves out to indefinite length to draw in all sorts of prey. Miss Willard seems . . . to reach out mental or spiritual arms to indefinite lengths, whereby to draw in everything and everybody that seem likely to help on the cause she has at heart. Hence I, who have felt the grip of those arms of hers, have come to call her in our private moments, 'My beloved Octopus,' and myself her contented victim."

Doubtless the most unfortunate compliment ever paid. Mrs. Smith also described the WCTU as "organized mother-love." Supposing mother-love incapable of minding its own business—which may be nearer the case than is usually admitted—there was much in this even though the prime organizer never knew motherhood.

The Temperance eagles, many of them former Crusaders, gathered that summer of 1874 in Old Orchard, Maine, and Chautauqua, New York, then just commencing as combined summer resort and center of mental uplift for the righteous. Miss Willard attended both powwows to sniff the air for an appropriate career. Apparently the overtones were propitious, for that fall, there she was in Cleveland accepting national office, soon seizing on the Illinois State WCTU to become its president and as such an *ex officio* member of the national executive. Presently she was national *corresponding* secretary—an opportunity like that exploited by Stalin as secretary of the Communist Party to found and reinforce his power within the Party while Lenin yet lived. She was soon known throughout the state and local branches as an untiring writer of letters of advice and a whirlwind on lecture and liaison tours. For some time she handled women's meetings for the world-shaking evangelists Moody & Sankey, but that was not far off line. Though against Prohibition, they were hot-Temperance and in their service she gained more experience in charming while inspiring large groups of women. She kept developing ideas about WCTU policies and organization, sometimes at odds with the Founding Mothers. After complex pullings and haulings, ladylike enough but fervent, the delegates at the WCTU's national convention of 1879 made her national president to carry out her notions. Thenceforth till her death, she and that post were identical, like Connie Mack and the Athletics.

In getting the WCTU to accept as motto "For God and Home and Native Land," she had already imposed her tactics on it. That "home" motif came to her, she said, on hearing a speech about Canada's policy of "home protection." Though aware that the context was economic, she suddenly saw the destiny of the WCTU as Protection of the Home, that locus of all things bright and beautiful—and womanly—through Temperance and, if she had her way, numerous other promising channels of moral Reform. The same convention that adopted her motto in 1877 had rejected her proposal to implement it by plumping for votes-for-women as the best way to get the Demon proscribed. "We do not propose to trail our skirts through the mire of politics," said her hoity-toity principal opponent. Miss Willard smiled thinly in sisterly charity and set about a three-year tug-of-war between Mrs. Wittenmyer's majority committed to the single-minded crusade specified in the WCTU's title and her own growing minority yearning to use this mighty weapon forged by the Crusaders for any cause likely to protect, or better still, exalt Woman. Though she won her presidency on organizational issues, her "Do-everything policy" came into office with her and was modified only after she died nineteen energetic years later.

It soon came to mean not only Women's Rights but support of the struggling labor movement; of kindergartens; of anti-tobaccoism; also No-Tight-Lacing and the version of vegetarianism taught at the crank Kellogg Sanitarium at Battle Creek, Michigan; also Temperance propaganda among lumberjacks and the tiny U.S. Armed Forces; also recruitment and supervision of the Loyal Temperance Legion, a juvenile auxiliary that attained an enrollment of 250,000. In the WCTU's great days these "departments" numbered close to forty. The soundest single achievement was forcing many municipalities to install police matrons. The most vapid was the "Flower Mission" that sent the ladies invading jails on Sundays to present dainty bouquets, each with a written Bible text, to the flabbergasted prisoners; surely Dr. Rush's watermelons were a better notion. And the most intimate was the "Social Purity Department," sometimes alias "The White Cross" after a similar British movement, that fought for chastity in that darkling plain where drink and sex are shamelessly entangled.

Its clearest purpose was to pledge boys to premarital chastity. The complementary White Shield promoted legislation against white-slaving and tried to help rehabilitate prostitutes and other "fallen women" whose disgrace was associated with drink. For Miss Willard had early determined that "intemperance and impurity are iniquity's Siamese twins . . . every house of ill-repute is a secret saloon and nearly every inmate an inebriate." Feelingly she warned of "the inflamed nature of men, let loose from the two hundred and fifty thousand saloons of the nation upon the weak and unarmed women, whose bewildering danger it is to have attracted [their] savage glances." She taught that far from being lesser evils, "malt liquors and wines have special powers to tarnish the sacred springs of being"; that is, to erode the true woman's natural instinct for purity. Some good came of it all as the WCTU harassed embarrassed legislators into raising scandalously low statutory ages-of-consent to levels better reflecting the facts of life. But that was not all gain, for it opened up a flourishing new field for blackmailers.

The brainwashing of American youth was, however, the important achievement of this mighty engine for God-and-Home-and-Native-Land. All authorities, from the *Encyclopaedia of Social Sciences* to the Anti-Saloon League, agreed on that. This was the work of the "Department of Scientific Temperance Instruction," special concern of Mrs. Mary Hannah Hunt of Hyde Park, Massachusetts. She had earned the job by persuading Hyde Park, a local option township near Boston, to impose on its public schools the *Temperance Lesson Book* of Dr. B. W. Richardson, which was sponsored by the National Temperance Society. Her assignment from Miss Willard was to expand this promising line of attack on "the sullen fortress of moderate drinking"—my favorite among all the Queen's great phrases—by conditioning the rising generation against the Demon. The first state-level victory, laws requiring "Temperance education" in all public schools, came in Vermont in 1882. Within twenty years—for Mrs. Hunt was almost as able as her chieftainess—every state and territory in the Union had given in to her Amazons hurling petitions and delegations and graphic representations of hobnailed livers at legislators and governors.

The "physiology instruction" that resulted usually used WCTU-inspired or -endorsed textbooks. The fragmentary general instruction about the human body that they provided was only sugar-coating for the main purpose of inculcating anti-alcohol propaganda, often irresponsible, sometimes wildly inaccurate. *Hygienic Physiology,* imposed on California high schools in 1887 taught that alcohol "impedes digestion, clogs the brain . . . turns the liver quickly from yellow to green to black . . . hardens and shrinks the liver . . . or else swells it to two or three times its normal size . . . much the same effect on the kidneys . . ." and had a new version of the old yarn—a Boston doctor bleeding a drunken patient and finding a match would set the drawn blood alight. These skillfully written works hammered it into their captive audiences that alcohol was categorically a poison in the same terms as arsenic; that to take a drink probably spelled alcoholic ruin; that beverage alcohol doomed the imbiber's offspring to hereditary taints. . . . Thus the millions of otherwise inaccessible children who had not the advantage of Temperance-minded parents or seldom if ever saw Sunday school—the accepted place for infecting small fry with Dry ideas—were soaked in intensive and apparently authoritative Temperance propaganda *at public expense.* It beat Cold Water Armies and Loyal Temperance Legions all hollow, and paid off admirably. For most of the boy-children thus worked over in the 1880's were well into voting age in the period 1905–1918, say, when Prohibition won its greatest victories at the polls, both state and national. It is a wonder that the Dry majorities were not greater. The immensely wide readership that *Uncle Tom's Cabin* got in the 1850's is believed by historians to have similarly readied the boys of the nation to be the young men who rushed to volunteer to fight the Southern slaveholder.

A prime reason why the WCTU did so well was that Miss Willard had reorganized it, placing her emphasis on high individual responsibility. Each member of a local Union was a committee of one with a year-round local responsibility: "Is an exposition to be held, or a state or county fair?" the Queen explained. "There is a woman in the locality who knows it is her business to see that the W.C.T.U. has an attractive booth with temperance literature and temperance drinks . . . [and to] secure . . . by-laws requiring the teetotal absence of intoxicants from the ground and buildings. . . . Is there a convocation of ministers, doctors, teachers, editors . . . there is a woman thereabouts who knows it is her business to secure . . . a resolution favoring the temperance movement. Is there a Legislature about to meet . . . there is a woman near at hand . . . making the air heavy with the white hovering wings of petitions . . . for prohibition . . . the better protection of girls and women . . . preventing the sale of tobacco to minors . . ."

This "Do-everything" policy was so like the Prohibition Party's eclectic adoption of good causes that it can have surprised nobody when Miss Willard allied her WCTU with it and wangled its statewide tickets of 1882 into using the name "Prohibition Home Protection Party" as acknowledgment of the marriage. For the nationwide campaign of 1884 "National Prohibition Party" was somewhat sheepishly resumed. Nevertheless it was Miss Willard, refined but prehensile as Mrs. Smith well knew, who seconded that year's nomination of St. John. In 1888 she suggested and secured adoption of the white rose as Party emblem, hence her lyrical references to the immaculate affinity between the white rose and the bow of white ribbon, the WCTU's badge. (With gracious whimsy she also named her new collie pup "Prohibition," Hibbie and Hib for short.) It was certainly no coincidence that this coalition closely preceded the Party's 2000 percent jump in national popular vote in 1884 with gratifying further accretions in 1888 and 1892. True, it was a time of rising

Populist feeling such as the Party's scattergun do-good program would appeal to. But a large proportion of those votes must imply that, though WCTU ladies lacked the franchise, they could nag at their husbands and sons pretty effectively.

Miss Willard seldom nagged. She had an immense fragile charm by all accounts and great eloquence of a sort on the platform. In tête-à-têtes faint overtones of teacher-is-such-a-darling doubtless stood her in good stead. In any case she was right when comparing her strength of will to that of Elizabeth I. In her time the WCTU had its minor schisms usually due to disputes over the wisdom of alliance with the Prohibition Party. But most of its ladies remained starry-eyed about their Queen, worked for her like dogs and saw to it that she had several monuments after death.

Her statue in the Capitol in Washington, gift of Illinois in 1905, made her the first woman there honored. Her bust in New York University's Hall of Fame was set up at the peak of the Temperance movement in 1921. She may well have died at the right time, for, though not yet sixty, she had been getting flighty—toying with the *Looking Backward* kind of socialism, with phrenology, spiritualism, theosophy, and along with her advisors managing to believe that an international WCTU had an important future. She aso let them embark on a grandiose scheme for a twelve-story Women's Temple— the narcissistic sex building a shrine for itself—in downtown Chicago for national and international headquarters, self-financed by renting office space in the upper floors. The project set off a flurry of small financial disasters. Yet when her progressive anemia finally carried the Queen off in 1898 there was the Temple's Willard Hall finished and ready for her to lie in state in. She had been brought back from the East in a special funeral car on the New York Central system arranged for by that ardent Dry, Chauncey M. Depew. She had wanted fame—and got it by the original method of carrying water on one shoulder and a chip of woman's self-esteem on the other.

The WCTU was never the same. Under her successor, a merely able lady from Maine, "Do-everything" dwindled and the political flavor grew Republican. Enrollment stayed high but did not match growing population. And prestige began to slip. Under Miss Willard the WCTU had been as much urban as small-town and distinctly right-side-of-the-tracks, particularly in the Middle West, its birthplace. Now, as Dr. Joseph Gusfield's recent study of its rosters shows, among its local leaders the wives of professional and managerial husbands began to disappear and those of clerical help and skilled workmen began to replace them. As recruiting fell off in cities and large towns, growth was confined to the outlying county seats and still smaller spots—poor culture-media for the sort of glory that the queen had always had in mind for her faithful. But there was a silver lining in that too: This shift did make sure that there would be plenty of militant Dryness among menfolks in the very freshwater settlements where the newborn Anti-Saloon League would make nation-shaking use of it.

෴

"When women walk to the polls, goodbye Mr. Booze!"
—Mrs. Florence D. Richard, president of the Ohio
State WCTU (1915)

In 1912 Jack London, at the height of his fame as a rugged author, rode into town from his California ranch and voted for woman suffrage. His wife, whom he called "mate-woman," found this curious—he had shown small zeal for Women's Rights. He explained that he did it because women were bound to use their new votes to "drive the nails into the coffin of John Barleycorn," and as one who had got little better than a draw in a bone-crushing struggle with that grim genie out of the bottle, he, Jack London, was all for anything, even woman-imposed Prohibition, likely to bury him deep once and for all.

On such implications of votes-for-women the frightened liquor interests had long agreed with him. So, we know, did Miss Willard and Mrs. Livermore, always with a foot in the feminist camp; so did old-line militants like Mrs. Stanton and Miss Anthony. Dr. Giele has shown a considerable "interlocking directorate" situation between the two movements involving second-echelon figures. This affinity had the strength of inner logic. Few respectable women drank, no decent ones frequented saloons, saloons were men's cultural fastnesses. Therefore whatever diminished drinking, particularly whatever undermined the saloon, weakened Man's world and relatively favored Woman's.

Yet, however natural this nexus, it grew uneasier as it neared the twentieth century. For Women's Righters the ballot was the main goal, and consequent ability to vote down the Demon only one of many status-improving blessings to result. But the WCTU's sights, particularly among the subalterns and rank-and-file, were primarily on annihilating the Demon, with potential beneficent side effects on Woman welcome but incidental. (Dr. Giele says that Suffragists were basically hoping to uplift women, whereas Temperance women had "hope in the improvement of men" first in view—a point worth thinking of.) Though the difference was partly one of emphasis it could cause grave frictions. Suffragists would be softening up a state to give women the vote on the sound grounds that they were as intelligent as men and on the specious promise that their votes would clean up politics—never so much as mentioning Prohibition—and then along would come the WCTU shouting for votes-for-women as the quickest way to reach Prohibition. Immediately the climate would change, legislators would begin to think it over, think twice, in fact. . . .

California had a classic example in 1896: Miss Anthony, shrewdly planning her campaign for a votes-for-women constitutional referendum, asked the WCTU to keep altogether out of things. Miss Willard promised that it would. But though the national organization kept to the letter of its word, too many Californian White Ribboners, too keen on Demon-hunting, openly promised that once the amendment carried, they would use women's votes to wipe out distilling and wine-making in the state.

"It was enough," Miss Anthony wrote bitterly. "The wine growers organized . . . the newspapers cooled perceptibly, and many of them, just before election, advised their readers

to vote against woman suffrage. So the amendment was lost.
. . ." Honing her pen on her temper, she told Miss Willard:
". . . if women ever get the right to vote it must be through
the consent of not only the moral and decent men . . . but
also that of the other kind. Is it not perfectly idiotic . . . to
be telling the latter class that the first thing we will do with
our ballots will be to knock them out of their pleasures and
vices? If you still think it wise to keep sticking pins in the
men, you will have to go on doing it. I shall certainly not be
one of your helpers in that particular line of work." Miss Anthony continued to maintain for the rest of her life that to
give women full political rights would suffuse politics with
new candor and honesty, eliminating subterfuge and manipulation.

Presently women themselves were making the WCTU look
a little tacky. Dr. Giele's researches lead her to suggest that
"the alert young woman" of some education—say a strong-
minded graduate of one of the fast-developing women's colleges or a coeducational Midwestern university—seeking a
cause to try her mettle, came to prefer Women's Rights to
Temperance because Temperance was becoming dowdy and
had nothing like glamorous Inez Milholland on her white
horse marshaling votes-for-women parades on Fifth Avenue.

It may be sadly significant that the most striking female
figure in Temperance after Frances Willard died was Carry
A. Nation, always corny, usually vulgar and intermittently
psychotic. The last term is well justified not only by her behavior but because there are known genetic factors in some
mental illnesses and the poor woman had a dismal family history—her daughter, a first cousin, her mother, her mother's
mother and sister, all developed severe mental troubles usually ending in institutionalization. That keeps Carry Nation
from being the figure of fun that many of her contemporaries
took her for.

But she did amount to a sort of painful travesty of the
Temperance Woman: Her childhood passed in Bluegrass
Kentucky; her Bible- and fantasy-haunted teens were spent in
Missouri in its viciously disturbed Civil War period. But her
mother's delusions of being Queen Victoria—no metaphor

but psychotic fact—ensured that her rearing was strict. At the age of nineteen the plain, tall, husky girl married a young physician who, having learned to drink and smoke too much in the federal army, did both so assiduously that he died in six months, leaving her pregnant. The rest of her life she hated alcohol, tobacco—and secret societies because her husband, a Mason, used the local Masonic Hall, from which she was barred, as a refuge during and after his sprees. In a low-grade Syndromism she also hated and shrilly denounced many other things and persons: William McKinley, Theodore Roosevelt, Republicans generally (though sometimes claiming to be one), tight corsets, foreign cooking, low-necked gowns. Some were connected with her disastrous marriage, some reflected the effect of her scrawny background on her bitterly sick temperament.

After a discouraging try at schoolteaching she met another war veteran—bearded, middle-aged David Nation, country newspaperman today, lawyer tomorrow, Campbellite preacher off and on—and by marrying him acquired the surname that she would make notorious. Taking along the doctor's small daughter and dependent mother—for Carry had streaks of quixotic benevolence—the couple went to Texas to raise cotton. When that failed to pay they made do bleakly with his newspapering and her dogged management of a cheap hotel with few resources and less help. Then they traipsed back north into southern Kansas to settle in a county seat named Medicine Lodge.

Kansas was already Dry by constitutional amendment but Prohibition was as slackly enforced there as in most places. Medicine Lodge, little more than a village, had seven blind pigs—"joint" was the local term—and a flourishing business smuggling liquor into Oklahoma Territory just over the county line. Already well into middle age, Carry stayed within normal bounds in combating the local Demon. She merely joined the Baptist minister's wife in forming a local branch of the WCTU and became its "jail evangelist," harassing the frowsy inmates of the lockup with prayer and Temperance reading matter. She also went in for other good works, distributing Christmas baskets and old clothes to the needy, riding herd on young folks' morals and throwing her weight around in the local Campbellite congregation. But emotional pressures must have been building up in her, for she experienced occasional seizures of what she called "a heavenly rapture" consisting of a sense of supernally exalted and personal communion with Christ. In her accounts they sound like authentic mystical experiences; or maybe the menopause played a part? Anyway they deeply impressed her and enhanced her sense of being important to the sinful world.

Hers was a Bible world and a self-pitying woman's world in terms that sound like satire of man-mistrusting feminism: From the Proverbs of Solomon she described "God's ideal of a woman" as "the overseer in her house to see that her husband is instructed in good ways" who won't "set a bad example by going to theatres and card parties . . . sees that her son and daughter are not out late . . . [take] no rich foods or drinks to inflame the animal passions, no thin extravagant dresses, no 'peekaboo' waists. . . ." She grasped at votes-for-women as a defensive weapon against men. Many a whore had told her, she said, that when her husband "drank and went with other women, I got discouraged or spiteful and went to the bad also." And she reduced the WCTU's motto to absurdity by putting the name "Home Defenders" on her own Kansas-wide organization of bar-smashing she-vigilantes. Her daughter's recurring psychosis she attributed to her husband's drinking combined with her own "distraction" at the time of conception due to his drinking. She had ominous tales about men who fell dead in their tracks soon after she denounced them for crossing her, and often guided her actions by opening the Bible at random . . . very like the Women Crusaders. They would certainly have approved the logic of her clearest statement of her position: "Anything that is sinful cannot be lawful, and anything that is lawful cannot be sinful. The saloon is not lawful because it is sinful."

In 1899 the sinfulness of those flagrantly unlawful joints in Medicine Lodge, reinforced by what she saw of the drunks in the jail, finally set her boiling over. With the Baptist minister's wife she took a portable harmonium into the streets and held casual hymn-and-prayer meetings outside the joints on Saturday afternoons. Then one afternoon she ventured inside a bar and made scenes that roused the local righteous women to mass behind her and close down the places that the authorities had been doing nothing about. Early the next summer she had a spell of praying at home in sackcloth and ashes—literally donning a gunnysack mantle and sprinkling ashes on her graying head—and soon a voice in the night woke her and told her to go clean out the joints in Kiowa, a sopping-wet village nearby.

She went alone armed with throwing-size stones wrapped in newspaper, invaded three bars and singing hymns the while, smashed up the bottles and the back-of-bar mirrors. The thunderstruck owners' protests got her threatened with arrest for destroying property. Her remarks in rebuttal about the utter illegality of the property she destroyed were so scathing that the cowed authorities let her leave town unhindered. The noise of those breaking decanters went all over the state. Reveling in righteousness and notoriety, she invaded Wichita, wettest and second largest city in Kansas. Her assault on the bar of its best hotel got her jailed for the first time. She disrupted the jail with her hymns, prayers and complaints of mistreatment, and emerged after some weeks on bail furnished by local Drys saying that she had assumed that "God intended to make me a sacrifice as He did John Brown"—a comparison that she frequently made. Late that winter she again invaded Wichita, mustering the most militant ladies of the local WCTU to help smash the joints again. Her disciples carried iron bars and newspaper-wrapped stones; but under her own cloak Carry Nation clutched a bright-edged hatchet which she used so devastatingly on the joints' stock and fixtures that it became her mascot-symbol, like Arthur's Excalibur. It put an extra touch on her revival of the mob techniques of the 1850's, making her immortal as the Harridan with the Hatchet like Florence Nightingale as the Lady with the Lamp.

Even before she took up smashing, her style had not been the ladylike, sweet-hour-of-prayer sort of thing affected by the Women's Crusade. Carry Nation strode in to sing and holler at the top of her considerable lungs. She adjured the rum-seller to cease and desist not as a dear, erring brother but as a besotted, law-breaking, booze-sodden, soul-killing, filth-smeared spawn of the Devil, or words to that effect. To the naked power of prayer she added umbrella, iron bar or hatchet—indeed, toward the end she carried three hatchets dubbed Faith, Hope and Charity. Her raiding outfit consisted of a high-cut, long-sleeved black dress with a white bow at the throat and a small white bonnet, the whole a rather Deaconess-like effect; a hatchet in hand; and over the shoulder a satchel containing a stock of toy-sized souvenir hatchets, sales of which were a principal part of her re-sources. . . .

It was a striking figure and show business soon noticed it. Lecture agents attracted by the national publicity created by her Wichita capers made offers. She needed money to pay off her accumulating court fines as well as to live on—her husband had ceased to mean much in her life—so she took to the platform both independently and as an attraction on Chautauqua circuits, where practically anything of Temperance flavor was welcome. Wherever she went she usually attracted crowds as if she had been a fire or a fight, and managed to get arrested often enough to guarantee continuing publicity—not only for hatchetizing bars but also for such antics as starting a riot in a Pittsburgh streetcar by vilifying a man wearing a Masonic emblem and for trying to scream her way into the White House to scold President Theodore Roosevelt for smoking cigarettes, as she had heard he did.

In late 1903 she was featured attraction of a revival of *Ten Nights* with a newly written-in role that gave her a bar-smashing scene. Sometimes the show was billed as *Hatchetation* as it slogged through one-night stands in the darkest Pennsylvania of Shamokin, Reading, Coatesville and so on. The newspapers give glimpses of her performance in Elizabeth, New Jersey: interpolating harangues in her stage scenes and making a curtain speech for what she called Pro-high-bition plus votes-for-women: "Who hath sorrow? Who hath woe? They can't deny it! They can't say No!" she would yell. "Women is the gardeen and pro-high-bition votes are the hatchets which will destroy the saloon! God gave Samson the jawbone! He gave David the sling, and he has given Carry Nation the hatchet!" After more and more such vociferous rigmarole seasoned with howlings about corsets and tobacco, she went among the audience to shake hands and sell souvenir hatchets.

The reporters had their fun with her, pointing out that the room where this production of *Ten Nights* had rehearsed was over one of the most notorious dives in New York's Tenderloin and describing her (in Baltimore, where the show broke in): "Carry is pudgy. Carry doesn't lace. Carry is aggressive. Carry has exactly enough nose to furnish a rest for her glasses —no more." She probably flinched a little but went on making a holy show of herself and selling hatchets, screaming down hecklers with her own non-obscene billingsgate and proclaiming—which was true—that the proceeds over her own Spartan living expenses went to pay off her fines and to the Home for Drunkards' Wives and Mothers that she was trying to found in Kansas City, Kansas. With such temperaments one never knows when the freewheeling delusion of grandeur slips over into deliberate hamming-it-up. In neither phase, however, was she half as funny as her contemporaries thought they were making her look.*

Her crudity made many Temperance ladies shy off. Susan B. Anthony censured her severely. Frances Willard probably would have done so too. But the Uncrowned Queen had passed on just before Carry began to show violent symptoms. Sometimes locally—at least once nationally if reluctantly—the WCTU lent some support. Her Home Defenders in Kansas seem to have been elite shock troops from local WCTU ranks and developed several subaltern-imitators whom Carry, in classic paranoid style, detested and mistrusted. When she died in 1911 she was fumbling with the notion of a training school for Dry crusaders. It is difficult to agree with the late Herbert Asbury that she was a principal factor in the victory of Pro-

---

* She was exhumed for a final fling on the stage in a biographical play, *Carry Nation*, at the Biltmore Theatre, New York, October 30, 1932, with Esther Dale, wife of the author (Frank McGrath) in the title role. The reviews make it sound pretty cumbrous. The most notable thing about it now is that minor roles were filled by Mildred Natwick and Joshua Logan.

hibition. In her time major credit certainly goes to the fast-stepping Anti-Saloon League; and by then the WCTU already had the bulk of Protestant, churchgoing women utterly convinced of the loathsomeness of the Demon and the iniquities of the saloon. Mrs. Nation did give the cause wide publicity but in terms so raucous as to do the image of Temperance Woman more harm than good. She was, however, interesting as another instance of a law of Reformism: the longer an organized good cause persists, the lower the tone of its tactics and exponents. Her most lasting monument has been the words of "The Eyes of Texas Are Upon You," composed in 1903 by students at the University of Texas after the president thereof, reproaching them for inviting "this poor, deluded woman" to speak on campus, said : "Remember . . . the eyes of Texas are upon you. You are expected to uphold her traditions and not act as hoodlums. . . ."

From the WCTU's point of view another misfortune of the 1900's was that the tide of No-Decent-Woman-Drinks began to recede. A snowballing increase in travel to Europe probably had much to do with it. Deep thinkers of the time saw in it either a symptom of decline in moral standards beginning as usual at the top of society; or a welcome hint that cracks in the rigidity of "Puritan" morals were gradually infecting the country with hedonistic values. Anyway, well before the end of the nineteenth century European visitors reported how liberally the girls at posh parties dipped their pretty beaks into the champagne and punch of the buffet. As the 1900's progressed, viewers-with-alarm scolded lady shoppers for taking "hot ginger"—highly alcoholic Jamaica ginger with boiling water—as a remedy for winter chill at the drugstore counter and deplored the readiness with which they discovered that the same store sold excellent liquors to take home. The rising custom of tea-dancing often saw tea ordered for the lady in the shape of sherry or claret lemonade. A *Life* cartoon of 1913 shows as "The Timid Debutante" a highly décolletée girl seated on a table with a cigarette hanging from her lip as she reaches out a cocktail glass which a handsome youth is filling from a shaker. The new country clubs saw "alcoholic girls . . . [wearing] silk stockings . . . shouting for highballs," years before Flaming Youth began officially even to glow. As early as 1903 the parson of a fashionable church in Philadelphia became alarmedly aware that at smart weddings and receptions "in families that for generations have been practicing total abstinence the punch-bowl is now coming in . . . wine is patronized by the church people to an alarming extent." Worse still, in some large cities women were openly ordering cocktails in public, and "not lewd women," the witness wrote bewilderedly, "[but] frequently . . . members of leading Protestant churches. Surely, it is time to call a halt."

Surely, surely. And here came the Anti-Saloon League to organize small-town "members of leading Protestant churches" to do just that.

13

THE SALOON
MUST GO!

The average self-respecting young man will shudder with disgust at the mere thought of hunting up a sneaking bootlegger.

—*Cyclopedia of Temperance and Prohibition* (1891)

FIVE years before Frances Willard died, a minister in Conneaut, Ohio, thus introduced a visiting preacher to his congregation: "There was a man sent from God whose name was John . . . there was a man sent from God whose name was Russell . . ." It verged on blasphemy but that probably never occurred to the Rev. Howard Hyde Russell, the subject of this extravagance. He had known he was God-piloted for years, ever since he had been holding tent revivals with strong Temperance overtones in Kansas City, Missouri, and daily passing a large brewery: "Always when I passed this devil's broth factory," he wrote for posterity, "I prayed to God to stay the tide of sin and shame flowing therefrom . . . and whenever I passed a saloon I sent up a prayer, 'O God, stop this! . . . [Finally] God plainly said to me, 'You know how to do it; go and help answer your own prayers!' "

Obedience was considerably delayed while Russell took over a slum-mission in Chicago financed by Philip Armour, the plutocratic meat packer. But all during that interval at ministerial and Temperance gatherings God's chosen instrument agitated for God's plan—a league of Protestant religious sects powerful enough to get Rum outlawed. And that was what he was authorized to create in 1893, when pious persons meeting in the First Congregational Church of Oberlin, Ohio—always a nest of hot-Temperance and keen Syndromism—formed the Ohio Anti-Saloon League destined to be the nucleus of the most ruthless good-cause lobby the United States ever saw. There and then the dream of nation-wide Prohibition first became potentially real. The League succeeded where others had failed because it learned to jettison scruples. "Why," it asked in effect, "should the Devil throw all the sneaky curves?"

Its achingly upright founder had been sired by an Episcopalian minister in Minnesota in 1855, the year when the Sons of Temperance first plumped for nationwide constitutional Prohibition far, far ahead of their time. Young Howard tried this and that here and there, eventually taking up law in Iowa, developing a promising practice and marrying his preceptor's godly-minded daughter. Temperance came naturally to Russell: He had had an alcoholic brother. His years in Iowa coincided with the state's most feverish Wet-vs.-Dry paroxysms. His last client in an Iowa court was a woman suing a barkeeper for selling liquor to her known-alcoholic husband. When Mrs. Russell discovered that he cherished a righteous dream of quitting the law for the pulpit, she so heartily encouraged it that at the age of twenty-eight he pulled up stakes and moved to Oberlin to study theology, very much as Miss Willard's father had in the generation before him. Whiskery good looks and an earnest, already professionally developed forensic skill brought him into high favor in both town and college. In due time ordained a Congregationalist minister, he took a pulpit in nearby Berea, a suburb of Cleveland, and was so active in a vigorous no-license contest there that a militant Wet knocked him down in the street. When no-license won and blind pigs sprang up, he resumed the practice of law to help prosecute them.

It was all admirable preparation for God's eventual command and the job of forging the newly created League into the irresistible weapon that He had in mind. Confidently he moved his family to Columbus, Ohio, to launch it with the very meager funds that were all his Oberlin sponsors could yet scrape together. Later he gloried in recalling how his wife—Spartan woman!—accepted the necessary economic comedown, actually put up with a ten-dollar-a-month house, "dismissed her maid and bravely did all the housework herself." She also put up several hundred dollars cash from a paternal legacy to keep the household eating until Russell's frantic organizing campaigns finally got some financial water under the League's keel.

In those trying first years "often the tears of parting [fell] as the father went forth" on organizing forays into rural Ohio, unflinchingly facing country boardinghouse biscuits, livery stable buggies with cracked storm curtains, and cindery day coaches. His small son asked: "Papa, why do you go so far away to fight saloons? There are some right here on the street. You can stay at home with us and fight them." The little shaver did not understand that at that stage in the League's development a large town like Columbus meant little except as seat of the legislature and hub of the railroad system that took Papa out into the sticks where first things came first. The turn of Columbus' rumsellers would come after the wide places in the road were organized.

Parallel efforts at "Anti-Saloon Leagues" had appeared in Massachusetts, Pennsylvania, and a few other states. These soon coalesced with the Ohio League into a national organization taking tone and tactics from Ohio and Russell. He worked God's scheme out from the grassroots up: He would descend on, say, Walnut Grove, Freshwater County, Ohio, and persuade the members of the two or three local churches, usually with their ministers' approval, to form local Leagues. Local duties were to collect and forward funds to headquarters; spread Dry propaganda supplied from headquarters; move heaven and earth for local no-license; vote as the League told them to in state local and county elections; send women and children also to the polls to picket and plead with all voters: "Mister, for God's sake, don't vote for whiskey!" Every year state headquarters arranged an Anti-Saloon League special service in each affiliated church with an outsider spellbinder shouting against The Saloon and securing renewed pledges of allegiance, zeal, money and votes. On request, Walnut Grove was also supplied with outside legal and detective talent to harass local rumsellers.

State headquarters' particular function was, however, to drive ahead on the state level, bullying legislators into passing stronger anti-Demon measures extending local-option to county level; or stiffening license requirements; or setting heavier penalties on violation of liquor laws . . . anything to keep the sins of The Saloon in the public eye, all of it working toward statewide Prohibition arrived at either piecemeal or by blanket state law. The several state-level "superintendents" were primarily responsible only to the national board, which was pretty much self-perpetuating. There was nothing democratic about the Anti-Saloon League. But that was in itself an advantage: it left each state-level viceroyalty an admirably free hand in wielding the League's weapons, chief among which was the minority bloc.

Avoiding the Prohibition Party's ingenuous mistake, the League went in for no extraneous good causes. (Occasional mild support for woman's suffrage on Jack London's principle was the sole exception.) It allowed no separate Dry tickets either. It had firmly in mind what the Prohibitionists had done to Blaine in 1884, but applied the lesson within the two-party framework, where its obedient minority bloc of Dry-pledged voters could be vital to the winning candidate in any given election. In a legislative district in central Indiana, say, where the total vote usually ran some 20,000, the Republican usually winning by 1,000, a stalwart phalanx of 3,000 Leaguers voting all one way at the word of command would mean win or lose.

To determine how to swing this whip the League regularly asked candidates for public office: "How do you stand on . . ." anti-Demon measures likely to come up during their terms of office. When both candidates meekly promised to vote against the Demon at every opportunity, the League stayed out of it, merely keeping a wary eye on subsequent actions. When one weasled or admitted Wet leanings and his opponent professed righteousness, the opponent got those captive League votes. If neither sounded satisfactory, the League might put up an entry of its own to be withdrawn before election in favor of whoever knuckled under in time. Democrat or Republican, the conscientious League voter made no distinction. These highminded minorities were like medieval mercenaries willing to fight on whichever side made it worth their while and implicitly obeying the orders of the chiefs who made the deals.

None of that was new in either highminded or corrupt politics: British Emancipationists combined this put-the-candidate-on-the-spot technique with a militant minority of voters to get the West Indian slaves freed in the 1830's. Wet politicians in large cities in New York had long used subtler versions of it. The Blaine episode had set several Dry groups trying it. But it took the League to get real mileage out of such "Nonpartisanship," as it called this cool exploitation of a basic flaw in representative government. Politicians still doubting the Anti-Saloon League's power got religion once and for all after the election of 1904 in Ohio. The incumbent Republican governor, Myron T. Herrick, had countenanced dilution of a local-option bill. The League secured 100,000 signatures on a petition opposing his renomination, but the State Republican convention, dominated by Wet-minded Cincinnati, put him back on the ticket. The League turned to the Democrats, jockeyed them into nominating a pious, Dry insurance executive and backed him all the way. Herrick had won by 113,000 his first term. This time he lost by 43,000 and ran far behind his ticket. "Never again," said the League's high command, "will any political party ignore the protests of the church and moral forces in [this] state." No more need to hark back to Blaine: "Remember what happened to Herrick" was thenceforth printed in invisible ink on every League letterhead.

It soon ceased to matter much whether League-endorsed candidates were themselves teetotal. It was better when they were so, true. But under the statehouse dome a vote was a vote. Many a frock-coated, string-tied legislator voting Dry and getting reelected by grace and favor of the League was just as rugged a drinker as his colleague at the next desk who voted Wet partly because he believed in booze but partly also because most of his campaign funds came from the distilleries in his district. The League's faithful had no scruples against voting in booze-fighting time-servers whose only recommendation was willingness to truckle, as against temperate, able rivals rejecting the League's soul-mortgaging compact written on Bible paper and signed in pure cold water. This was flagrant disregard of the general welfare in favor of a single fanatic scheme. But it got the League the best of both worlds—exploiting democratic election of legislators in order to further undemocratic manipulation in the statehouse. Significantly the League usually preferred to seek Dry laws from

legislatures rather than put the issue up to statewide referenda, as was the growing political fashion of the day.

Those tactics, which some called hypocritical, were one
cause of the enmity between the League and the less supple-
minded Prohibition Party. (Another was the Party's sulky
conviction that the intrusion of the League in the mid-1890's,
just when the future looked rosy, had stunted its growth.)
But the League hardly bothered to apologize for its cynicism,
any more than the veterans' lobby does now, and its members
went on dutifully voting for known heavy drinkers whenever
God asked it. That was the triumphant fruit of those scores of
years of dinning Temperance into the young of Methodists
and Baptists—the double backbone of the League—making
the Demon out so hideous and the rumseller so vicious that
any means to do them down was altogether holy and righteous.

Not all churches countenanced these methods. The Episcopalians, Lutherans and certain minor sects were usually
lukewarm and often drew hard language from the League for
refusing the use of their pulpits to its spellbinders. But many
Congregationalist, Presbyterian and other congregations followed Methodists and Baptists in letting the League have its
way with them. Funds thus raised were used for, among other
things, the creation of a large publishing house at Westerville, Ohio, near Columbus, eclipsing the old National
Temperance Society and Publication House with *The American Issue,* a paper with split-run state editions, and tons of
other propaganda.

The League's command were mostly former preachers and
pretty able men. So were most of its state superintendents.
And though the nation was emerging from the period when,
to judge from the results of elections, Presidents of the
United States had to come from Ohio, it was significant of the
League's marked freshwater flavor that most of its leaders
were Midwesterners, and most of those from Ohio.

Ablest of Russell's Ohioan recruits was Wayne B. Wheeler,
demure, self-admiring hatchet man primarily responsible for
the humbling of Herrick and many another before and after
him. A farm boy, Wayne began first to dislike the Demon
when a tipsy neighbor accidentally speared him in the leg

with a hayfork. After high school he turned teacher till he had saved enough to get a start at Oberlin College, where he worked his way through as janitor, waiter, and book-agent in vacations—the usual story of the ambitious, tireless strive-and-succeeder. He also had time for debating, class football and the bicycle cult of the day. The nascent Anti-Saloon League's organizational meeting found him in the front row of the gallery where Russell, speaker of the evening, happened to single him out, as orators often do, as the specific person to talk at. Overwhelmed, Wayne pledged a quarter a month from his meager resources to support God's new agency. As the end of his senior year approached it was he whom the Oberlin faculty proposed when Russell asked for a youngster "tireless, tactful, optimistic, resourceful, a good speaker, a good mixer, a loving-spirited, self-sacrificing soul" to become a League district manager. The career that ensued made Wheeler as well known in his time as William Jennings Bryan. He loved being conspicuous—and conspicuously denounced, which he soon was by both persons of liberal common sense and politicians aghast at the ruthless skill with which he used the minority-vote weapon. He loved power, which was good because the League never paid well. Half what he did so cleverly for it would have made him a small fortune as a corporation lawyer in Cleveland.

He broke in as scourge of The Saloon by infiltrating rural areas on his bicycle, doing as much as anybody to shape the League's blackjack, blandly defining its purpose as "to make it safe for [legislators] to vote right." When the League needed a legal staffer, he studied law on trains and in the evenings and had a law degree within four years. Eventually national counsel for the League, he not only helped to prosecute over 2,000 Dry-law cases but continually drafted and promoted such laws. Neat-mustached, starchily dressed, he looked like the cashier of a middle-sized bank, not at all the umbrella-brandishing, black-gloved, stovepipe-hatted, gaunt ascetic whom Rollin Kirby, great cartoonist of the New York *World,* made the national symbol of the Dry cause. Yet he remained a hayseed at heart. In his view the war on the Demon was basically righteous-country-vs.-vicious-city. He called cities "un-American, lawless and wet." William Cowper's line about "God made the country and man made the town" was always in his mouth. His rustic rearing and early battles with the liquor interests of Cincinnati account for the intensity of his feeling. His efforts to use Ohio's rural Dry minority—never over a third of the voting population even on his estimate—to impose crossroads ideas about drink on the whole state trained him in how to dominate national politics.

Throughout he had the born operator-politician's zest for the hidden ball and the stolen signal. He specialized in infiltrating meetings of the counter-organizations set up by Ohio's brewers and distillers. On one occasion he managed it by falling into conversation on the train with a delegate to such a "Personal Liberty League," finding him uncertain what to say in a speech he was to make—and earning his gratitude and an admission badge by writing an eloquent anti-Dry speech for him. Russell soon lagged far behind this dapper Mephistopheles whom he had conjured up from the academic shades of Oberlin. When he objected to Wheeler's cultivation of the Foraker crowd of Wet-minded Ohio politicians, the young fellow said maybe the League would need a friend in that camp sometime. When the press gleefully pointed out that the League-endorsed candidate for mayor of Cincinnati owned two saloons, Wheeler, aware how firmly the gentleman was bound to Dry chariot-wheels, said evenly that "owning saloons doesn't have anything to do with his official actions." Neal Dow might well have gone along with that. But it would have been near the death of that sounder Quaker, Anthony Benezet.

The prohibition law sprang from the soil and soul. It germinated in remote and sacred places where mothers pray and fathers think.
    —GENERAL EVANGELINE BOOTH of the Salvation Army

The League's doctrine of city-vs.-country had a good deal in it. There really was a sharp, significant contrast between

the Old-White-Protestant-American, farm-oriented, preacher-
ridden, culturally Temperance-minded tank towns where the
League best flourished and the industrialized cities that con-
tained the bulk of the new immigrant population. That climate was mostly Catholic, its politics were saloon-based, most
of the barkeeps were Irish or German, and the premises often
harbored prostitutes and gambling. In those neighborhoods
the idea that beer and wine—or whiskey on payday evening—
were immoral poisons struck the Poles and Italians of Pittsburgh or Chicago as just another crazy American notion.
And on the right side of the tracks ornate private clubs and
fancy hotels kept lively the notorious affinities (in the rural
mind) between sin and drink on another and equally alien
level. Thus, resentment of high-toned urban extravagance
blended with hostility toward Sabbath-breaking furriners
with their beer gardens and rumselling precinct leaders. It
bulked large among the emotions that had written Reform
planks of the Prohibition Party's platforms and now kept
monthly contributions fattening the League's war chest.

The cleavage was not as clean, however, as is sometimes
represented. The sinful big city's well-off suburbs were utterly unrural, yet they often voted Dry on local-option because saloons were low and attracted undesirables. That was
part of the upper-vs.-lower-orders flavor that had always been
strong in Temperance. Many of the middle-aged persons
flocking to Southern California in the "Pullman migration"
of the early 1900's were of that same fat-cat stripe and had
much to do with making Los Angeles a large city that was
also a nest of Dry sentiment. Before the battle culminated in
Prohibition, the American Medical Association and the General Federation of Women's Clubs, both essentially urban,
had endorsed the Dry cause. The city-vs.-country contrast was
further blurred when, as the League's muscle began to show,
many founders of great city-based fortunes lent it heavy support. The Rockefellers, John Wanamaker, J. L. Hudson, S. S.
Kresge, Andrew Carnegie and other industrialists and merchants only slightly less redoubtable gave money and personal encouragement. They could readily do so because, un-
like the Prohibition Party, the League had no truck with

wild-eyed ideas except suffrage—and that only on Tuesdays and Thursdays.

Some such benefactors of great wealth, like Wanamaker, contributed heavily at least partly because of their copybook-maxim, Sunday-school kind of piety. The approach of others was largely economic: That saloon at the factory gate meant hangovers, hence injuries and breakdowns that were increasingly expensive as machinery in steel mills, food-processing plants and so forth grew complicated. Then Workmen's Compensation laws making employers liable for most accidents forced them to insure and to campaign for on-the-job safety—which led to further discouragement of off-the-job drinking. An undercover man for the United States Brewers' Association also heard from an officer of the Iron and Steel Institute that employers were backing the Drys because drinking employees meant pressure for higher wages—taking booze-money out of the pay envelope left too little to buy the round steak the wife wanted. In any case, saloons, alien riffraff and labor agitation had long gone together in the boss's mind, as is made clear in T. S. Arthur's *The Strike at Tivoli Mills* (1879). The bomb scares of the 1880's left the impression that beer saloons were the typical haunts of bearded, German-reared, Anarchist assassins. In many industrial neighborhoods saloonkeepers found it good business to maintain an upstairs meeting hall for the use of union locals.

So industrialists moved from merely subsidizing the League to active help in getting its anti-Demon propaganda into the men's hands. "Read and heed this or else" was often the angle. Pay envelope slips showed a flour sack and a beer keg: "Which do you buy?" Before a statewide Prohibition referendum in Ohio, employees of a minor automobile manufacturer got a letter from the boss:

> Vote "Yes" for State Prohibition . . . Alcohol destroys the efficiency of man . . . the character and reputation of man . . . the happiness and prosperity of the home. Alcohol corrupts politics. Alcohol cheats the coming generation of an honest inheritance. Statistics show that the saloon is responsible for 75% of all crimes.
> Therefore THE SALOON OUGHT TO DIE . . .

Zealously Dry management might rule that only known non-drinkers would be promoted; or only such would be hired; or even, particularly on railroads, that known drinkers would be weeded out. Railroad directors financed "railroad YMCAs" to provide Dry away-from-home quarters for train crews. New company-created towns like Pullman, Illinois, wrote a legal ban on saloons into the buyers' title deeds. As pay checks replaced cash, saloons obligingly cashed them with the implied return obligation to do a little drinking, so Dry-minded employers might take to marking the checks void if cashed in a saloon. . . .

All such support from powerful and distinctly non-rural elements was vital to the future of Prohibition. Drys and Wets both recognized it. By 1911, John G. Woolley, famous Temperance spellbinder and former Prohibition Party candidate for President who defected to the League, was saying: "The present turn of the tide [toward Prohibition] came when the Blucher of 'business' brought its burly reenforcements into action." By 1914 Hugh F. Fox, secretary of the United States Brewers' Association, was warning his industry that though churchgoers' support for the League might be slacking off, "this deficit is made up many times by the new contributions . . . from large corporations."

At the same time, the intellectual standing of Prohibition was improving. Temperance had not yet lost its acceptability as a good cause—it took Prohibition to effect that. But it had been growing corny. Now, in the early 1900's, the atmosphere of the muckraking era rehabilitated its social standing. The times deplored unscrupulous Big Business, and the distilling and brewing interests were as noisome as any. Social service had become a profession, and the social worker's nose—often that of a fairly strait-laced lady—was often rubbed in misery attributable to The Saloon. There was a new wave of medical slander of the Demon and a shaky but flashy sociology of the same tenor, weaving alcoholism firmly into the family trees of the famous Kallikak and Jukes strains of degenerates.

When much of Big Business and most of urban Reform thus threw in with Chautauqua lecturers and crossroads deacons—John D. Rockefeller, Upton Sinclair, William Jennings Bryan and Carry Nation all in the same camp—the rumseller was a gone goose. In *The Nigger* by the brilliant young Edward Sheldon, the New York theatre saw whiskey depicted as the detonator of Negro lust and violence in the South and heard its noble politician-hero call Prohibition "the only way in which we can attack the niggah problem." Magazines were full of the scientific and social horrors of drink. Their publishers closed the advertising columns to the Demon: *Collier's, The Saturday Evening Post, The American, Harper's, The World's Work, The Review of Reviews,* most such shapers of opinion among the educated in cities and suburbs joined the juvenile and religious presses in scorning money with liquor on its breath. *Life* (a comic weekly, remember?) was one of the few holdouts. But then it was a little "fast," with smirking cartoons about above-the-knee bathing suits and a swipe at Mr. Bryan's grape juice every few months. A growing number of daily newspapers found it advisable to refuse liquor advertising. Even the new motion pictures worked in the Demon's disfavor: They gave the workingman an inexpensive evening recreation that tended to keep him out of the saloon and with his wife; and the drift of the scenarios was overwhelmingly Dry, heavy with the curse of drink, the foulness of saloons and the association of sin with wine on the table.

ᴏᴏ

"You have a nice village . . . but . . . three saloons to damn your boys. What license do they pay? . . . You have sold your boys and girls to hell and yourselves to the devil for forty cents a head."
— THE REV. SAM JONES (of Georgia)

The motif of city-vs.-country persisted, however, in the League's collective mind and was useful where it fitted—most notably in the conquest of the South. Dixie was long a special case where Temperance had not done too well. Certain Virginians had organized Southern counterparts of Northern societies. The Washingtonians and Sons of Temperance took temporary root. Father Mathew fared well in spite of threatening omens, and eminent Southerners identified with the cause before the Civil War included Augustus Baldwin Longstreet and fire-eating Senator Howell Cobb. But the coziness between Temperance and antislaveryism made many Southerners uneasy, and the area lacked a strong native Reformist tradition. Indeed the most striking Temperance development down there before the war was highly individual and significantly futile: John Jacobus Flournoy of Georgia, who tried his hand at a Temperance-based third party thirty years before the Prohibition Party.

"Deaf Flournoy," as he sometimes called himself, was "quality"—his was a known Southern name, his mother was a Cobb, he inherited a sizable plantation and slaves. Severe mental troubles shook the boy up thoroughly in his late teens. He developed speech defects and progressive deafness, and neither the famous Hartford (Conn.) School for the Deaf nor a mental asylum in North Carolina helped him much. Eventually prayer brought him round, though he remained subject to strange convulsions, had a wildly incoherent speaking style and exhibited marked eccentricities, such as riding a donkey when he could afford good horses and wearing a rubber raincoat in all weathers—which, in Georgia's steaming summers, was eccentric indeed.

An instinctive Syndromist, he espoused the "peace movement"; phrenology; Temperance, though he drank heavily when things got too much for him; defense of the Indians against the cynical oppressions of the state of Georgia; and solution of the Negro problem by sending it back to Africa. In the mid-1830's he appeared as a politics-flavored Reformer announcing for the state legislature as member of both parties. He got 10 votes. Next time a strong no-license appeal to "cold water men" raised it to 15; his third attempt netted him 25 in some 2,500 cast. He had considerable success, however, with a subsequent no-license petition in his neighborhood, and when the politicians of both factions among Georgia Democrats tried to slow down his petition-campaign, he persuaded some local Temperance groups to set up their own

Dry-pledged aspirants for the legislature. All he accomplished was to make bitter enemies in both factions. Indeed the consequent flood of abuse was so vicious that Flournoy's preacher son-in-law credited it with plunging him into greater depths of eccentricity than ever.

In the late 1850's he tried to cajole President Buchanan into appointing him ambassador to somewhere, finally offering to settle for accreditation to the Utah Mormons. He was simultaneously writing a book advocating "trigamy"—three wives for each man—and once when his wife was away, demonstrated the notion by "marrying" a thirteen-year-old girl as Wife No. Two. He also invented Flournoy's Medical Headbands "concentrating, in abstraction, the hidden virtues of Animal Magnetism, Mesmerism, Electrisity [sic], Magic, and the Manifestations of the Spirits—together with impulses from the Aurora Borealis."* The more one sees of him the less one admires the Temperance historians who treated him as a hero with no hint that the poor devil obviously suffered from the most severe mental illness ever to afflict a Temperance leader—and that is saying a great deal.

It was Frances Willard who, well after the Civil War, breached the hedge of thorns between North and South and kissed the Sleeping Beauty of Southern Temperance awake. She was apprehensive lest her Yankee-ness get her snubbed when she went touring from Maryland to Texas in 1881. But by then Reconstruction had been pretty much abandoned and her rather birdlike charm could secure her proper welcome. Mrs. Jefferson Davis was cordial though her husband took a dim view of Prohibition. The parson who introduced Miss Willard to her enthusiastic audience at Charleston, South Carolina, the former commander of a battery firing on Ft. Sumter, wound up his speech construing WCTU to mean "We Come To Unite" North and South. Maybe he picked that up from her. She actually had hopes that because her "Home Protection" revision of the Prohibition Party lacked the bitter connotations of the regular national parties, it

* The above owes much to E. Morton Coulter's monograph on Flournoy published by the Georgia Historical Society, 1942.

might take root South as well as North and itself become nationwide.

She was equally astigmatic in failing to see how much of her welcome was due to the South's problem with the former slaves. Their new freedom made it awkward to keep liquor away from them legally. Southern ladies and their husbands too concluded that local or state no-license barring the open sale that tempted both Negroes and white trash to get dangerously drunk would be well worth trying. They even allowed formation of some local Negro WCTUs. So when the Anti-Saloon League went into Dixie after 1895 the WCTU had done quite as much to make straight its way as it previously had in the Middle West.

As one consequence of the Demon's rising ill repute the South made the nation's first sizable experiments in cleaning up rumselling by putting it in government hands. By 1890 Athens, Georgia, seat of the University of Georgia, had had seven years of no-license with the usual trimmings—speakeasies, bootleggers and moonshining *ad lib.* The disgusted city fathers set up a municipal monopoly of liquor-selling with restrictions meant to suppress sale-by-the-drink and the undue public temptation of the bar: Nothing sold under half a pint; the buyer had to take his purchase away at once and not open it till well away from the store; any kind of private resale was forbidden; so were sales to minors or university students. In that close-knit community it worked well enough to sound promising to loudmouthed Governor "Pitchfork Ben" Tillman of South Carolina, where successive variations of local option had been working no better than anywhere else. Tillman persuaded his legislature to set up the Athens system statewide, only with two ill-advised changes: rules against drinking near the "dispensary" were loose, and the pay of the state-employed "dispenser" was not fixed but depended considerably on commission on gross sales.

Inevitably dispensers eager to encourage sales winked at convivial groups in the store next door or the backyard or anywhere handy for clandestine resale-by-the-drink. Their jobs were soon lucrative enough to become political plums.

The system was bound to turn political as more dispensaries opened, creating new state jobs and—also inevitably—as the state set up a special constabulary to keep down speakeasies and bootleggers. Peevish resistance to these officers, many of them clumsy political hacks, led to shooting and a few corpses with local militia refusing riot-duty. Then there were scandals about graft in out-of-state procurement of the dispensaries' liquor. After Repeal several states set up and still maintain some form of state monopoly of bottled goods. But it works best when combined with some sort of sale-by-the-drink. Since South Carolina never tried that, her dispensary system was soon a hissing and a byword. All over the nation militant Drys could point to its noisomeness as warning against any kind of paltering with the Demon. See! not even government could keep him clean! Society could make no terms with him, nothing could reform him, the only cure for his ingrained wickedness was the gallows.

A more striking consequence of Dixie's Dryness was the aforementioned Richmond Pearson Hobson of Alabama, a type dismally familiar among us of late—the able professional officer of the armed forces who becomes a hero, leaves the service and launches on a career of half-baked ideas. Hobson showed signs of egocentric ugliness earlier than most such self-sent prophets. At Annapolis he saw fit to take literally the rules requiring midshipmen to report their mates' breaches of discipline. Naturally he was well and truly ostracized. But it affected him so little that when, after two years, it was hinted that he might be forgiven if penitent, he said never mind, I've been getting along well enough as lone wolf. After Annapolis he specialized in hull construction and then came to glory in the Spanish-American War as the lieutenant who volunteered to scuttle the collier *Merrimac* in the narrow gut of Santiago harbor to keep the blockaded Spanish squadron from slipping out.

The mission was highly hazardous, for it took the ship right into range of everything the Spaniards had that would go bang. Indeed, this heavy fire smashed her steering gear and sank her in the wrong place, so she failed to impede the squadron's subsequent dash for freedom. But that bad luck

did not affect the home public's well-taken judgment that
Hobson was a hero. On his return, millions of panting admirers saw a rangy, handsome young fellow, looking much
like one of Frederic Remington's popular pictures of heavy-
mustached cowboys. When a girl-cousin of his turned up at
his welcome in Chicago, he kissed her in public. Other girls
demanded equal treatment and so forth. During his ensuing
nationwide tour he was kept as busy kissing as a debutante at
a charity bazaar, a curious career for a man so prim.

Much more in character was his retiring from the Navy in
1903 to give the nation the benefit of his views on The Yellow Peril; the Navy's role in international peace; the allied
rackets of dope and white slavery—and the Demon Rum, his
lecture on whom was called "The Great Destroyer." His recent fame assured him ample bookings. He got elected to
Congress from Alabama; and soon the Anti-Saloon League
hired him at a handsome salary to campaign against the Demon. When the League formed a troop of spellbinders to
hold Prohibition powwows in key cities, Hobson was one of
its stars and supplied its dashing name—"The Flying Squadron." In 1914 he offered the House resolution for a national
Prohibition amendment to the Constitution and with its
Senate sponsor, Morris Sheppard of Texas, received on the
Capitol steps the throng of delegates from the League and the
WCTU celebrating that momentous if as yet abortive step.
By 1920 he was heading an American Alcohol Education
Association based on his euphonious theory that alcohol is a
"protoplasm poison." . . .

"Dry Southerner" and "U.S. Navy" had been more cred-
itably coupled in the public mind when, the summer before
Hobson took the WCTU's white-handkerchief salute at the
Capitol, the famous General Order 99 abolished the officers'
so-called "wine mess" throughout the fleet. The Secretary of
the Navy issuing the order was Josephus Daniels, of Raleigh,
North Carolina, able politician and newspaper editor. As a
fair-minded civilian, he took a dim view of the Demon's
status in Navy vessels: Enlisted men had long been forbidden
all intoxicants in any installations, but officers were still per-
mitted to procure and ship wines for the wardroom. By long-

standing custom precious little actual juice of the grape was involved. "Wine A" on the list meant Bourbon, "Wine B" Scotch, and so on; and it troubled Daniels that the same messman who fetched that case of Wine A aboard went to the brig if a bottle of beer was found in his bunk. A devout Methodist, hence with no use for the Demon, the Secretary naturally redressed that situation not by letting the men have at least beer within reason but by making the Demon walk the plank. For that he had the confidential approval of his chief, Woodrow Wilson, and the explicit backing of the Navy Surgeon General.

The order struck the fleet during the blockade of Vera Cruz in Uncle Sam's fumbling skirmish with Mexico in 1914. The horizon off the port was crowded with several American battleships, numerous American cruisers and smaller support vessels, and seven observer-warships of various classes under five European flags. June 30, the day when the order went into effect, was lively in those waters. Several of the Americans staged elaborate burials-at-sea for the Demon, duly sewing up a bottle of booze in shotted canvas and sliding it overside with all traditional ceremony. Barges were continually taking officers of six nations from ship to ship to drink still another toast to the Demon's dishonorable discharge and make conscientiously sure that none of him would be left in any U.S. Navy vessel to violate the Secretary's order. It had already done for Daniels what the grape juice had for Bryan, making him another jokesmith's darling. During the rest of his honorable and useful career in politics and diplomacy the one thing first recalled by mention of his name was that he was the man who dried up the Navy. Yet it appears that nobody relished more than he the cartoon showing him as Sir Josephus, Admiral of U.S.S. *Grapejuice Pinafore,* singing:

> When I was a lad I pondered some
> On the horrible effects of the Demon Rum;
> I scorned to dally with the dread highball
> And I never saw a bottle of champagne at all.
> I kept away from guzzling men
> And now I am the ruler of the U.S.N.

A much more significant Southerner because far more astringent in his zeal was the Rev. James Cannon, Jr., a Methodist too, of course, who sometimes referred his early hatred of the Demon to the sad case of an uncle who died of blood poisoning after a drunkard's dog bit him. It probably meant more that the boy's mother was organizer of the WCTU in the family's Eastern Shore hometown of Salisbury, Maryland. Her only ornament was the White Ribbon she was buried with, and she always made a point of taking son James with her on her weekly rounds of the drink-sodden poor. Dry as a Rechabite, James went to Randolph-Macon, thence into the Methodist ministry, doubling in school administration and in religious journalism, and was in on the ground floor of the Virginia Anti-Saloon League when it organized in Richmond in 1901. As state superintendent, then national legislative representative of the League in Washington, he earned a name for toughness and cunning rivaling that of Wheeler himself. It was principally he, for instance, who bamboozled Warren G. Harding, then Senator from Ohio, into going along with the Eighteenth Amendment. Thanks to his sort, Virginius Dabney, great editor and appalled chronicler of Cannon's career, called the League in the South "virtually a branch of the Methodist and Baptist Churches."

The South seemed destined to be the League's oyster: It had few and small ill-assimilated alien groups to resist the doctrine that alcoholic drinks are evil *per se*. Yet what depressed strata it had—Negroes and white trash—struck the ruling class of whites as such poor drinking-risks that drastic action was advisable. Then the God-made-the-country appeal paid off because country folks were greatly in the majority in all Southern states. For such reasons by 1907 Tennessee's Four-Mile Law—no liquor sold within four miles of a school—had been applied to larger municipalities until only three cities remained Wet. That same year, Georgia's adoption of statewide Prohibition set off a third epidemic of state Dryness, which imposed nominal Prohibition on most of the South by 1915. Mr. Dooley had long been alarmed enough to tell Mr. Hennessy:

". . . it ain't goin' to be very long before this here wave iv

Prohybition comes up here and deluges you an' me . . . I see
. . . portints iv th' times. Th' day was whin ivry wan that
wanted a pollytickal job asked th' privilege iv hangin' a
litthygraft iv himsilf in me window . . . nowadays be Hivens,
no wan wants his pitcher hung in a saloon. They're thryin' to
get thim pasted up in th' churches."

The frequenters of dram-shops . . . are generally attracted
far more by the light, warmth, and good-fellowship, than by
the rum.

        —Dio Lewis, *A Story of the Ohio Crusade*

Throughout the League's war of attrition its name was its
basic asset. "Saloon" began as an elegant, French-derived
term for a sort of super drawing room; then sank to commercial pretentiousness as in "dining-saloon," "billiard-sa-
loon," "beer-saloon" of fancy intentions; then as American
rumsellers exploited it, it dropped the adjectives and came to
mean "barroom independent of an inn" with implications
ranker every decade. The sidewalk outside The Saloon as
Little Willie Leavitt was shown it smelled smotheringly of
beer in hot weather and was ornamented with loafers, some
drunk and recumbent, some tipsy and noisy. Decent women's
reluctance to walk past it was often well advised. It consistently violated ordinances about no screens, large windows
and bright lighting. Its operator was a corrupt power in the
precinct, using the place to recruit illegal voters at election
time and at all seasons to cater to local gamblers and pimps.
Its ventilation was poor, its liquor phony, its décor dingy or
shinily strong on pseudo-rococo carving, mirrors and the
usual "barroom nude."*

By no means all places were that bad, of course. Big-city
saloons often had special clienteles—newspapermen or print-

* In today's English pubs, "saloon-bar" marks the most elegant of the
house's several divisions. "Saloon-deck" is still occasionally seen in British
ships, meaning not the deck with the ship's bar but that reserved for "saloon"
(i.e., first class) passengers.

ers or leather dealers or hack drivers—with the tone of the place reflecting the respectability of the typical customers and the quality of the free lunch, to which anybody buying a drink had access within reason. The content ranged from the oyster stew-Welsh rarebit-cold game-Smithfield ham sort of thing in silkhat places to rat cheese, crackers and salt herrings in the lowest ones. (It seems to have been only the very lowest that set out only items intended to provoke thirst and stimulate sales of beer.) The eminence of baked beans in the canning industry of sixty years ago, particularly the Van Camp brand, testifies to the popularity of the item in average saloon free lunches. A certain large Chicago bar daily used 150 pounds of meat, 50 loaves of bread, 35 pounds of beans, 500-odd hardboiled eggs. . . .

Such generosity was a way to compete with the place down the street without disturbing the delicate structure of drink prices. The brewery holding the mortgage or paying the license fee often picked up at least part of the grocery bills to keep the customers coming and the beer flowing. Low-paid big-city clerks counted on saloons for thrifty midday meals, since purchase of a beer or two entitled them to heavy raids on the soup, beef stew, sardines, pickles and cheese. The house lost money on that but recouped some when they dropped in for a snort on the way home to the boardinghouse at night, and hoped to more than recoup on the regular lushes who spent the evenings drinking much and eating little.

Alert saloonkeepers early installed a telephone for the convenience of the customers. They also offered bathing and washroom facilities, often the only public accommodations of the sort in the neighborhood. They took messages and mail, kept ears open for jobs for the unemployed or dissatisfied, cashed checks in a day when banks looked down on wage earners—all in addition to supplying warmth for the chilled, cheer for the gloomy and at least a pretense of sympathetic listening for the troubled. Temperance men sneered at the phrase "the poor man's club." But many saloons in several strata were exactly that—a low-stake card game in the backroom, knots of cronies arguing or swapping lies at the tables, a few local politicians talking low at the far end of the bar. The small-time drummer in town for a few days used practically all its facilities while gleaning local information from the barkeep or the man drinking Old Popskull at his elbow. The saloon he chose probably saw many small businessmen and supervising clerks and was fairly decently run. But as competition stiffened and growing populations festered in larger centers, Little Willie's picture came to be all too true of more and more saloons—which was why the League's motto, "The Saloon Must Go!" was its single greatest propaganda stroke.

A few shrewd Drys saw the validity in "the poor man's club" and hoped to undercut the Saloon by creating "saloon-substitutes" performing most of its functions—except the serving of alcohol. Here was the genesis of the quick-lunch industry. The WCTU ladies of San Francisco, where saloons were about the only inexpensive lunch places, made a great success with coffee-tea-and-snack rooms serving thousands of downtown employees a day. The first year, they made a $1,500 profit which they promptly reinvested in a free Temperance reading room next door. The Women's Crusade of Washington, D.C., had set up a "Holly Tree" lunchroom of the same sort in 1874. Simultaneously one Joshua Bailey of Philadelphia founded a chain of bone-dry quick-lunchrooms where neat waitresses served, at a few cents each, generous portions of hot cereals, soups, corned beef, eggs, pies, and fresh fruits in season. The idea spread to New York City. Earnest philanthropists in Washington, D.C., even tried a Temperance counterpart of a barroom—table games, billiards, newspapers and magazines, a shirt-sleeved barkeep serving the soft drinks over an ornate, polished bar with a footrail—presumably everything but that voluptuous nude. The place actually drew considerable patronage but never quite enough to make ends meet.

The notion of cheap, good food for white-collar lunchers went vigorously off on its own, however, eventually begetting such profitable variations as Philadelphia's Automats, New York's Exchange Buffets and the Middle West's Thompson Dairy Lunches. But substitutes-for-the-saloon as such had no future. It was too clear that, as a Boston social worker sadly explained, though the saloon did have clublike functions, "The secret of [its] influence consists in the opportunity . . . for producing alcoholic drinks. . . . A 'temperance saloon' is and can be but an imperfect substitute." One might think he could have figured that out beforehand. But then the modern "key club" prospers on just that basis, looking and acting like a brothel but serving only pseudo-sex. Maybe our grandfathers were less tolerant of absurdity than we are.

> Free from taverns I will make it—
>   This my model town—
> Naught to tempt the coming settler
>   Or to break men down. . . .
> For I never knew a pauper
>   Made of sober men;
> They are ever always breeding
>   In a liquor den. . . .
>   —BESSIE AYERS ANDREWS, commemorating
>   the fiftieth anniversary of Vineland, N.J.

The grape-juice industry too, as well as the baked-bean, quick-lunch and Ohio wine industries, came into being as an indirect consequence of the Demon. It was born in Vineland, New Jersey,* a community, innocent of liquor from scratch, created by Charles K. Landis, a righteous Philadelphia land-developer. In the early 1860's he bought a huge tract of land in thinly settled South Jersey, laid out a mile-square town and persuaded the state legislature to give it the privilege of voting itself no-license at will. As soon as the first settlers had unpacked, they did just that at Landis' behest. The place grew fast as his propaganda attracted sobersided and indus-trious types from the Midwest and also from Europe, largely experienced fruit growers from England, France, Germany

* I can find no mention of why Landis chose this name so unsuitable for a town destined to be Dry. He seems to have had general fruit-growing in mind all along; but "Fruitland" would have been better for that.

and Italy. First of a subsequent number of such born-Dry towns, Vineland became famous as a showcase of no-license: The local jail was usually empty, poor-relief funds went untouched, dwelling-fires were almost unknown and, as its Board of Trade still boasted in 1904, "School children are spared the necessity of witnessing saloon brawls and seeing drunken men stagger along the streets . . . no doubt hundreds of [Vineland] men are now living strictly temperate lives who might have yielded to the curse of drink had open saloons existed."

The local Methodist church had been substituting an infusion of raisins in water for fermented wine at communion. A godly dentist, Dr. Thomas B. Welch, chosen as the church's recording steward in 1869, thought he could improve on that. Mustering his whole family to work on it, he developed a sterilized bottled grape juice that kept well without fermenting and satisfied not only Vineland's Methodists but also similarly squeamish congregations all over the nation. As the business grew it got into the national advertising that enabled it to go beyond the communion market, exploiting the secular possibilities of purple Temperance punches and summer-hammock soft drinks. It did much to confirm the economic success of the community until disease attacked South Jersey vineyards and forced a move to the grape country of western New York State, where Welch's Grape Juice still flourishes though Vineland went off the wagon forty years ago.

It was partly Vineland's example, partly that of the Mormons with communal irrigation in Utah, that caused Nathaniel C. Meeker, farm-editor of Horace Greeley's New York *Tribune,* to found the born-Dry colony of Greeley, Colorado, in the early 1870's. He laid it out like a New England village of the seventeenth century. Each householder-settler got a large farming plot outside town and a small dwelling plot in town, and the deed to both banned liquor-selling forever. It naturally followed that as soon as the community had gained any size an unrighteous opportunist set up a saloon in a sod-hut just across the boundary line to, as it were, irrigate the settlers. News of its existence first came to the leaders at church one Sunday morning. After the concluding hymn they marched the congregation off to expostulate with this rumseller and, having done so, returned to town leaving his hut accidentally set on fire.

Greeley prospered, sugar beets and potatoes doing well thereabouts under efficient irrigation. In the 1880's Bill Nye described it as "a fertile island dropped from heaven in a boundless stretch of buffalo grass" where "all the water not used for irrigating purposes is worked up into a light, nutritious drink for the people." By then, however, though the town stayed firmly Dry—still is, in fact—the Demon had gained a toehold. Strangers might have trouble getting liquor, Nye reported, but residents sneaked it in freely and on Sunday mornings hotel washrooms, where social drinking mostly occurred, were usually full of empties "sucked dry and the cork half gnawed up."

That motif of the town Demon-free from birth kept recurring: General Fisk, the Prohibition candidate in 1888, was a principal founder of Harriman,* Tennessee, created as part of a land-development scheme of the 1890's. For a time an American Temperance University existed there. In its turn-of-the-century boom southern California saw the birth of several such bleakly Dry and sunny settlements. In the late 1880's, Staten Island, still countrified and not yet part of New York City, was afflicted with a Temperance summer colony, Prohibition Park, as haven for Manhattan Drys nearer at hand than the already flourishing Methodist-inspired Ocean Grove, New Jersey. Its founders were the Rev. William Boole, Methodist preacher spouse of Ella Boole, a high priestess of the WCTU; Isaac K. Funk of the Funk & Wagnalls publishing house; and William T. Wardwell, a top-echelon figure in the Rockefellers' Standard Oil Company. Wardwell found the money to build the place a gimcracky hotel with a veranda full of rocking chairs and a Chautauqua-type auditorium with seating for 4,000. As Dry-minded fami-

---

* Named not, as is often supposed, for E. H. Harriman, railroad-magnate, but for Col. Walter H. Harriman, post-Civil War governor of New Hampshire, who had an interest in the land company.

lies bought plots—with no-booze clauses in the deeds, of course—and built cottages, the project became a year-round enclave for Dry commuters in the middle of beer-happy Staten Island, home of fourteen breweries. The area is now known as Westerleigh. Hotel and auditorium are gone, but not the Dry-flavored street names: Here is the corner of Maine and Willard. Nearby are avenues named Jewett, Dow, St. John, Fisk, Livermore, Dakota—because South Dakota entered the Union with Prohibition already imbedded in its constitution. I asked a passing mailman who was this Willard the street was named after. He said he had no idea. *Sic transit.* . . .

ഉ

The whole gave him quite a sensation . . . that Nature was always making quite mysterious jokes.
—G. K. CHESTERTON, *The Man Who Was Thursday*

In 1913 the League suddenly dropped its exclusive emphasis on extinguishing The Saloon and coolly stole the Prohibition Party's thunder, coming out solidly for federal constitutional Prohibition. Three years later its high command smirkingly admitted that that had always been in the back of their minds even while they were berating the Prohibitionists for openly demanding it. That fits the League's taste for underhandedness. And it had been implicitly foreshadowed by the gradual apostasy from the Party of John G. Woolley, last of the great reformed-drunk spellbinders.

Successors of Hawkins and Gough had almost disappeared in this culminating era of Temperance eloquence. William Jennings Bryan had never been a drinker. Neither had the Rev. Clinton W. Howard, "The Little Giant" of Rochester, New York, the Mickey Rooney-sized parson who converted Bryan to outright Prohibitionism. Before he got religion, Billy Sunday had ingested his share of alcohol but had been no problem-drinker, and his famous "Booze Sermon" was only one aspect of his hot-gospel preaching. But Woolley was classic: Down-and-out drinking had ruined a brilliant career as courtroom lawyer in Minnesota and he had hauled himself up by the moral bootstraps from far down in the alcoholic's slough. So when as Prohibition Party presidential candidate in 1900 he pulled out all the stops and let his eagle scream, his old-timey virtuosity soared all the higher because he knew the emotions of the burned child as well as of the evangelist.

In 1908 he was already calling for reconciliation between League and Party. Hear him as keynote orator of the Centennial Congress at Saratoga celebrating the birth of that first viable Temperance Society:

> "It has been a great fight and there is glory enough for us all. . . . The enemy has read the writing on the wall, and his line is all but panic-stricken. . . . Formerly the liquor-dealers hunted the voters, but the quarry has become the chase. The trade runs like a scared wolf, ears low, tail between its legs. Local option presses hard upon it, and the deep sea of National Prohibition roars in front. Let us have an end of factions and divisions, and in the consciousness of quiet power administer the daily victory until the chariot of final triumph enters the National Capitol dragging the arch traitor of Christendom at its heel!"

He had just previously called the Prohibition Party "the voice crying in the wilderness" and the Anti-Saloon League "the engineer corps" of Temperance, words of most unusual kindness. Three years later he had openly crossed to the League's side of the narrowing chasm and told its annual meeting:

> ". . . the Prohibition Party fails in these constructive days. It was first to get a sure grip on the keynote . . . that the liquor trade must go. . . . It was pious, passionate, intelligent, altruistic. . . . But it became blindly and savagely partisan . . . scorned the lowly but necessary notches and circuits and zig-zags of the upward trail. It won promptly and splendidly a noble following of pastors, prophets, apostles and others who had felt the adder tooth of drink and

got away. But it never touched the mixed, refractory multi-
tude. . . . It could not get the voters. . . . The American
Anti-Saloon League is Prohibition with the people behind
it and in this land of democracy and liberty the people can
rule, ought to rule and are going to rule."

Actually, of course, the League did not yet have "the
people behind it" if that means, as it must, a majority of
adults in either the nation as a whole or the dozen most pop-
ulous states. That was only one of the considerations making
it look as if the League's policy-switch in 1913 was a serious
error. As of then it was likely to alienate many fence-sitters
without attracting any more of the susceptible righteous, who
had already been practically all taken into camp. Further,
Votes-for-Women, which was widely thought likely to put
Prohibition across in many wavering states, had yet to conquer a majority of state legislatures. It might have been
wiser for the League to wait a few years more before unmask-
ing to get heavier advantage from upcoming new millions of
women voters.

Foolish or not, however, the die was cast. The WCTU
eagerly allied its fortunes with the League's in a new National Temperance Council to take in all Dry organizations,
so did the Prohibition Party in an understandably mixed
frame of mind, and the final battle was joined under fairly
dubious auspices in that heady first year of Woodrow Wilson's first term. Maybe the haste with which Western and
Southern states had been going Dry had gone to the League's
collective head. Maybe the unbalancing item was its recent
success in bullying federal legislators into passing the Webb-
Kenyon Act, which forbade express shipments of private
liquor across the boundaries of Dry states. And soon came the
miracle: Whether the head-shakers or the League's high
command were right can never be known. For little more
than a year later came World War I to stack the deck
flagrantly in favor of the League's new program. Never had
the League's opportunistic genius blazed brighter than now
as fast talking persuaded a distracted people that national
security and Prohibition were mutually essential. And never

had it been clearer that the Wets' stupidity was the Drys' most effective secret weapon.

Whom the gods would destroy they first make mad.
—LONGFELLOW, *The Masque of Pandora*

The Demon had remained his own worst enemy. He persisted in preferring frowsy associates. A monstrous complacency kept him from serious countermeasures till too late; and when taken they were often miracles of ineptitude. The best of good causes could hardly have survived such bungling, and his cause was neither good nor bad. In fact, it was not a cause at all. From any commonsense point of view Rum was a chronic emotional-economic-medical problem incapable of pat solution, impossible to eliminate, susceptible only to rule-of-thumb adjustment. Nor, from a tactician's point of view, could the Demon do much in his own behalf except trust in social inertia and popular dislike of shrillness—neither of which was much use against the minority vote.

Rowdyism, usually spontaneous, had marked the Demon's first reactions—as ever since the 1850's when, for preaching Prohibition, the Rev. William H. Bird of DuQuoin, Illinois, had hogs turned into his yard, his house stoned, firecrackers tossed into open windows, and the town drunks dropping their pants and lewdly exhibiting themselves to his womenfolks—probably the best Prohibition propaganda ever dreamed of. Occasionally, as we have seen, rumsellers or their suppliers sued Temperance zealots. Win or lose, that helped little: The Salem deacon-distiller who had the law on the parson who wrote *Deacon Giles' Distillery* got him jailed. But the Salem ladies furnished his cell comfortably, plied him with delicacies and brought him out a hero at the end of his sentence. A Westchester County innkeeper sued the printer of a Sons of Temperance paper for libel and won a verdict—paid off by a subscription so large that the balance went to fatten a prize for a Temperance essay. Defensive organization in the shape of the United States Brewers' Association in 1862 had the purpose not of improving the Demon's public relations but of lobbying against higher federal taxes on beer. Clandestine economic organization in the scandalous shape of the Whiskey Ring of the 1870's and the menacing shape of the Whiskey Trust of the 1880's proved to be worse than no publicity when its nature became public knowledge.

Actually the Demon's most useful friends would have indignantly rejected being called such. We have already met Temperance-minded or personally abstemious public figures mistrusting Prohibition, some on grounds of public policy, others for moral or religious reasons: Jefferson Davis, Dio Lewis, John A. Andrew, Dwight L. Moody, Horatio P. Seymour. John Fiske, philosopher-historian at Harvard, clung to the light-wines-and-beer theory of regulation. So did Arthur Brisbane, editor-columnist-publisher of the Hearst newspaper empire. In the 1890's certain august sociologists, publicists and such formed a Committee of Fifty under men like Charles W. Eliot, president of Harvard, to explore the actual facts of the Demon's case. They hired expert investigators and eventually published elaborate social, legislative and medical findings that greatly irked Prohibitionists. The gist of them was: Much Temperance propaganda was half-baked nonsense. So far, widely restrictive laws had effected little but impairment of public morals. Some sort of regulation was indispensable, however; and in many contexts local option might do less harm than outright Prohibition.

By then, however, Prohibition's bandwagon was rolling on its final foray, and for every weighty name on the Committee of Fifty, the Drys could whistle up three of equal weight: Luther Burbank, famous (though sub-scientific) wizard of plant breeding; David Starr Jordan, brilliant first president of Stanford; Irving Fisher, imaginative economics professor at Yale; Dr. Charles H. Mayo, chief of the great Mayo Clinic; Dr. Harvey W. Wiley, father of the momentous Federal Pure Food & Drug Act; William Allen White, nationally renowned "grassroots" editor of the Emporia, Kansas, *Gazette.* . . .

There was also plenty of testimony from unqualified witnesses whose impertinent fame got them a hearing anyway: Lillian Russell, reigning stage-beauty of 1900—Mark Twain said most men would rather see her naked than the Second Coming—warned that drink not only ruins a girl's complexion but also afflicts her with "indigestion, headache, biliousness, Bright's disease, nervousness, bad temper, loss of common sense." Athletic public idols were trotted out: Ty Cobb was quoted as saying that ballplayers who drank were usually dropped because it impaired their skills. Connie Mack attributed much of his teams' prowess to the total abstinence of which he approved. An intimate of Jess Willard's said that if he had his way, "there would not be a drop of liquor made or sold in America." John L. Sullivan had already astounded all who knew him by going militantly teetotal, a great day for the cause. But this propaganda triumph went sour in 1913 when aged Gen. Nelson A. Miles, hero of the Indian wars and bloodless conqueror of Puerto Rico, booked to preside at a national convention of the Anti-Saloon League, heard that the Boston Strong Boy was to be there too and refused to sit on the same platform with so uncouth a figure. Advised of this, Sullivan telegraphed to the League that he wanted no part of anything sponsored by such an "arrogant, prejudiced, self-centered, strutting old peacock now in his dotage . . . yours for Temperance, John L. Sullivan."

Technological and financial changes accounted for some of the Demon's later troubles: In the 1880's the advent of artificial refrigeration more than doubled the breweries' capacity to age beer. Production skyrocketed and though beer consumption per capita had been growing fast, while that of hard stuff slacked off, drinkers could no longer keep pace with brewing. Overproduction intensified competition. Sharper competition lowered the industry's business standards. To keep his own beer flowing at all costs the brewer resorted to securing control of saloons to make them exclusive outlets for Brand X or Y. Sometimes he bought the place outright, leaving the former owner in charge on salary; or, as pressure mounted, bought or leased likely sites and created new saloons. Oftener, however, he merely paid the rumseller's license fees in high-license territory or lent him money for the bar and fixtures on mortgage—on condition that he sell only Brand X. Such financing without genuine control proved a great mistake, as the United States Brewers' secretary, Hugh F. Fox, sadly admitted by 1918. Then the industry got worse entangled in the chain-saloon business when British capital began buying dozens of Stateside breweries for consolidation into syndicates that played the Brand X game intensively. So large cities saw more and more saloons in wolfish competition, giving The Saloon still higher visibility and, since it sold quantities of hard stuff too, loading on its brewer-landlords the onus of all the noisome troubles associated with saloon-bought booze. Gleefully the Anti-Saloon League leaped at the opportunity to tar brewers with the same stick, lumping them with the rumsellers as targets of "The Saloon Must Go!"

The League's victories with local no-license or statewide Prohibition usually hurt brewing more than they did distilling. Beer is bulkier than spirits, hence harder to smuggle. So bootleggers supplying a newly Dry state rather neglected it and assumed—correctly—that most serious drinkers would readily turn to a steady diet of whiskey. Hence when a given state went Prohibition, national sales of beer fell more markedly than those of hard stuff. For that reason—also because certain brewers finally began to sense where history was taking them—the United States Brewers belatedly tried to slow the League down. They hired publicity men; increased pressure on urban politicians and newspapers taking beer advertising; and cooperated on one basis or another with the trade organizations of distillers and rumsellers.

The cleanup program of the consequent "Joint Harmony Committee" of 1914 would have been admirable had it been launched twenty years sooner. It called for restricting number of saloon licenses to match population; licenses issued only to American citizens of repute; no wholesaling to bootleggers or speakeasies; no sales to chronic drunkards; no use of free lunch as special customer-bait; discouragement of "rushing the growler." . . . It was assumed that the liquor interests themselves, working from within and below, could effect such reforms where government had always failed. The question who was to ride herd remained. A tactless Cincinnati distiller insisted that since it was the brewers who sponsored most saloons, it was up to them to control the individual rumseller. But he stretched his point beyond the working facts when he said: "The saloon is the property of the brewing industry." That was true of many saloons but not of many others. The actual rumsellers tended to be hard-nosed ruffians recruited by sponsoring brewers more for their ability to keep their heads above water in a tough business than for honesty or liking for discipline. And in order to cajole or cuff them into good behavior the brewer needed complete ownership, not just a mortgage on the mahogany bar, the beer pump and the genuine oil-painting of Cleopatra all asquirm-o.

So what cleanup there was had barely begun when Prohibition struck. There was more Joint than Harmony about it anyway. The brewers outraged the distillers when, seeking to establish beer as an innocent family treat, belonging in every icebox and picnic basket, they tactlessly advertised it as nonintoxicating, hence not to be confused with alcohol-heavy whiskey. In rowdy cities like San Francisco hard-liquor interests hesitated to help the brewers clean up The Saloon because speakeasies and the very plugugly-run joints that were under fire bulked too large among the wholesale liquor dealers' customers. California's brewers developed a promising program of outlawry for The Saloon with plenty of light-wines-and-beer for home and restaurant. But the state's important wine industry failed to support it because restriction to light wines would have bankrupted the vineyards. Too much of their profit came from coarse, cheap, highly fortified port and sherry meant largely for getting drunk on.

California did develop a fraternal order of reputable rumsellers, the Knights of the Royal Arch (Officers: Grand Valiant Commander, Grand Captain of the Guard, *et al.*), sworn to keep their own premises and noses clean, inform against speakeasies and back local law favoring responsible operation. Though effective in some places, the Order remained sporadic and never caught on outside the state.* Another sound notion was advertising to reconcile women to beer, rather like that cigarette-smoking Quakeress of Chesterfield's thirty years ago. It was clever if not scrupulous to buy up newspapers and to subsidize, at least in part, anti-Prohibition articles by known writers like Albert Jay Nock. But it was poor judgment for the brewers to go to war on large businesses supporting the League either directly or through Dry-minded executives.

Against minor firms, threats sometimes succeeded. The advertising manager of the Packard Motor Company was only using the tone prevalent in 1909 when he publicly reproached his fellow advertising men with being "the hired megaphones of brewing interests, which run all the dives in the country and successfully conduct . . . drunken darkies' orgies and white slavery." The brewers bethought themselves that Packard made trucks and brewers bought them; their collective screams persuaded Packard's president to see to it that the speaker apologized profoundly and never opened his trap on the subject again. Despite its considerable size and wide ramifications, however, the brewing industry was obviously giving away too much weight when setting out to blacklist Western Union, the Pennsylvania Railroad and several subsidiaries of United States Steel for one form or another of Temperance-minded policy. The very attempt looked arrogantly absurd and fitted too well with the long-standing image of The Brewer's Big Horses and the aura of thick-necked, tunnel-visioned German-ness that had hovered round brewing since the 1850's.

Historically that was unavoidable. The German immigrants' lager had long been far and away the dominant beer, and nine out of ten American brewers were still named something like Schultz or Dorfenheimer. German alien-ness readily merged, as we have seen, into disregard of Sunday, women's drinking (as in family-type beer gardens) and general big-town looseness that was anathema to the Temperance mind. The danger thus presented seems never to have

---

* The above owes much to Dr. Gilman A. Ostrander's admirable monograph, *The Prohibition Movement in California, 1848–1933.*

come home to the USBA. With exquisite lack of tact they tied up with the German-American Alliance, which sought to richen American life with *kultur*, install German as the only foreign language taught in public primary schools and proliferate *Männerchors* and *Turnvereins*. When the USBA sent an anti-Temperance play touring the Middle West it was called *The Passing of Hans Dippel** and seems to have depicted—no script survives—the sorrows of a lovable old German barkeep overwhelmed by local option. Such conspicuous German orientation was bad enough medicine before 1914. Then World War I set up a natural and by no means wholly imaginary identification of Germans and Irish—the two "hyphenated" groups that dominated rumselling—with the cause of the Central Powers, which grew steadily less popular as the war proceeded. In 1917–18 the fat really dripped into the fire when it came out that the USBA had kept up secret relations with the German American Alliance right up to its suppression in 1916; and had clandestinely financed the purchase of the Washington (D.C.) *Times* by Arthur Brisbane, who wanted an organ of his own in which to shout for light-wines-and-beer.

Well before those disclosures, however, practically all the essential data had been fed into the political computer. The late Herbert Asbury, who studied these matters with bleak shrewdness, believed that the battle for nationwide constitutional Prohibition was won in the elections of 1916 when the League greatly extended its already formidable grip on majorities in both state and national legislatures. (Later complaints that the Drys had put Prohibition over while millions of voters were overseas in uniform certainly had small foundation, for they had all been home when the Congress that voted the Eighteenth Amendment was elected.) Anyway, wherever the League's strategy may have misfired, the fact of the war made up for it. Particularly wartime shortages of food and transport enabled the Drys to deplore use of grain and rolling stock for beer and whiskey as close to treason.

* They would have done better to revive Charles H. Hoyt's *A Temperance Town*, the only successful anti-Dry play I know of, produced in 1893. The hero is a Yankee rumseller with a heart of gold; one of the several hypocritical villains is named Kneeland Pray.

Between that and the German tag on beer the Demon was readily made out to be the Kaiser's bosom friend, a popular impression gaining such momentum that the Dry-bullied Congress passed an alleged wartime-emergency Prohibition bill ten days after the Armistice of November 11, 1918, had already ended the war.

The Eighteenth Amendment, imbedding Prohibition in the Federal Constitution, had already got through Congress and was seeking ratification in the states. The promptness with which Dry-bullied legislators approved it dismayed the many Wets who had given ground in the belief that the necessary thirty-six states would never ratify within the stipulated seven years. They had not grasped how deep and wide the League's infiltration was. Here was a triumph for long, fervently intensive preparation topped by amazing luck in the outbreak of war at the right time.

It went into effect at midnight, January 16–17, 1920—a milestone where the Drys' opponents stumbled and fumbled as usual, as inept in defeat as they had been in battle. They let Rum go into exile not with a bang, not even with much of a whimper. There had been much gay talk of mass-bacchanalia for that historic evening, a nationwide wake for the Demon. But the unregenerate had already staged a premature minor farewell to booze on the previous July 1, when wartime Prohibition had gone nominally into effect, very nominally; and then on the recent New Year's Eve they had widely dedicated the usual guzzling and squealing to the same gloomy purpose. Now the edge was dulled, the spark of spontaneity gone. From coast to coast, press and police reported that efforts to work up appropriate carousings had hung fire or soon fizzled out. Certain elaborate, long-planned mock-funeral ceremonies in expensive New York cabarets seem to have been about the only goings-on that were not lackadaisical as well as anticlimactic.

This apathy is not easy to account for. Some have laid it to postwar confusions distracting people from what was already an old story, nothing like as piquant as Red scares and the "Old Ironsides" scandal about girls leaving off corsets. It may well be that people staying home sober that night had a vague sense of relief that this overbelabored Temperance issue was finally promising to quiet down. Much of the nation certainly neglected to recall that Prohibition had always failed at state-level, and managed to half believe the Drys' promises that federal enforcement would be prompt and airtight. Tin Pan Alley was wryly playing it that way in songs about "Goodbye, whiskey, goodbye gin . . ." and "Sahara, Sahara, we're just as dry as you! . . ." And many who were by no means teetotalers but suspected that booze was so wrong for so many that nobody should insist on his right to have it—a very decent point of view—tried to accept Prohibition in good faith as probably a constructive thing.

The militantly righteous made a contrastingly great success of their well-earned celebration. They greeted that January 17 with the same kind of pious rejoicings that their grandparents had accorded the Emancipation Proclamation. Their great church meetings were awash with tears of sincere thanksgiving and thunderous with joyful hymns. The League's high command in Washington joined with its outstanding politician-allies to hear from William Jennings Bryan a lay sermon on a text from the Gospel according to St. Matthew: ". . . for they are dead who sought the young child's life." Josephus Daniels, one of his hearers, said that the great Amendment "will last as long as the preamble [to the Constitution] . . . no man living will ever see a Congress that will lessen the enforcement of that law! The saloon is as dead as slavery!" In Norfolk, Virginia, the Rev. Billy Sunday, preparing the same gimmick as the New York cabarets but with better omens, preached the funeral of a twenty-foot effigy of John Barleycorn attended by a chief mourner impersonating the Devil, and gloatingly predicted that "Hell will be forever for rent."

Our 20/20 hindsight makes it clear that he should have known his Burns better:

> . . . the cheerful spring came kindly on,
>   And showers began to fall;
> John Barleycorn got up again,
>   And sore surprised them all . . .

as moonshiner, rumrunner and bootlegger set in action nationwide the skills and tactics they had already learned on the local and state levels. None were more surprised than the Anti-Saloon League and the WCTU, who were already laying the keel of an international Prohibition movement with all ingenuous hope of success. History has no finer example of zeal overreaching itself because it believes every syllable of its own propaganda nonsense.

14

POST-MORTEM
FOR THE DEMON

In those days, they shall say no more, the fathers have eaten
a sour grape, and the children's teeth are set on edge.
—*Jeremiah, XXXI, 29*

SCIENTISTS who seek cycles in everything should look into the recurrence of thirteen- to fourteen-year intervals in the ups and downs of Prohibition laws. Finland tried Prohibition in 1919 and repealed it in 1932 because rumrunning and kindred enterprises were making it look foolish. The Eighteenth Amendment was repealed for the same reason, of course, in 1933. In 1964, the state of Majarashtra (including Bombay) in India abandoned Prohibition after fourteen years because . . . Nevertheless, nominal Prohibition may stay on the books forever in the state of Mississippi because bootlegging is so well entrenched in the economy and pays such gratifying "black market" taxes to the collusive state.

Among the other forty-nine states (and minor civic units) can probably be found surviving versions of all the odd legal devices, from suburban no-license to state liquor stores, so hopefully created in the past that this book has explored. Texas remains a "bottle state" allowing local option. Virginia forbids sale of hard liquor by the drink. In a restaurant in Charleston, South Carolina, I recently found that I could buy a cocktail on Sunday but not wine or beer because, it was explained, bar sale of wine or beer is illegal on Sunday, whereas hard liquor is illegal seven days a week. All such laws fail more or less in their purposes, as we have been seeing. But though no form of public control of booze can ever conceivably make unflawed sense, no control at all would make still less. And none of this crazy quilt of legislative experiments, not even Mississippi's dogged persistence in absurdity, implies any possibility of federal Prohibition's reviving in the foreseeable future.

Shreds of the old Temperance organizations survive, however, still hoping somehow to square the circle. When a European of my acquaintance recently took the oath as a new U.S. citizen in a small-town courthouse, a member of the local WCTU was there to give him a leaflet calling drink sinful, hence un-American. WCTU war parties still occasionally raid Capitol Hill when a proposed measure has a pertinent angle such as regulation of liquor advertising. The National Temperance League, successor to the Anti-Saloon League, still has a Washington office with a Methodist minister from Texas as president, still publishes a rickety ghost of *The American Issue,* and still has for stated purpose "ultimately [to] eliminate the traffic in alcoholic beverages." The Prohibition Party had a presidential candidate in 1964. The Good Templars persist in miniature decay. . . .

The National Temperance and Prohibition Council, a league of such agencies, claims twenty-six member organizations. But the downbeat that began with the Repeal movement of the 1920's holds its own and to spare: The National Council of Churches of Christ eschews the Prohibitionist approach to the problem of alcohol. Methodism still speaks kindly of legislation "to outlaw beverage alcohol." But it has long since watered down the name of its Board of Temperance, Prohibition and Public Morals to "Temperance and General Welfare," and apparently finding many current communicants lukewarm toward the traditional teetotalism, is even muttering informally about how, after all, it was only distilled spirits that John Wesley really execrated. And though states usually retain those laws requiring public schools to warn pupils against drink, responsible study materials on the topic are at last coming available.

In proportion as the United States has come to see alcohol as something society must learn to live with, the Demon has been fading. By now he has all but vanished. Indeed it has become clear that he was never there at all. Our ancestors had unwittingly to invent him so they could bring to bear on the matter of alcohol-vs.-man their habitual ways of feeling and thinking: black/white; right/wrong. They were cramped and led astray by a too simple psychology heedless of subrational motives and a chronic belief that clear enough views of wrong lead to upright behavior, a delusion that they shared with Plato. Their alarm at what distilled spirits were certainly doing to people's welfare in this world and probably to their souls in the next was understandable. But remedial schemes were perverted by pharisaical cults eager to see wickedness in the drinker and cynical evil in the supplier; and by presumptuous savants sounding off long before they could possibly know what they were talking about. Actually all that the unco' guid and the frock-coated doctors had in their sights was a mere biochemical accident—the coincidence that C_2H_5OH, a rather simple compound of carbon, hydrogen and oxygen, happens intimately to affect human and other organisms. To keep things in proportion, reflect that an even simpler compound, hydrogen oxide (alias water, which incidentally has a marked physical affinity for alcohol), acts in its own right as solvent for life itself, carries off your internal wastes, invigorates or soothes or flays depending on its temperature, and will drown you down among the dead men if you don't watch out.

Prohibition was certainly a ravaging ailment, however, and among the scars and bodily impairments it left were things even worse than the perpetuation of a newly powerful underworld. Thirty years after repeal most of us seventy million Americans who "drink" retain from the excesses of Temperance doctrine what was recently described at an interdisciplinary scientific meeting as "a sort of societal guilt feeling about alcohol." The same family now able to speak candidly of relatives afflicted with cancer or tuberculosis, once obscurely disgraceful diseases, still shy from saying much about alcoholic kin. The reason is a cultural residue more and more diluted as time passes but still pungent. It derives from the millions still among us who go back to otherwise not highly straitlaced households that never saw liquor from one year's end to the next—not because Pa and Ma had signed the pledge, which they probably hadn't, not because Pa voted the Prohibition ticket, which he would have thought silly, but because alcohol was under taboo, automatically rejected as The Unclean Thing. That our culture should be so ill at ease about the ghost of the Demon is natural in view of the harsh and sometimes unfair things that our forebears said about him. And those old slanders still make it difficult for us to handle alcohol on its own merits, which are considerable.

Temperance did us a particular disservice by focusing attention on the alcoholic. The big spotlight stayed on the drinker ruined by alcohol. The moderate drinker was allowed onstage only as an apprentice alcoholic or as heedless tempter of his weaker brother. Then after Repeal came a spate of publicity about Alcoholics Anonymous. It was well deserved and the movement has accomplished much. But by inevitably misplaced emphasis it tends to shore up the old Temperance position that the significant drinker is the self-destructive one. Far more constructive is the point of view recommended in 1944 to the Yale Summer School of Studies on Alcohol by the Rev. A. J. Murphy of the Catholic Charities Bureau of Cleveland, Ohio:

"A man who can drink moderately and who can use [alcohol] as one of the forces that contribute toward life is, to my notion, probably better organized than [the teetotaler]." The late Dr. Howard W. Haggard of Yale's Laboratory of Applied Physiology told the same group: "For the moderate man alcohol is not used as crutch against life as much as for the enjoyment of life."

It is high time that the 65,000,000 American drinkers who are not self-destructive got some of the study customarily lavished on the 5,000,000 who are. That feeling was understandably widespread at a symposium held at the University of California in 1961* at the instance of the state Wine Advisory Board. For instance, Dr. Giorgio Lolli, head of the International Center for Psychodietetics, suggested that the marriages that alcohol ruins, the fights it starts, the business deals it clogs, may be more than made up for by the deals it lubricates, the fights it cools off, the marriages it preserves when she and he have a nightcap and stop picking at each

* Proceedings published as *Alcohol and Civilization*, New York, McGraw-Hill Book Co., 1963.

other. This reverts to St. Paul's "good creature of God" notion. It can be overdone: Dr. William M. Dock of the State University of New York lovingly listed alcohol's versatile uses as tranquillizer, sedative, anesthetic, diuretic, appetite-stimulant, promoter of fat-absorption; whereas I am assured that, though alcohol serves all those purposes, modern medicine has a better drug or drugs for each of them. Indeed Dr. Selden D. Bacon of the School of Alcoholic Studies at Rutgers University has called alcohol "a second-rate food and a fourth-rate medicine." But on the whole the symposiasts concurred when Dr. Chauncey D. Leake of Ohio State University, a past president of the American Association for the Advancement of Science, called Rum "like fire or nuclear energy, a most sharp and powerful double-edged sword" for good as well as ill.

The above estimates—70,000,000 drinkers, 5,000,000 alcoholics—are much more accurate than Temperance's wild swings. But they remain guesses, for today's experts fail disconcertingly to agree on how to define an "alcoholic." Dr. Lolli told the symposium that definition is impossible. Dr. Leon A. Greenberg, Professor of Physiology and Biochemistry at Rutgers, said: "Trying to define alcoholism has become in itself a disease," but had a crack at it anyway: "If a person drinks so much and so frequently that he gets into trouble health-wise, economically or socially . . . has no control of his drinking, to me this man is suffering from alcoholism." But though the sense of the meeting was that alcoholism *is* a disease—Dr. Greenberg thinks that "illness" conveys the point better to laymen—and though that notion grows more useful yearly, some doubt, largely between the lines, was cast on even that.

The more these experts talked, in fact, the greater the number of disciplines weighing in, the less was definitely stated about the tricky mixture of alcohol and people. With a sort of rueful zest George C. Drew, M.A., Professor of Psychology at University College, London, said that science was probably not within some hundreds of years of discovering what really underlies alcoholism—why A can take it or leave it and poor old B can't. Indeed Dr. Karl M. Bowman,

Professor of Psychiatry (Emeritus) at the University of California, suggested that alcoholism may well not necessarily come from a single cause nor "the same set of causes in every person . . . certainly we don't know much about them."

Shades of Drs. Rush and Richardson! From such cautious, flexible approaches—and from such responsible and stimulating admissions of ignorance—will eventually come genuine knowledge enabling us better to live with both the risks and the benefits of alcohol. Talk like that is the best omen possible. For interim encouragement consider current responses to medicine's appalling findings of the last few years, culminating in 1964, about cigarettes. Twenty-five years ago when I wrote a small book about why and how to stop smoking, responsible medicine had little to say against the habit: Irritating to the upper respiratory tract, yes; inadvisable in certain heart conditions perhaps; but little if any association with cancer. . . . It looked as if Henry Ford, Lucy Page Gaston, Carry Nation and the other cranks screaming against "coffin nails" in my childhood had actually much less of a case against them than against Rum. Now, as grave risks of emphysema and heart trouble expand the new picture of lung cancer, it seems they hadn't guessed the half of it. They were, in fact, as occasionally happens to such crackpots, meaninglessly right for the wrong reasons.

No serious movement to outlaw cigarettes has appeared, however. Not even the Bible-pounders whose counterparts before World War I made possible the Anti-Saloon League's triumph have been heard from. Government action to modify cigarette advertising and more intensive anti-cigarette propaganda in schools are in motion. But nobody has yet reached for the panic-button marked PROHIBITION. Could it really be we have learned something from experience? That would greatly increase our chances of constructively living with alcohol, as we must. The late Dr. Abraham Myerson, a great psychiatrist, laid down the blueprint a generation ago:

> . . . alcoholic beverages serve useful functions in society
> . . . the moderate drinker shows no inferiority in any respect
> whatever to the total abstainer and in general he is probably

a more personable fellow, easier to get along with, and having a better time out of life. . . . There are times when, and places where, that chemical physiological compound known as man needs chemicals to alter his reactions. Alcohol is a sort of chemotherapy for undue stress, for the overdeveloped purpose, for the effect of those social organizing forces which become too onerous. It releases exuberance, good fellowship, and friendliness, all of which are exceedingly valuable to man. The synthesis of temperance, of the wise use of alcoholic beverages, is a necessary part, I think, of the battle against alcoholism.

The sensible thing is to bury the Demon in the empty grave that John Barleycorn vacated.

ACKNOWLEDGMENTS

Institutions to which this book is indebted for research facilities include first and foremost the Princeton University Library; then the New York Public Library, the Harvard College Library, the library of the Harvard Club of New York City, the Flemington (N.J.) Free Library, the Women's Archives of Radcliffe College, the Libraries of the University of Georgia, the University of Texas Library, the Museum of the American Indian, the Alderman Library of the University of Virginia.

Information or good offices were helpfully supplied by the Federal Bureau of Investigation, the Kansas State Historical Society, the Staten Island Historical Society, the Historical and Philosophical Society of Ohio, the McGraw-Hill Book Company, the F. A. Bartlett Tree Expert Company, the American Tract Society, the New York Central Railroad. . . . I also should acknowledge various degrees of runaround from the Woman's Christian Temperance Union, the National Temperance League and the Division of Temperance and General Welfare of the General Board of Christian Social Concerns of the Methodist Church.

For material help from individuals, grateful thanks to Helen Papashvily, George I. Bushfield, Freeman Lewis, Albert Q. Maisel, Marjorie Lawrence Street, Ernest K. Lindley, André L. Simon, Gordon S. Haight, Janet Z. Giele, Arlin Turner, Marjorie Barstow Greenbie, Captain F. Kent Loomis, USN (ret.), Glyndon G. van Deusen, Dr. Morton E. Tavel, Dr. Leon A. Greenberg. . . . The author is sure numerous other obliging people should have been included.

WORKS CONSULTED

The following is not a bibliography of Temperance, or intended to be one. It is merely a check list to indicate the character of sources used, their scope, and to give informal aid to anybody caring to read further. Fictional and stage materials are listed separately after general works. An asterisk identifies books well worth reading for their own sakes.

Adams, P. R., *A Treatise on the Prohibitory Law of Michigan.* Romeo, Mich., Peninsular Herald Office, 1866.

Adams, Samuel Hopkins, *The Great American Fraud.* Fourth Edition. Chicago, Press of the American Medical Association, n.d. [1907].

An Address to the Citizens of New Orleans on the Subject of Temperance. Published by order of the New Orleans Temperance Society, New Orleans, Office of the Lafayette City Advertiser, 1841.

*Ade, George, *The Old-Time Saloon: Not Wet—Nor Dry—Just History.* New York, Richard R. Smith, 1931.

The Alarm Bell [Alfred Gibbs Campbell, ed.]. Paterson, N.J., July 4, 1851 et seq.

Alcohol, Science and Society. Twenty-nine Lectures with Discussions as Given at The Yale Summer School of Alcoholic Studies. New Haven, Quarterly Journal of Studies on Alcohol, n.d. [1945].

Allen, John, *An Address Delivered Before the Washington Total Abstinence Society of Rockport,* [Mass.] February 22, 1842, n.p. Published by the Society, 1842.

American Temperance Society, *Fifth Report of the . . .* presented at the meeting in Boston, May, 1832. Boston, Aaron Russell, 1832.

————, *Permanent Temperance Documents of . . .* Vol. I. Boston, Seth Bliss . . . and Perkins, Marvin and Co., 1835 [Includes Reports IV, V, VI, VII, VIII].

American Temperance Union, *Ellsworth and His Zouaves.* Prepared for the Camp, $2.00 per Thousand, n.p., n.d.

American Tract Society, *The Temperance Volume,* embracing the Temperance Tracts of the . . . New York, Published by the Society, n.d. [1835?].

Anderson, Oscar E., Jr., *The Health of a Nation:* Harvey W. Wiley and the Fight for Pure Food. Published for the University of Cincinnati by the University of Chicago Press, n.d.

Andreae, Percy, *The Prohibition Movement* in its Broader Bearings . . . Addresses and Writings of . . . Chicago, Felix Mendelsohn, n.d. [1915].

Andrews, Bessie Ayars, *Vineland:* A narrative poem by . . . Vineland, N.J., 1911.

Anonymous, *The Origin of the Maine Law and of Prohibitory Legislation;* with a brief memoir of James Appleton. New York, The National Temperance Society and Publication House, 1886.

―――――, "The Experiences and Observations of a New York Saloon-Keeper," as told by himself. *McClure's,* January, 1909.

The Anti-Prohibition Manual: A Summary of Facts and Figures Dealing with Prohibition. Cincinnati, National Wholesale Liquor Dealers Association, n.d. [1917].

Armstrong, Lebbeus, *The Temperance Reformation:* Its History from the organization of the first temperance society to the adoption of the Liquor Law of Maine, 1851; and the consequent influence of the promulgation of that law on the state of New York, 1852 . . . New York, Fowler & Wells, 1853.

Arthur, T. S., *Grappling with the Monster,* or, The Curse of Strong Drink. New York, International Book Company, n.d. [1877].

*Asbury, Herbert, *Carry Nation.* New York, Alfred A. Knopf, 1929.

*―――――, *The Great Illusion:* An Informal History of Prohibition. Garden City, Doubleday & Co., 1950.

―――――, *A Methodist Saint:* The Life of Bishop Asbury. New York, Alfred A. Knopf, 1927.

―――――, *Up From Methodism.* New York, Alfred A. Knopf, 1926.

Ayres, Mrs. Edwin B., Jr., *The Hillsboro Story:* 150 Years of Progress 1807–1857. Springfield, Ohio, H. K. Skinner & Son, 1957.

Baird, R., *Histoire des Sociétés de Temperance des Etats-Unis d'Amérique,* avec quelques détails sur celles de l'Angleterre, de la Suède et autres contrées. Paris, L. Hachette . . . , 1836.

Baldwin, Hanson W., "The End of the Wine Mess," *Proceedings U.S. Naval Institute,* August, 1958.

Ballou, Jenny, *Period Piece:* Ella Wheeler Wilcox and Her Times. Boston, Houghton Mifflin Company, 1940.

Banks, Rev. Louis Albert, *The Lincoln Legion:* The Story of its Founder and Forerunners. New York, The Mershon Company, n.d. [1903].

Barnard, Harry, *Rutherford B. Hayes and His America.* Indianapolis, The Bobbs-Merrill Company, n.d. [1954].

*Barnum, P. T., *Life of* . . . Written by Himself, including his Golden

Rules for Money-Making. Brought up to 1888. Buffalo, The Courier Company, Printers, 1888.

————, *The Wild Beasts, Birds and Reptiles of the World:* The Story of Their Capture. Chicago and New York, R. S. Peale & Company, 1888.

Baron, Stanley, *Brewed in America:* A History of Beer and Ale in the United States. Boston, Little, Brown and Company, n.d. [1962].

Barrows, Samuel J., "The Temperance Tidal Wave," *Outlook,* July 4, July 11, 1908.

Bassler, Robert E., "Splice the Main Brace," *Proceedings U.S. Naval Institute,* November, 1937.

Beck, Lewis C., M.D., *Adulterations of Various Substances Used in Medicine and the Arts.* New York, Samuel S. and William Wood, 1846.

Beecher, Henry Ward, *Lectures to Young Men on Various Important Subjects.* Boston, John P. Jewett & Co., 1846.

Beecher, Lyman, *Autobiography, Correspondence, Etc. of . . . D.D.* Edited by Charles Beecher. New York, Harper & Brothers, 1864.

————, *Six Sermons* on the Nature, Occasions, Signs, Evils and Remedy of Intemperance. New York, American Tract Society, n.d. [1827].

Benezet, Anthony, *The Mighty Destroyer Displayed,* in some account of the Dreadful Havock made by the mistaken Use as well as Abuse of Distilled Spirituous Liquors. By a Lover of Mankind. Philadelphia, Joseph Cruikshank, 1774.

————, *The Pennsylvania Spelling-Book,* or Youth's Friendly Instructor and Monitor . . . The Second Edition, Improved and Enlarged. Compiled by . . . Philadelphia, Joseph Cruikshank, 1779.

Benson, Luther, *Fifteen Years in Hell;* An Autobiography. Indianapolis, Tilford & Carlon, n.d.

Billings, John Shaw, *Physiological Aspects of the Liquor Problem;* investigations made for and under the direction of . . . The Committee of Fifty . . . Boston, Houghton, Mifflin and Company, 1903.

Billington, Ray Allen, *The Protestant Crusade:* 1800–1860. A Study of the Origins of American Nativism. New York, The Macmillan Company, 1938.

Black, James, *The Cider Question.* By Hon. . . . , G.W.C.T. of Pennsylvania [Good Templars], n.p., n.d.

Blackwell, Alice Stone, *Lucy Stone:* Pioneer of Woman's Rights. Boston, Little, Brown, and Company, 1930.

Bode, Carl, *The American Lyceum:* Town Meeting of the Mind. New York, Oxford University Press, 1956.

Boole, Ella A., *Give Prohibition Its Chance.* New York, Fleming H. Revell Company, n.d. [1929].

Brace, Charles Loring, *The Dangerous Classes of New York,* and Twenty Years' Work Among Them. New York, Wynkoop & Hallanbeck, 1872.

Bradford, Gamaliel, *D. L. Moody:* A Worker in Souls. Garden City, Doubleday, Doran & Company, 1928.

Bradford, S. B., *Prohibition in Kansas and the Kansas Prohibitory Law.* By . . . Ex-Attorney-General of Kansas. Topeka, Kansas, The Geo. W. Crane Publishing Company, 1889.

Brink, Carol, *Harps in the Wind:* The Story of the Singing Hutchinsons. New York, The Macmillan Company, 1947.

Brookes, George S., *Friend Anthony Benezet.* Philadelphia, University of Pennsylvania Press, 1937.

Broun, Heywood and Margaret Leech, *Anthony Comstock,* Roundsman of the Lord. New York, Albert & Charles Boni, 1927.

Brown, Joe David, "A Kind Word for Drink," *Saturday Evening Post,* May 25, 1963.

Bungay, George W., *The Maine Law Museum;* and Temperance Anecdotes, Original and Selected. Boston, Stacy and Richardson, 1852.

Burdick, Francis M., *Can Saloons Be Closed on Sunday in Large Cities?* Address Delivered before the City Club of Chicago by Prof. . . . of the Columbia University Law School and a Member of the Committee of Fourteen of New York City. Published by the Literary Bureau of the National Liquor League, U.S.A.

Burton, Jean, *Lydia Pinkham Is Her Name.* New York, Farrar, Straus and Company, 1949.

Byrne, Frank L., *Prophet of Prohibition:* Neal Dow and His Crusade. Madison, The State Historical Society of Wisconsin, 1961.

Cain, Arthur H., "Alcoholics Anonymous: Cult or Cure?" *Harper's Magazine,* February, 1963.

Calkins, Raymond, *Substitutes for the Saloon:* An investigation made for the Committee of Fifty under the direction of Francis G. Peabody, Elgin R. L. Gould and William R. Sloane. Boston, Houghton, Mifflin and Company, n.d. [1901].

Cambridge [Mass.], Citizens' Committee of . . . *Ten No-License Years in Cambridge.* A Jubilee Volume. Cambridge, Mass., 1898.

Cannon, James, Jr., *Bishop Cannon's Own Story:* Life as I Have Seen It. Edited by Richard L. Watson, Jr. Durham, Duke University Press, 1955.

*Carson, Gerald, *Cornflake Crusade:* From the Pulpit to the Breakfast Table. New York, Rinehart & Company, n.d. [1957].

Carter, Jacob, *My Drunken Life,* and Original Songs. By . . . of Philadelphia. Boston, Printed for the Author, 1848.

*Cartwright, Peter, *Autobiography of* . . . The Backwoods Preacher. Edited by W. P. Strickland. New York, Nelson & Phillips, n.d. [1856].

Catechism on the Twin Evils, Intemperance and Tobacco. New York, R. H. McDonald Drug Co., Publishers.

Cherrington, Ernest Hurst, *The Anti-Saloon League Year Book.* 1915. An Encyclopedia of Facts and Figures Dealing with the Liquor Traffic and the Temperance Reform. Compiled and Edited by . . . Editor of the American Issue . . . Westerville, Ohio, The American Issue Press, n.d.

————, *The Evolution of Prohibition in the United States of America:* A Chronological History of the Liquor Problem and the Temperance Reform in the United States from the Earliest Settlements to the Consummation of National Prohibition. By . . . General Secretary of the World League Against Alcoholism. Westerville, Ohio, The American Issue Press, n.d. [1920].

————, *Standard Encyclopedia of the Alcohol Problem.* . . . Editor-in-Chief . . . Westerville, Ohio, 1925.

Chester, Giraud, *Embattled Maiden.* The Life of Anna Dickinson. New York, G. P. Putnam's Sons, n.d. [1951].

Chipman, Samuel, "Report of an Examination of Poor-Houses, Jails &C. in the State of New-York . . . *American Quarterly Temperance Magazine,* No. II, May, 1834.

Clubb, Henry S. [Rev.], *The Maine Liquor Law* . . . Including a Life of Hon. Neal Dow. New York, Fowler and Wells, 1856.

Cochran, Thomas C., *The Pabst Brewing Company:* The History of An American Business. New York, New York University Press, 1948.

Colvin, D. Leigh, *Prohibition in the United States.* A History of the Prohibition Party and of the Prohibition Movement. New York, George H. Doran Company, n.d. [1926].

Committee of Fifty, *The Liquor Problem.* A Summary of Investigations Conducted by . . . 1893–1903. Prepared for the Committee by John S. Billings, Charles W. Eliot, Henry W. Farnam, Jacob L. Greene, and Francis G. Peabody. Boston, Houghton Mifflin Company, n.d. [1905].

Conaty, Thomas J., *Temperance and Total Abstinence.* By Rev. . . . Vice President of the Catholic Temperance Association Union of America. Worcester, Charles Hamilton, 1887.

Congressional Total Abstinence Society, *Proceedings of the* . . . at a meeting held in the hall of the House of Representatives, Friday, February 25, 1842. From the Washington edition. New York, Office of the American Temperance Union, 1842.

Conwell, Joseph A., *Religious Forces and Other Activities* in the History of Vineland, N.J. . . . , n.p., n.d. [c. 1904].

Cory, Earl Wallace, *Temperance and Prohibition in Ante-Bellum Georgia.* A thesis submitted to the Graduate Faculty of the University of Georgia . . . Athens, Ga., 1961. [Typescript]

Coulter, E. Merton, *John Jacobus Flournoy:* Champion of the Common Man in the South. Savannah, The Georgia Historical Society, 1942.

————, *A Short History of Georgia.* Chapel Hill, University of North Carolina Press, 1933.

Crafts, Rev. Wilbur F., Ph.D., *Why Dry?* Briefs for Prohibition Local, State National and International. Washington, D.C., International Reform Bureau, n.d. [1918].

Crusade Temperance Almanac, 1875 [R. H. Macdonald & Co., . . . New York].

The Cyclopaedia of Temperance and Prohibition, New York, Funk & Wagnalls, 1891.

*Dabney, Virginius, *Dry Messiah:* The Life of Bishop Cannon. New York, Alfred A. Knopf, 1949.

Danforth, J. N., *An Alarm to the Citizens of Washington:* or an Exposure of the Evils of Intemperance . . . Washington, Way and Gideon, 1830.

Daniels, Josephus, *The Wilson Era:* Years of Peace, 1910–1917. Chapel Hill, University of North Carolina Press, 1944.

Daniels, Rev. W. H., ed., *The Temperance Reform* and Its Great Reformers. New York, Nelson & Phillips, 1878.

Davis, Alexander S., *A Loud Call to the Citizens of this Nation* . . . A True, Honest and Impartial Investigation of the Present Temperance Question. Hanover, Pa., Published by Alexander S. Davis, 1842.

Davis, Mrs. Edith Smith, *A Compendium of Temperance Truth.* Compiled by . . . Superintendent of the Scientific Temperance Department. n.p., National Woman's Christian Temperance Union, n.d.

Day, Holman, "Does Prohibition Pay?" *Appleton's,* August, 1908.

————, "Maine Faces Bitter Facts," *Appleton's,* February, 1909.

Deardorff, Merle H., "The Religion of Handsome Lake." *Smithsonian Institution, Bureau of American Ethnology, Bulletin CXLIX, No. 5.* Washington, Government Printing Office, 1951.

de Chambrun, Clara Longworth, *The Making of Nicholas Longworth,* Annals of an American Family. New York, Ray Long & Richard R. Smith, 1933.

Delavan, Edward Cornelius, ed., *Temperance Essays,* and Selections from Different Authors, collected and edited by . . . , South Ballston, N.Y. Also a *Treatise on Tobacco* by General John H. Cocke, of Virginia, late president of the American Temperance Union. Albany, Van Benthuysen's Steam Printing House, 1865.

————, *Temperance Essays,* and Selections from Different Authors. Collected and edited by . . . New York, The National Temperance Society and Publication House, 1869.

Devereux, George, Ph.D., "The Function of Alcohol in Mohave Society," *Quarterly Journal of Studies in Alcohol,* September, 1948.

Donovan, William F., Jr., "Real Estate Speculation in Cardiff and Harriman, 1890–1893," *Tennessee Historical Quarterly,* September, 1955.

Dorr, Rheta Childe, *Susan B. Anthony:* The Woman Who Changed the Mind of a Nation. New York, Frederick A. Stokes Company, 1928.

Dow, Neal, "Prohibition and Persuasion," *North American Review,* August, 1884.

————, *The Reminiscences of* . . . Recollections of Eighty Years. Portland, Maine, The Evening Express Publishing Company, 1898.

————, *The Results of Twenty-Five Years of Prohibition in Maine,* n.p., n.d.

Dugdale, Robert L., *The Jukes:* A Study in Crime, Pauperism, Disease and Heredity. Fourth Edition. New York, G. P. Putnam's Sons, n.d. [1877].

Dunn, Rev. James B., *Band of Hope Manual.* New York, National Temperance Society and Publication House, n.d.

————, ed., *Moody's Talks on Temperance* with Anecdotes and Incidents in connection with the Tabernacle Temperance Work in Boston. Compiled and edited by . . . New York, National Temperance Society and Publication House, 1878.

Dutcher, George M., *Disenthralled:* A Story of my Life. A Vivid Portrayal of the Evils of Intemperance . . . Hartford, Conn., Columbian Book Company, 1873.

Earhart, Mary, *Frances Willard:* From Prayers to Politics. Chicago, University of Chicago Press, n.d. [1944].

Eastman, Mary F., *The Biography of Dio Lewis, A.M., M.D.* prepared at the desire and with the co-operation of Mrs. Dio Lewis. New York, Fowler & Wells Co., 1891.

Eckenrode, H. J., *Rutherford B. Hayes:* Statesman of Reunion. New York, Dodd, Mead & Company, 1930.

Eddy, Richard, *Alcohol in Society.* New York, The National Temperance Society and Publication House, 1888.

Edwards, Justin, *Letter to the Friends of Temperance in Massachusetts.* By . . . , Corresponding Secretary of the American Temperance Society. Boston, Seth Bliss, 1836.

————, *The Temperance Manual.* New York, American Tract Society, n.d.

Eliot, Charles Warren, "A Study of American Liquor Laws," *Atlantic Monthly,* February, 1897.

Estabrook, Arthur H., *The Jukes in 1915.* Washington, The Carnegie Institution of Washington, 1916.

Eubanks, John Evans, *Ben Tillman's Baby.* The Dispensary System of South Carolina. 1892–1915, n.p., n.d.

Fehlandt, August F., *A Century of Drink Reform in the United States.* Cincinnati, Jennings and Graham, n.d. [1904].

Fifteen Gallons, or The Tyranny and Injustice of Sumptuary Law. An Appeal to the Good Sense of the People of Massachusetts. Boston, 1838.

Finch, John B., *The Great Speech of Hon. . . . .* of Illinois on Temperance and Prohibition at Macon, Georgia, January 25th, 1887. Macon, Ga., J. W. Burke & Co., 1887.

Finley, James B., *Autobiography of Rev. . . . .* or, Pioneer Life in the West. Edited by W. P. Strickland, D. D. Cincinnati, Cranston and Curtis, n.d. [1853].

Fiske, John, M.A., LL.B., *Tobacco and Alcohol.* New York, Leypoldt & Holt, 1869.

Fowler, O. S., *Temperance Founded on Phrenology and Physiology,* or The Laws of Life, and the Principles of the Human Constitution, as developed by the sciences of phrenology and physiology, applied to total abstinence from all alcoholic and intoxicating drinks. By . . . Practical Phrenologist. Twenty-fourth Edition Enlarged and Improved. . . . New York, Fowler & Wells Phrenological Cabinet, 1846.

Friend, Llerena, *Sam Houston the Great Designer.* Austin, University of Texas Press, 1954.

Funk, Charles Earle, "Prohibition Park, Staten Island," *The Staten Island Historian,* July–September, 1952.

Giele, Janet Zollinger, *Social Change in the Feminine Role:* A Comparison of Woman's Suffrage and Woman's Temperance, 1870–1920. A thesis presented by . . . to the Department of Social Relations . . . Radcliffe College, Cambridge, Mass., April, 1961.

Glad, Paul W., *The Trumpet Soundeth:* William Jennings Bryan and His Democracy, 1896–1912, n.p., University of Nebraska Press, 1960.

Gladden, Washington, *Moral Gains and Losses of the Temperance Reformation:* An Address by Rev. . . . D.D., of Columbus, Ohio. Delivered upon request of Managers of the University Temperance Hall at the University of Virginia, May 14th, 1895. Charlottesville, Va., Progress Print., 1895.

Goodman, Nathan G., *Benjamin Rush,* Physician and Citizen. 1746–1813. Philadelphia, University of Pennsylvania Press, 1934.

Goodspeed, E. J., *A Full History of the Wonderful Career of Moody and Sankey,* in Great Britain and America, embracing also the best portion of Mr. Moody's sermons . . . New York, Henry S. Goodspeed & Company, n.d. [1876].

Gordon, Anna, A., *The Beautiful Life of Frances E. Willard:* A Memorial Volume by . . . For twenty-one years her private secretary. Introduction by Lady Henry Somerset. With Character Sketches and Memorial Tributes . . . Chicago, Woman's Temperance Publishing Association, n.d. [1898].

Gordon, Sloane, "Booze, Boodle, and Bloodshed in the Middle West," [tearsheets from unidentified magazine in library of United States Brewers' Association].

Gough, John B., *Autobiography and Personal Recollections of . . .* with Twenty-Six Years' Experience as a Public Speaker. Springfield, Mass., Bill, Nichols & Co., 1869.

————, *An Autobiography by . . .* Thirty-First Edition. Boston, J. B. Gough, 1852.

————, *Platform Echoes:* or, Living Truths for Head and Heart . . . With a history of Mr. Gough's Life and Work by the Rev. Lyman Abbott, D. D. Hartford, Conn., A. D. Worthington & Co., 1887.

————, *Sunlight and Shadow,* or Gleanings From My Life Work. Hartford, Conn., A. D. Worthington & Company, 1881.

*Greeley, Horace, *Recollections of a Busy Life.* New York, J. B. Ford and Company, 1868.

Greenbie, Marjorie Barstow, *Lincoln's Daughters of Mercy.* New York, G. P. Putnam's Sons, n.d. [1944].

*Griffin, Clifford S., *Their Brothers' Keepers:* Moral Stewardship in the United States, 1800–1865. New Brunswick, Rutgers University Press, n.d. [1960].

Grimké, Thomas S. *Address on the Patriot Character of the Temperance Reformation:* . . . by . . . President of the Charleston Temperance Society. Charleston, Observer Office Press, 1833.

Gusfield, Joseph R., "Social Structure and Moral Reform: A Study of the Woman's Christian Temperance Union," *American Journal of Sociology,* November, 1955.

Hadley, Henry H., *The Blue Badge of Courage.* Akron, Ohio, The Saalfield Publishing Co., 1902.

Hadley, Samuel H., *Down in Water Street.* London, Fleming H. Revell Co., n.d.

Hale, William Harlan, *Horace Greeley:* Voice of the People. New York, Harper & Brothers, n.d. [1950].

Hargreaves, William, M.D., *Our Wasted Resources;* The Missing Link in the Temperance Reform. New York, National Temperance Society & Publication House, 1878.

Harlan, Rolvix, *John Alexander Dowie and the Christian Catholic Apostolic Church in Zion.* A Dissertation submitted to the faculty of the Graduate Divinity School . . . Evansville, Wis., Press of R. M. Antes, 1906.

Harrington, Fred Harvey, *Fighting Politician:* Major General N. P. Banks. Philadelphia, University of Pennsylvania Press, 1948.

*Harrison, Harry P., *Culture Under Canvas:* The Story of Tent Chautauqua. By . . . as told to Karl Detzer. New York, Hastings House, n.d. [1958].

Hay, James Jr., "The Side-Shows of Drink," *McClure's Magazine,* October, 1917.

*Henderson, Yandell, *A New Deal in Liquor.* A Plea for Dilution. By . . . Professor of Applied Physiology, Yale University. Also a Reprinting of an Inquiry into the Effects of Ardent Spirits upon the Human Body and Mind by Dr. Benjamin Rush. New York, Doubleday, Doran & Company, 1934.

Hertell, [Judge] Thomas, *An Exposé of the Causes of Intemperate Drinking,* and the means by which it may be obviated. By . . . of the City of New York. New York, Printed by E. Conrad, 1819.

*Hibben, Paxton, *Henry Ward Beecher:* An American Portrait. With a Foreword by Sinclair Lewis. New York, The Press of the Readers Club, n.d. [1942].

Hobson, Richmond Pearson, *Alcohol and the Human Race.* New York, Fleming H. Revell Company, n.d. [1919].

———, *The Great Destroyer:* Speech of Hon. . . . of Alabama in the House of Representatives, February 2, 1911. Washington, 1911.

Hopkins, Alphonso A., Ph.D., *Profit and Loss in Man.* New York, Funk & Wagnalls Company, 1909.

Hopkins, Samuel M., and Gerrit Smith, Rev. Dr. Justin Edwards and

Rev. Samuel H. Cox, *Correspondence on the Principles of Right Reasoning Applicable to Temperance and to the Effects of Fermented and Distilled Liquors* between . . . Geneva, N.Y., John C. Merrell, 1836.

Horton, Donald, Ph.D., "The Function of Alcohol in Primitive Societies; A Cross-cultural Study," *Quarterly Journal of Studies in Alcohol*, September, 1943.

Humphrey, Heman, *Miscellaneous Discourses and Reviews*. Amherst, J. S. and C. Adams, 1834. "Extracts From an Address on Temperance in 1812."

————, *Parallel Between Intemperance and the Slave-Trade*. By . . . , D.D., President of Amherst College. New York, John P. Haven, n.d.

Hunt, Thomas P. *The Cold Water Army*. By . . . , the Drunkard's Friend. Boston, Whipple and Darrell, 1841.

Hutchinson, John Wallace. *Story of the Hutchinsons* (Tribe of Jesse) by . . . Compiled and Edited by Charles E. Mann. With an Introduction by Frederick Douglass. Boston, Lee and Shepard, 1896.

Iglehart, Ferdinand Cowle, D.D., *King Alcohol Dethroned*. Westerville, Ohio, The American Issue Publishing Company, n.d. [1919].

Ingraham, Charles A., "The Birth at Moreau of the Temperance Reformation," Proceedings of the New York State Historical Association, VI, n.p. Published by the . . . , 1906.

————, *Elmer E. Ellsworth and the Zouaves of '61*. Chicago, Published for the Chicago Historical Society by the University of Chicago Press, n.d. [1925].

Jackson, Rev. James C., M.D., *How to Cure Drunkards*. By . . . , Physician-in-Chief of "Our Home on the Hillside," the Largest Hygienic Infirmary in the World. Dansville, N.Y., Austin, Jackson, 1868.

Jewett, Charles, *A Forty Years' Fight with the Drink Demon,* or *A History of the Temperance Reform as I Have Seen It, and of my labor in connection therewith*. By . . . M.D. New York, National Temperance Society and Publishing House, 1876.

————, *Speeches, Poems and Miscellaneous Writings* on Subjects connected with Temperance and the Liquor Traffic. Boston, John P. Jewett, 1849.

————, *The Youth's Temperance Lecturer*. Boston, Whipple and Damrell, 1840.

Johnson, William E., "I Had to Lie, Bribe and Drink to Put Prohibition Over in America," by Pussyfoot Johnson. *Hearst's International-Cosmopolitan,* May, 1926.

————, *The South Carolina Liquor Dispensary*. Westerville, Ohio, The American Issue Publishing Company, n.d. [1919].

Keeley, Leslie E., M.D., LL.D., *The Non-Heredity of Inebriety*. Chicago, S. C. Griggs and Company, 1896.

Kirk, John, *Medicinal Drinking*. New York, National Temperance Society and Publication House, 1869.

Kitchel, Rev. H. D., *An Appeal to the People for the Suppression of the Liquor Traffic*. A Prize Essay. Middlesbro'-on-Tees, John Jordison, 1852.

Koren, John, *Alcohol and Society*. New York, Henry Holt and Company, 1916.

―――――, *Economic Aspects of the Liquor Problem*. An Investigation Made for the Committee of Fifty . . . Boston, Houghton, Mifflin and Company, 1899.

―――――, *The Prohibition "Crusade."* Factitious Character of the Present Agitation—Evils of Recent Liquor Legislation—Local Option and the Saloon Question. Address Delivered at a Convention of the United States Brewers' Association, Atlantic City, N.J., June 2, 1909.

*Krout, John Allen, *The Origins of Prohibition*. New York, Alfred A. Knopf, 1925.

Landis, Charles K., *The Founder's Own Story* of the Founding of Vineland, New Jersey, n.p., Vineland Historical and Antiquarian Society, 1903.

Lemert, Edwin M., *Alcohol and the Northwest Coast Indians*. University of California Publications in Culture and Society. Volume 2, No. 6, pp 303–406.

Lewis, Dio, *Prohibition a Failure: or, True Solution of the Temperance Question*. Boston, Charles R. Osgood and Company, 1875.

―――――, *Our Girls*. New York, Harper & Brothers, 1871.

―――――, "Prohibition and Persuasion," *North American Review*, August, 1884.

Livermore, Mary A., *The Story of My Life, or, The Sunshine and Shadow of Seventy Years*. By . . . Teacher, author, wife, mother, army nurse, soldier's friend, lecturer, and reformer . . . to which is added six of her most popular lectures. Hartford, Conn., A. D. Worthington Co., 1899.

Lockhart, Sir Robert Bruce, *Scotch*: The Whisky of Scotland in Fact and Story. London, Putnam, n.d. [1951].

Loeb, Edwin M., Ph.D., "Primitive Intoxicants," *Quarterly Journal of Studies in Alcohol*, December, 1943.

Logan, Olive, "About the Drunken Drama," in *Apropos of Women and Theatres*. With a Paper or Two on Parisian Topics. New York, Carleton, Publisher, 1870.

*London, Jack. *John Barleycorn*. New York, The Century Co., 1913.

Long, J. C. *Bryan*: The Great Commoner. New York, D. Appleton & Company, 1928.

Longworth, Nicholas. *A Letter From . . .* , to the Members of Cincinnati Horticultural Society, on the Cultivation of the Grape and Manufacture of Wine . . . Cincinnati, Published by Order of the Society, 1846.

*Lucia, Salvatore Pablo, ed., *Alcohol and Civilization*. New York, McGraw-Hill Book Co., n.d. [1963].

Lutz, Alma, *Susan B. Anthony:* Rebel, Crusader, Humanitarian. Boston, The Beacon Press, n.d. [1959].

Maguire, John Francis, M.P., *Father Mathew:* A Biography. London, Longman, Green, Longman, Roberts & Green, 1863.

Marsh, John, *Hannah Hawkins,* The Reformed Drunkard's Daughter. By Rev. . . . New York, American Temperance Union, 1844.

————, *The Napoleon of Temperance.* Sketches of the Life and Character of the Hon. Neal Dow . . . author of the Maine Liquor Law. New York, American Temperance Union, 1852.

————, *Temperance Recollections.* Labors, Defeats, Triumphs. An Autobiography. New York, Charles Scribner & Co., 1866.

————, Rev. *The Triumphs of Temperance.* New York, John P. Prall, 1855.

Marshall, Thomas Francis, *Speeches and Writings of* . . . Edited by W. R. Barre. Cincinnati, Applegate & Company, 1858.

Martyn, Carlos, *John B. Gough:* The Apostle of Cold Water. New York, Funk & Wagnalls Company, 1893.

Massachusetts, Legislature of, *Reports on the Subject of a License Law,* by a Joint Special Committee of the . . . ; together with a stenographic report of the Testimony taken before said committee. Boston, Wright & Potter, State Printers, 1867.

McAuley, Jerry, *Jerry McAuley:* His Life and Work . . . Edited by Rev. R. M. Orford. Second Edition. New York, Published by the New York Observer, n.d. [1885].

*McCarthy, Raymond G., ed., *Drinking and Intoxication:* Selected Readings in Social Attitudes and Control. New Haven, Yale Center of Alcohol Studies, n.d. [1959].

McGlinchee, Claire, *The First Decade of the Boston Museum.* Boston, Bruce Humphries, Inc., n.d. [1940].

McLoughlin, William G., Jr., *Billy Sunday Was His Real Name.* n.p., The University of Chicago Press, n.d. [1955].

McMullen, Thomas, *Hand-book of Wines.* New York, D. Appleton & Co., 1852.

*Merz, Charles, *The Dry Decade.* Doubleday, Doran & Company, Inc., Garden City, 1931.

Milner, Duncan C., *Lincoln and Liquor.* New York, The Neale Publishing Company, 1920.

Mitchell, Stewart, *Horatio Seymour of New York.* Cambridge, Harvard University Press, 1938.

Monaghan, Jay, *The Great Rascal.* The Life and Adventures of Ned Buntline. [E. Z. C. Judson] Boston, Little, Brown and Company, 1952.

Monahan, M. [ed.], *A Text-Book of True Temperance.* Second Edition. Revised and Enlarged. New York, United States Brewers' Association, 1911.

Mott, Frank Luther, *Golden Multitudes.* New York, The Macmillan Company, 1947.

Moynihan, James H., *The Life of Archbishop Ireland.* New York, Harper & Brothers, n.d. [1853].

Münsterberg, Hugo, "Prohibition and Social Psychology," *McClure's Magazine,* August, 1908.

Nation, Carry A., *The Use and Need of the Life of Carry A. Nation.* Written by herself. Revised Edition. n.p., n.d. [1908].

The National Temperance Almanac and Teetotaler's Yearbook for the Year of Our Lord 1878. New York, The National Temperance Society and Publication House, n.d.

National Temperance Society and Publication House, *Temperance Tracts* issued by the . . . Vol. 1. New York, J. N. Stearns, 1874.

Nichols, Ray Franklin, *Franklin Pierce,* Young Hickory of the Granite Hills. Philadelphia, University of Pennsylvania Press, n.d. [1958]

Nixon, Raymond B., *Henry W. Grady:* Spokesman of the New South. New York, Alfred A. Knopf, 1943.

Nott, Eliphalet, *Lectures on Temperance.* New York, Cheldon, Blakeman & Co., 1857.

*Odegard, Peter H., *Pressure Politics:* The Story of the Anti-Saloon League. New York, Columbia University Press, 1928.

Opinions and Facts from Eminent Physicians, Chemists and Others in Favor of Ale and Beer as Light Wholesome Beverages. Boston, Press of Rand, Avery & Co., 1872.

Organ, Thomas W., *Biographical Sketch of General Neal Dow.* New York, National Executive Committee of the Prohibition Reform Party, n.d.

Ostrander, Gilman M., *The Prohibition Movement in California, 1848–1933.* University of California Publications in History, Vol. 57. Berkeley and Los Angeles, University of California Press, 1957.

Parker, Arthur C., "The Code of Handsome Lake, the Seneca Prophet," *New York State Museum Bulletin,* No. 163. Albany, University of the State of New York, 1913.

*Parker, Robert Allerton, *The Transatlantic Smiths.* New York, Random House, [1959].

Pearson, Edmund Lester, "Temperance Novels," *Scribner's,* November, 1924.

Pearson, Henry Greenleaf, *The Life of John A. Andrew,* Governor of Massachusetts, 1861–65. Boston, Houghton Mifflin and Company, 1904.

Pennsylvania Society for Discouraging the Use of Ardent Spirits, *The Third Anniversary Report of the Managers of* . . . Read on the 22nd May, 1832, and ordered to be published by the Society. Philadelphia, John Clarke, 1832.

Phelps, C.A., "Liquor's Fight Against Prohibition," *Broadway Magazine,* August, 1908.

The Pocket Encyclopedia of Temperance. Topeka, Kansas, Published by the Temperance Society of the Methodist Episcopal Church, Revised and Enlarged. 1916.

Potter, A., *Drinking Usages,* being the substance of a Lecture . . . in the Masonic Hall, Pittsburgh . . . April 3, 1852, by . . . D. D. Bishop of the Diocese of Pennsylvania. Philadelphia, Published by the Pennsylvania State Temperance Society, n.d.

Powell, Frederick, *Bacchus Dethroned.* Prize Essay. New York, National Temperance Society and Publication House, 1875.

Prime, Nathaniel S., *The Pernicious Effects of Intemperance in the Use of Ardent Spirits* and the Remedy for that Evil. A Sermon . . . Brooklyn, Alden Spooner, 1812.

Prohibitionists' Text-Book, Comprising Arguments, Appeals, and Statistics, showing the iniquity of the license system, and the right and duty of Prohibition. New York, National Temperance Society and Publication House, 1880.

Rand, Festus G., *Autobiography of . . . A Tale of Intemperance,* with a . . . Recommendation by John B. Gough. Montpelier, [Vt.], J. and J.M. Poland, 1868.

Randall, Ruth Painter, *Colonel Elmer Ellsworth:* A biography of Lincoln's friend and first hero of the Civil War. Boston, Little, Brown and Company, n.d. [1960].

Reese, David M., A.M., M.D., *A Plea for the Intemperate* by . . . , late professor of theory and practice of physic, Albany Medical College. New York, John S. Taylor, 1841.

Richards, William C., *Great in Goodness:* A Memoir of George N. Briggs. Boston, Gould and Lincoln, 1866.

Richardson, Benjamin Ward, *The Temperance Lesson Book.* A Series of Short Lessons on Alcohol and its Action on the Body. Designed for reading in schools and families. By . . . M.A., M.D., LL.D., F.R.S. New York, National Temperance Society and Publication House, 1880.

*Rowntree, Joseph, and Arthur Sherwell, *The Temperance Problem and Social Reform.* London, Hodder & Stoughton, 1901.

Rush, Benjamin, M.D., *An Inquiry into the Effects of Ardent Spirits upon the Human Body and Mind,* with an Account of the Means of Preventing and of the Remedies for Curing Them. The Eighth Edition, with Additions . . . [Appendix I in Yandell Henderson, A New Deal in Liquor, pp. 185–221].

————, *Letters of . . .* Edited by L. H. Butterfield. American Philosophical Society, Princeton University Press, 1951.

*Schlesinger, Arthur M., *The American as Reformer.* Cambridge, The Harvard University Press, 1951.

Scomp, H. A., *King Alcohol in the Realm of King Cotton,* or, A History of the Liquor Traffic and of the Temperance Movement in Georgia from 1733 to 1887 . . . n.p., Press of the Blakeley Printing Company, 1888.

Sheppard, John H., "Lucius Manlius Sargent," in *Memories of Several Deceased Members of the New England Historic, Genealogical Society,* Published by . . . , Boston, 1878.

*Sinclair, Andrew, *Prohibition:* The Era of Excess. Boston, Little, Brown and Company, n.d. [1962].

*Sinclair, Upton, *The Cup of Fury.* Great Neck, New York, The Channel Press, n.d. [1956].

Smith, Gerrit, *Speech of . . . On Sale of Intoxicating Drinks in the City of Washington:* In Congress, July 22, 1854.

Smith, Logan Pearsall, ed., *Philadephia Quaker:* The Letters of Hannah Whitall Smith. Edited by her son . . . With a biographical preface by Robert Gathorne-Hardy. New York, Harcourt, Brace and Company, n.d. [1950].

Smith, Randolph Wellford, *The Sober World.* Boston, Marshall Jones Company, 1919.

Smith, W. L. G., *The Life and Times of Lewis Cass.* New York, Derby & Jackson, 1856.

Stanton, Elizabeth Cady, Susan B. Anthony, and Matilda Joslyn Gage, *History of Woman Suffrage.* Edited by . . . New York, Fowler & Wells, 1881.

State Temperance Committee [of Massachusetts], *Address of the . . .* to the Citizens of Massachusetts on the Operation of the Anti-Liquor Law. n.p., n.d.

Stearns, J. M., *National Temperance Almanac* for 1871. New York, National Temperance Society and Publication House, n.d.

Stelzle, Charles, *Why Prohibition?* New York, George H. Doran Company, n.d. [1918].

Steuart, Justin, *Wayne Wheeler, Dry Boss:* An Uncensored Biography of Wayne B. Wheeler. New York, Fleming H. Revell Company, n.d. [1928].

Stone, Rev. A. L., Oration Delivered Before the Sons of Temperance at Charlestown, N.H., July 4, 1850. Boston, John P. Jewett & Co., 1850.

Story, Dr. Charles A., *Alcohol: Its Nature and Effects.* Ten Lectures by . . . of Chicago. New York, The National Temperance Society and Publication House. 1879.

Stout, Charles Taber, *The Eighteenth Amendment* and the Part Played by Organized Medicine. New York, Mitchell Kennerley, 1921.

Stuart, George R., *The Stump Digger.* By . . . The Great Temperance Evangelist. Westerville, Ohio, The American Issue Publishing Company, n.d. [1896].

Swansea, A. Scholfield, *Notes on Canada and the United States of America.* London, Printed at the "Cambria Daily Leader" Office, 1888.

Talmage, T. De Witt, *High License:* The Monopoly of Abomination. A Sermon by . . . New York, The National Temperance Society and Publication House, 1884.

A Temperance Physiology for Intermediate Classes and Common Schools prepared under the direction of the Department of Scientific Instruction of the Women's National Christian Temperance Union . . . with a preface and endorsement of scientific accuracy by A. B. Palmer, M.D., LL.d., professor of pathology and practice of medicine . . . in the University of Michigan . . . New York, A. S. Barnes & Company, n.d. [1884].

*Thomas, Benjamin P., *Theodore Weld:* Crusader for Freedom. New Brunswick, Rutgers University Press, 1950.

Thompson, Mrs. Eliza Jane Trimble, *Hillsboro Crusade Sketches and Family Records* By . . . , Her Two Daughters, and Frances W. Willard. Cincinnati, Jennison and Graham, 1906.

Thompson, Vance, *Drink.* A Revised and Enlarged Edition of "Drink and Be Sober." New York, E. P. Dutton & Company, n.d. [1918].

*Timberlake, James H., *Prohibition and the Progressive Movement.* 1900–1920. Cambridge, Harvard University Press, 1963.

Train, George Francis, *My Life in Many States and in Foreign Lands.* Dictated in my Seventy-Fourth Year. New York, D. Appleton and Company, 1902.

Trotter, Thomas, M.D., *Essay, Medical, Philosophical, and Chemical, on Drunkenness and Its Effects on the Human Body.* London, Longman, Jurst, Rees and Orme, 1810.

Tucker, Glenn, *Tecumseh, Vision of Glory.* Indianapolis, The Bobbs-Merrill Company, 1956.

*Turner, E. S., *Roads to Ruin:* The shocking history of social reform. London, Michael Joseph, n.d. [1950].

U.S. Senate, *Brewing and Liquor Interests and German Propaganda:* Hearings Before a Subcommittee of the Committee on the Judiciary United States Senate Sixty-fifth Congress Second Session . . . Washington, Government Printing Office, 1919.

van Deusen, Glyndon G., *Horace Greeley:* Nineteenth-Century Crusader. Philadelphia, University of Pennsylvania Press, 1953.

Vrettos, Theodore, "Rockport's Hatchet Gang," *Yankee,* November, 1962.

Wallace, Anthony F. C., "Handsome Lake and the Great Revival in the West," *American Quarterly,* Summer, 1952.

Wallace, Irving, *The Fabulous Showman.* London, Pan Books, n.d. [1962]. [Hutchinson, 1960].

Weems, Mason L., *Three Discourses:* 1. Hymen's Recruiting Sergeant. 2. The Drunkard's Looking Glass. 3. God's Revenge Against Adultery. New York, Random House, 1929.

*Werner, M. R., *Barnum.* New York, Harcourt, Brace and Company, n.d. [1923].

White, P. S., and Pleasants, H. R., *The War of Four Thousand Years:* being a connected history of the various efforts made to suppress the vice of intemperance in all ages of the world; from the foundation of the class of Nazirites by Moses, to the institution of the order of the Sons of Temperance. Philadelphia, Grifft & Simon, 1846.

*Whitlock, Brand, *The Little Green Shutter.* New York, D. Appleton and Company, 1931.

Wilberforce, Rev. Basil, *Doctors and Brandy.* London, W. Tweedie, Co., 1874.

Willard, Frances E., *Glimpses of Fifty Years:* The Autobiography of an American Woman . . . Written by order of the National Woman's

Christian Union. Introduction by Hannah Whitall Smith. Chicago, H. J. Smith & Co., n.d. [1889].

Willett, Rev. J., *The Drunkard's Diseased Appetite,* What is it? if curable how? by miraculous agency or physical means—which? Fort Hamilton, Printed at the Inebriates' Home for Kings County, 1877.

Wines, Frederick H., and John Koren, *The Liquor Problem in Its Legislative Aspects.* An Investigation Made Under the Direction of Charles W. Eliot, Seth Low and James C. Carter, sub-committee of fifty to investigate the liquor problem. Second Edition. Boston, Houghton Mifflin and Company, 1898.

Wittenmyer, Annie [Turner], *History of the Woman's Temperance Crusade.* A Complete Official History of the Wonderful Uprising of the Christian Women of the United States Against the Liquor Traffic, which culminated in the Gospel Temperance Movement. Introduction by Miss Frances E. Willard. Philadelphia, Published at the Office of the Christian Woman, 1878.

Woodbury, N. F., *Prohibition in Maine,* n.p., Auburn, Maine, 1920.

Woodend, Rev. W. W., *Yayin the Death-Dealing Monster* with Serpent Teeth and Adder Stings. Pittsburgh, 1869 [no publisher given].

Woodman, Charles T., *Narrative of . . . ,* A Reformed Inebriate. Written by Himself. Boston, Theodore Abbot, 1843.

Woolley, John G., *A Hundred Years of Temperance:* An Address Delivered at the International Centennial Congress at Saratoga, June, 1908. Westerville, Ohio, The American Issue Publishing Company, n.d.

————, *Prohibition: With the People Behind It.* An address delivered at the National Convention of the American Anti-Saloon League, December 11th, in Washington, D.C. Westerville, Ohio, The American Issue Publishing Company, n.d. [1912].

————, *The Wounds of a Friend.* Westerville, Ohio, The American Issue Publishing Company, n.d.

Young, James, ed., *Lights of Temperance,* Edited by Rev. . . . , Late Grand Chaplain of the Grand Division of the Order of the Sons of Temperance in Kentucky. Louisville, Morton & Griswold, 1851.

*Young, James Harvey, *The Toadstool Millionaires.* Princeton, Princeton University Press, 1961.

Fictional and Stage Materials

Adkisson, Noble, *Ruined by Drink*. An Original Temperance Drama in Four Acts. No. CCCCIV French's Standard Drama. . . . New York, Samuel French, n.d.

Alden, Isabella, pseud. [Pansy], *Three People*. Cincinnati, Western Tract and Book Society, 1873.

Allen, John H., *Fruits of the Wine Cup*. A Drama, in Three Acts. As performed at the Old Bowery, in 1858. New York, Clinton T. De-Witt, n.d.

Anonymous, *Mapleton; or, More Work for the Maine Law*. Boston, Jenks, Hickling and Swan, 1853.

Arthur, T. S., *The Bar-Rooms at Brantly; or, the Great Hotel Specula-tion*. Philadelphia, Porter & Coates, n.d. [1877].

————, *The Crystal Fount for 1851*. New York, Cornish, Lamport & Co., n.d. [1850].

*————, *Danger; or, Wounded in the House of a Friend*. New York, John W. Lovell Company, n.d. [1875].

————, *Illustrated Temperance Tales*. With an autobiography and a portrait of the author. Philadelphia, J. W. Bradley, 1850.

————, *Six Nights with the Washingtonians*. With Nine Illustrative Engravings designed by George Cruikshank, and engraved by Tudor Horton. Philadelphia, T. B. Peterson & Brothers, n.d. [1865].

————, *The Sons of Temperance Offering for 1851*. New York, Cornish, Lamport & Co., n.d. [1850].

————, *The Strike at Tivoli Mills, and What Came of It*. Philadel-phia, Garrigues Brothers, 1879.

*————, *Ten Nights in a Bar-Room, and What I Saw There*. Phila-delphia, G. G. Evans, 1858.

————, *Three Years in a Man-Trap*. By the Author of "Ten Nights in a Bar-Room." Philadelphia, J. M. Stoddart & Co., 1872.

————, *Woman to the Rescue*. A Story of the New Crusade. Phila-delphia, J. M. Stoddart & Co., n.d. [1874].

Baker, George M., *A Drop Too Much*. A Farce. The Amateur Drama. Boston, Lee & Shepard, 1866.

Bradley, James A., *Clayton Berry*. Or, New Year's Calls. A Temperance Story. New York, McDonald Bros., 1871.

Bradley, Mrs. Nellie H., *Marry No Man If He Drinks: or, Laura's Plan and How It Succeeded*. New Temperance Dialogues. New York, J. N. Stearns, 1868.

————, *Wine as a Medicine:* or, Abbie's Experience. New Temperance Dialogues. Rockland, Maine, L. Pope Vose & Co., 1873.

Brown, Thurlow Weed, *Minnie Hermon:* or, The Curse of Rum. A Tale for the Times. Embracing also the Life and Work of Francis Murphy and Dr. Henry A. Reynolds. By George T. Ferris, A.M. New York, Henry S. Goodspeed & Company, 1878.

Burleigh, William H., *Poems.* With a Sketch of His Life by Celia Burleigh. New York, Hurd & Houghton, 1871.

————, *The Rum Fiend,* and other Poems. New York, National Temperance Society and Publication House, 1871.

Cable, George W., "Gregory's Island," *Scribner's Magazine,* August, 1896.

Cary, S. F., ed., *The National Temperance Offering,* and Sons and Daughters of Temperance Gift. Edited by . . . M.W.P. of the Sons of Temperance of North America. New York, R. Vandien, n.d. [1850].

*Chambers, Robert W., *The Fighting Chance.* New York, A. B. Burt Company, n.d. [1906].

Cheever, George Barrell, *The Dream:* or, The True History of Deacon Giles' Distillery, and Deacon Jones' Brewery, Reported for the Benefit of Posterity. New York, Printed for the Publishers, 1846.

Colman, Julia, *Readings on Beer.* Union Handbill No. 42. New York, National Temperance Society and Publication House, 1887.

————, *Readings on Cider:* An Annual Course of Readings for local unions or other Temperance organizations. New York, National Temperance Society and Publication House, 1887.

Erickson, Matilda, *Temperance Torchlights* . . . Studies, Songs, Poems, and useful information on Temperance Topics, for the use of Individuals, Churches, Schools, Temperance and Young People's Societies. Review and Herald Pub. Assn., Washington, D.C., n.d. [c. 1909].

Fillmore, A. D., *Temperance Musician:* A Choice Collection of Original and Selected Temperance Music . . . With an Extensive Variety of Popular Temperance Songs Designed for the People. Cincinnati, Applegate & Co., 1854.

Gordon, Anna A., ed., *The White Ribbon Birthday Book.* A Selection for Each Day from the Best Writers Among Women. Woman's Temp. Pub. Association, Chicago, 1887.

*Habberton, John, *The Barton Experiment.* By the Author of "Helen's Babies." New York, G. P. Putnam's Sons, 1877.

*Hale, Edward Everett, *Our New Crusade.* A Temperance Story. Boston, Roberts Brothers, 1875.

*Hall, Eliza Calvert, pseud. [Mrs. Eliza C. Obenchain], "The Reformation of Sam Amos" in *The Land of Long Ago.* Boston, Little, Brown & Company, 1909.

*Hoyt, Charles H., *Five Plays By* . . . Edited by Douglas L. Hunt. Princeton, Princeton University Press, 1941.

————, *Lyrics of the Maid and the Moonshiners.* Written by . . . Composed by Edward Solomon. First produced at the Standard Theatre, New York, August 16, 1886, under the management of Mr. Jas. C. Buff. New York, E. F. McBreen, Printer, n.d. [1886].

Hutchinson Family, *Books of Words of the* . . . New York, Baker Godwin & Co., 1851.

Ingraham, J. H., *Edward Austin:* or, The Hunting Flask. A Tale of the Forest and Town. Respectfully dedicated to John B. Gough, Esq., a thrilling passage in one of whose addresses suggested this tale. Boston, F. Gleason, 1842.

Jerrold, Douglas, *Fifteen Years of a Drunkard's Life.* A Melodrama in Three Acts. No. CCCXLCII French's Standard Drama. New York, Samuel French, n.d.

Judson, E. Z. C. ["Ned Buntline"], *The B'Ways of New York.* A Sequel to the Mysteries and Miseries of New York. New York, W. F. Burgess, 1850.

————, *The Mysteries and Miseries of New York:* A Story of Real Life. New York, Bedford & Co., 1848.

Kirton, John William, ed., *One Thousand Temperance Anecdotes,* Jokes, Riddles, Puns and Smart Sayings, suitable for speakers, readings and recitations. Collected and edited by. . . . New York, National Temperance Society and Publication House, 1877.

Livermore, Mary Ashton [Rice], *Thirty Years Too Late:* A True Story; and *One in a Thousand.* Boston, Lockwood, Brooks & Co., n.d. [1878].

Marsh, John, D.D., ed., *The Temperance Speaker.* Compiled from various sources for the use of Bands of Hope . . . etc. by . . . New York, the National Temperance Society and Publication House, 1868.

Massachusetts Sabbath School Society, *Benjamin, the Temperance Boy.* Written for the . . . , and approved by the Committee of Publication. Boston, . . . n.d. [1853].

Newton, Newkirk, *Recollections of a Gold Cure Graduate.* Boston, H. M. Caldwell Co., [1906].

*Powers, Mrs. O. A., *The Maple Dell of '76.* Philadelphia, Lippincott & Co., 1883.

Pratt, William W., *Ten Nights in a Bar-Room.* A Temperance Drama in Five Acts. Founded on Mr. T. S. Arthur's Novel. New York, Samuel French, n.d.

*Robinson, Solon, *Hot Corn:* Life Scenes in New York Illustrated. Including the Story of Little Katy, Madalina, Rag-picker's Daughter, Wild Maggie, etc. New York, DeWitt and Davenport, 1854.

Sargent, Lucius Manlius, *Nancy Le Baron* . . . *Kitty Grafton.* Boston, Whipple and Damrell, 1837.

*————, *The Temperance Tales.* Boston, John P. Jewett & Company, 1856.

Shepard, Isaac F., copyrighter, *Confession of a Female Inebriate,* or Intemperance in High Life. By a Lady. Boston, William Henshaw, 1842.

Sigourney, Mrs. L. H., *Water-Drops*. Third Edition, Revised by the Author. And Illustrated by Rowland. New York, Robert Carter & Brothers, 1850.

Smith, William H., adaptor, *The Drunkard, or, The Fallen Saved. A Moral Domestic Drama in Five Acts.* Adapted by. . . . New York, Samuel French, Inc., n.d.

Southworth, Mrs. S. A., *The Inebriate's Hut; or, The First Fruits of the Maine Law.* Boston, Phillips, Samson, and Company, 1854.

Stowe, Harriet Beecher, *Betty's Bright Idea.* Also, Deacon Pitkin's Farm, and The First Christmas of New England. New York, J. B. Ford & Company, 1876.

Taylor, C. W., *The Drunkard's Warning.* A Temperance Drama in Three Acts . . . French's Standard Drama No. CCCLV. New York, Samuel French, n.d.

Taylor, T. P., *The Bottle.* A Drama in Two Acts. Founded upon the Graphic Illustrations of George Cruikshank, Esq. . . . New York, John Douglas, 1847.

Tom Starboard and Jack Halyard, A Nautical Temperance Dialogue. New York, The American Tract Society, n.d.

Walker, Mary Spring, *The Rev. Dr. Willoughby and His Wine.* New York, National Temperance Society and Publication House, 1876.

*Wheeler, Ella [Wilcox], *Drops of Water.* New York, National Temperance Society and Publication House, 1886.

Whitman, Walt, *Franklin Evans,* or The Inebriate. A Tale of the Times. By a Popular American Author. New York, J. Winchester, 1842.

Willard, Frances E., *Werner's Recitations and Readings* No. 18. Frances E. Willard Recitation Book. New York, Edgar S. Werner Publishing & Supply Co., 1898.

Woodward, T. Trask, *The Social Glass;* or, Victims of the Bottle. The Great Sensational Temperance Drama. In Five Acts. French's Standard Drama No. CCCLXXXV. New York, Samuel French, n.d. [1887].

*Wright, Julia McNair, *Nothing to Drink:* A Temperance Sea Story. New York, National Temperance Society and Publication House, 1873.

INDEX